Pathways to Change

Pathways to Change

Brief Therapy with Difficult Adolescents

SECOND EDITION

MATTHEW D. SELEKMAN

THE GUILFORD PRESS
New York London

A Division of Guilford Publications, Inc.
72 Spring Street, New York, NY 10012
www.guilford.com

Printed in the United States of America

This book is printed on acid-free paper.

Last digit is print number: 9 8 7 6 5 4 3 2 1

Library of Congress Cataloging-in-Publication Data

Selekman, Matthew D., 1957–
Pathways to change : brief therapy with difficult adolescents / Matthew D. Selekman.—2nd ed.
p. cm.
Includes bibliographical references and index.
ISBN 1-57230-959-8 (trade cloth)
1. Brief psychotherapy for teenagers. I. Title.
RJ504.3.S45 2005
618.92′8914—dc22

2005009476

To the two most special women in my life,
Asa and Hanna, who have been there with
undying support and love, and light up my life

About the Author

Matthew D. Selekman, LCSW, MSW, is a couple and family therapist in private practice and the codirector of Partners for Collaborative Solutions, an international family therapy training and consulting firm in Evanston, Illinois. Mr. Selekman received the Walter S. Rosenberry Award from The Children's Hospital in Denver, Colorado, in 1999 and 2000 for his significant contributions to the fields of psychiatry and the behavioral sciences. He is the author of numerous family therapy articles and three other professional books: *Living on the Razor's Edge: Solution-Oriented Brief Family Therapy with Self-Harming Adolescents*, *Solution-Focused Therapy with Children: Harnessing Family Strengths for Systemic Change*, and *Family Therapy Approaches with Adolescent Substance Abusers*. Mr. Selekman has presented workshops on his solution-oriented brief family therapy approach with challenging children and adolescents throughout the United States, Canada, Mexico, South America, Europe, and Australia.

Preface

Ralph Waldo Emerson once said, "Unless you try to do something beyond what you have already mastered, you will never grow." In this spirit, since the first edition of *Pathways to Change* was published in 1993, I have continued to allow my solution-oriented brief family therapy model to evolve considerably in terms of model expansion, becoming even more collaborative, and carefully targeting and intervening in the multisystems levels of the adolescent's social ecology to produce long-lasting systemic changes. Being a diehard integrationist, I continue to develop and look for new and old therapeutic ideas that can logically fit together and help build in more therapeutic flexibility and choices with therapeutic experiments and rituals. Another important dimension to this second and expanded edition is my placing a stronger emphasis on the engagement process and relationship building throughout the book, particularly in the new chapters. Our ability to establish meaningful connections with challenging adolescents and their families at the start of treatment can greatly contribute to positive treatment outcomes. This is supported by many psychotherapy outcome research studies that have consistently demonstrated how relationship factors were highly rated by clients as greatly contributing to their treatment success (Hubble, Duncan, & Miller, 1999).

The first edition of *Pathways to Change* theoretically was quite heavy on the solution-focused brief therapy side (de Shazer, 1988, 1991). Although this important therapeutic approach has shown favorable clinical results with a wide range of adolescent behavioral difficulties, I came to discover over the past decade some of its limitations with much more complex adolescent case situations that had experienced multiple treatment failures. At times, in staying too wedded to the basic solution-focused brief therapy approach (de Shazer, 1988, 1991), I found myself naturally favoring the kinds of solution-determined stories I wanted to coauthor with my clients and inadvertently minimizing their problem-saturated tales of oppression and demoralization that featured chronic difficulties and negative past treatment experiences. Nylund and Corsiglia (1994) refer to this way of interviewing and staying true to the base model as "solution-focused forced" therapy. I still find the practical formulas, decision trees, major therapeutic categories of questions, and tasks of the basic solution-focused approach to be quite useful in my clinical practice. But earlier I found myself becoming too dependent on these features of the model for therapeutic guidance, robbing myself of the opportunity to tap my own inventiveness, creativity, and strengths, or to borrow ideas from other therapeutic approaches in the interviewing process and with therapeutic experiment selection and design. Another major gap in the brief therapy literature and a weakness of the first edition of *Pathways to Change* is the lack of discussion about and sensitivity to social injustice—the cultural, gender, and wider societal aggravating factors relating to the development and maintenance of adolescent difficulties.

Today's youth are overscheduled, have oppressive homework loads, and are faced with having to make far too many choices about everything, which is largely attributable to our media-driven and consumerist cultural landscape; peer group life has become more high-pressured, and young people are struggling to cope with excessively high levels of stress. Other than turning to substance abuse or self-harming and eating-distressed behaviors, emotionally vulnerable adolescents often are at a loss for more healthy coping strategies. In this volume, I present a variety of useful therapeutic coping strategies such as mindfulness meditation (Hanh, 2001, 2003a), visualization, and disputation skills (Seligman, 2003; Seligman, Reivich, Jaycox, & Gillham, 1995)—to name a few—that adolescents can easily learn and use to help themselves cope with stress.

In this new edition of *Pathways to Change*, readers will find more creative and powerful ways of involving the services of key members of the adolescent's social network, such as concerned peers and inspirational others (Selekman, 2002, 2004) in family therapy. Given the push in the mental health and juvenile justice fields for the use of "best-practice" empirically validated treatment approaches with troubled youth, it is important that we become much more familiar with these approaches and see how we can incorporate what current research is indicating works in our clinical practices with youth and their families. Along these same lines, we need to be sensitive to—and maximize—the four common factors or major elements that 40 years of psychotherapy outcome research studies have indicated count the most for positive treatment outcomes (Hubble et al.,1999); they are extratherapeutic factors, relationship factors, hope and expectancy factors, and models and techniques.

Furthermore, the positive psychology movement (Peterson & Seligman, 2004; Seligman, 2002, 2003; Keyes & Haidt, 2003; Snyder & Lopez, 2002; Fredrickson, 2002, 2003; Csikszentmihalyi, 1990, 1997, 2003) has recently produced some groundbreaking research and therapeutic ideas that may eventually revolutionize our mental health delivery system. I present the innovative multiple intelligences framework of educational psychologist Howard Gardner (1993, 1999, 2004) and discuss how we can use this framework as a guide for matching what we do in the interviewing process and with therapeutic experiment design and selection with the key intelligence areas of the clients.

Finally, there are three new chapters—on the improvisational use of self, engaging and creating possibilities with difficult parents, and dealing with no-problem problem mandated families—and a greatly revised and expanded chapter on the solution-oriented parenting group. Readers will find these new chapters to be filled with many practical guidelines and therapeutic tools that can be put to immediate use with their clients.

OVERVIEW OF THE BOOK

This book is specifically designed to provide clinicians with the practical "how to's" for conducting solution-oriented brief family therapy with difficult adolescents and their families. Chapter 1 describes how our media-driven and consumerist cultural landscape and treatment-related system-aggravating factors have contributed to how adolescents develop difficulties. I discuss the various ways I have expanded the solution-oriented brief family therapy approach by incorporating innovative ideas from the fields of psychology and family therapy and integrating what we know works from psychotherapy and family therapy outcome research into our clinical practices. Chapter 2 presents helpful assumptions about difficult adolescents, their families, and brief therapy. In Chapter 3, I present several creative ways therapists can use their own improvisational skills in sessions to create possibilities with their most challenging adolescents and their families. Chapter 4 discusses how to co-create a context for change, beginning in the first family interview. Several categories of therapeutic questions and guidelines for therapeutic experiment selection and implementation are presented.

Chapter 5 presents practical guidelines for engaging and treating parents who are angry and hostile, highly pessimistic, laissez-faire, or mental health and substance abuse impaired. In Chapter 6, I present 10 effective and empirically based engagement strategies with difficult adolescents. Chapter 7 provides helpful guidelines for engaging and treating no-problem problem mandated families. Many therapists find these families to be the most difficult to engage, let alone treat. Difficult adolescents attract helping professionals from larger systems like a magnet. In Chapter 8, I discuss how to co-create with the family and involved helping professionals a safe and respectful collaborative context in which facilitating transformative dialogues can open up space for possibilities.

In Chapter 9, I present a variety of strategies for amplifying changes and consolidating therapeutic gains in the second and subsequent therapy sessions. Several solution-oriented therapeutic experiments, team strategies, and other therapeutic options for more challenging case situations are discussed. Guidelines for matching and selecting therapeutic experiments with key client intelligence areas and the family members' unique cooperative response patterns in the second and subsequent sessions are covered as well.

Chapter 10 presents a greatly updated version of my solution-oriented parenting group. This eight-session parenting group is designed to capitalize on the strengths and resources of parents to co-construct solutions. Parents learn a number of tools that they can put to immediate use to help strengthen their relationships with their kids, bring out the best in their behavior, and serve as their advocates in the various larger systems in which they are experiencing difficulties. A detailed session-by-session description is provided. Finally, Chapter 11 summarizes the major themes of the book and offers some implications for the future.

Contents

One

An Evolving Solution-Oriented Brief Family Therapy Approach with Difficult Adolescents

Do not go where the path may lead, go instead where there is no path and leave a trail.

—RALPH WALDO EMERSON

THERAPIST: What would you like to change today?

MEREDITH: Well, Jimmy has been abusing drugs, getting into trouble at school, and not listening to me or following my rules. I think he has an "attitude" problem.

T: How long has the "attitude" been pushing you and him around for?

M: I would say for the past three years. I've taken him to a lot of therapists . . . but nothing seems to work.

T: Do you think the "attitude" had sabotaged his work with all of those counselors?

M: Yeah, probably. I always had to drag him to those meetings, and he would never cooperate or talk much with those counselors. They would end up giving up on him.

T: The funny thing about "attitudes" is they are quite skilled at training kids to frustrate their parents and other adults. Tell me, Meredith, have there been any times lately where the "attitude" was lurking about and you and Jimmy joined forces and did not allow it to make the two of you lock horns with each other?

In order to protect client confidentiality, all names and client identifying background information have been changed in the case examples described within this book.

JIMMY: Yesterday, you know . . . I started to cop an attitude with you, and I didn't. We were talking without you bitching at me.

T: Jimmy, are you aware of how you did that?! What did you tell yourself to pull that off?!

J: I don't know, dude. I just wanted things to be chilled, I guess.

T: Have you used that "I just wanted things to be chilled" tape in your head with your mother other times lately or with any of your teachers on your case?

Many therapists would have stopped Meredith in her tracks when she mentioned that her son was "abusing drugs" and may have jumped to the conclusion that they were "causing" Jimmy's "attitude" problem and other behavioral difficulties. The school social worker who had referred Jimmy to me had indicated that she thought he had an "attitude" and "substance abuse" problem. She described him as being "anti-authority" when he would "mouth off" to his teachers and the dean. Jimmy had been suspended twice for being "verbally abusive toward the dean" and for "fighting with peers." Apparently, his former therapists had labeled him with "oppositional defiant disorder," "conduct disorder," and "intermittent explosive disorder." In our first family session, the mother seemed to think that the real problem with her son was that he had an "attitude problem." For 3 years the "attitude problem" had been getting the best of them and the school staff. I decided to take a risk and externalize the "attitude" (White & Epston, 1990). Much to my pleasant surprise, this therapeutic move paid off. We were able to identify "newsworthy" exceptions (de Shazer, 1985) or "sparkling moments" (White, 1995) when both Meredith and Jimmy were quite successful at standing up to the "attitude" and not allowing it to push them around. At Jimmy's school, I met with success using this same externalization of the "attitude" problem strategy with his teachers. Combining narrative and solution-oriented therapy ideas helped to co-create possibilities with this family and the school helping system, all of whom were being oppressed by "the attitude problem" for a long time.

The approach I was utilizing with Jimmy and his mother is my solution-oriented brief family therapy approach, which is an expansion of the solution-oriented brief therapy approaches developed by O'Hanlon and Weiner-Davis (1989) and Steve de Shazer and his colleagues (de Shazer, 1985, 1988, 1991; Berg & Miller, 1992; Berg & Gallagher, 1991; Gingerich & de Shazer, 1991; Gingerich, de Shazer, & Weiner-Davis, 1988; Lipchik, 1988; Molnar & de Shazer, 1987; Lipchik & de Shazer, 1986). Expanding the original solution-oriented brief family therapy model (Selekman, 1993) through integrating ideas from other individual and family therapy approaches, ideas from Howard Gardner's multiple intelligences framework (Gardner 1993, 2004), important research findings from positive psychology (Peterson & Seligman, 2004; Seligman, 2002, 2003; Snyder & Lopez, 2002; Fredrickson, 2002), psychotherapy (Hubble et al., 1999), and family therapy outcome research findings (Henggeler & Sheidow, 2002), and actively collaborating with key members of the adolescent's social network, has helped make the model even more flexible and an effective treatment option for adolescents presenting with such serious problems as self-harming, aggressive and violent, delinquency, substance-abusing, eating-distressed, school disruptive behavior, and depression difficulties (Selekman, 1989a, 1989b, 1991b, 1993, 1995, 2002, 2004; Berg & Miller, 1992; Berg & Gallagher, 1991).

In this chapter, I provide a discussion of some major wider societal and treatment system-related aggravating factors that play a role in how adolescents develop problems and become difficult to treat, and present a variety ways in which I have expanded the original solution-oriented brief family therapy model to make it more comprehensive and effective with challenging adolescents and their families presenting with serious and chronic behavioral difficulties.

THE TEEN ANGST BLUES: HOW OUR MEDIA-DRIVEN AND CONSUMERIST CULTURAL LANDSCAPE BREEDS TROUBLED YOUTH

There are six major wider societal and cultural aggravating factors that I believe greatly contribute to the emotional and behavioral difficulties adolescents are experiencing today. The identification of these key aggravating factors grew out of a critical analysis of our media-driven and consumerist cultural landscape, from therapeutic conversations with adolescents and their parents, and collaborations and consultations with therapists and representatives from larger systems regarding the stressors and challenges youth face today. Therapists need to be sensitive to the roles these aggravating factors play in the development and exacerbation of young people's difficulties.

The Demonization and Criminalization of Youth

A growing trend in the United States is for school officials to have police officers and the juvenile justice system discipline youth for behavioral misconduct that previously was managed on-site at their schools. According to Rimer (2004), "the juvenile detention center has become an extension of the principal's office" (p. 1). In response to the rise in school-related cases in his courtroom, James Ray, the administrative judge for the Lucas

County juvenile court in Toledo, Ohio, says, "We're demonizing children" (in Rimer, 2004, p. 15). Ray is not alone in his concern; judges from the states of Virginia, Kentucky, and Florida have had similar concerns about how schools are mismanaging the student behavioral misconduct situation. Adolescents are being arrested and charged with misdemeanors for such minor infractions as "being loud and disruptive," "cursing at school personnel," and "dress code violations." At the heart of the criminalization of student misbehavior are the zero-tolerance policies of the mid- to late 1990s, which were created in response to a series of school shootings and other youth violence (Rimer, 2004; Aronson, 2000).

As Michael Moore accurately pointed out in his Academy Award-winning documentary *Bowling for Columbine*, if you are an African American youth or adult, you will be the first to be targeted and subsequently arrested (Moore, 2002). A recent example of unjust treatment and what appeared to be racial profiling of African American youths took place at a high school in Goose Creek, South Carolina. The school administration arranged with the local police department to make a surprise raid on a group of African American students suspected of using marijuana on school grounds. The timing of the raid, at 6:45 A.M., was the exact time that most of the African American students were brought to the school by their buses. The students were handcuffed and forced to kneel down, facing the wall, by the police. No marijuana was found (Lewin, 2003). Clearly, these youth and their parents believed that their civil rights had been violated and that the whole incident had occurred because of racial bias.

Many schools across the country have installed metal detectors, hidden surveillance cameras, and security guards to check kids when they enter the school and to help track suspicious students, all designed to relieve the school staff's fears and maximize overall school safety. Thus, schools have increasingly become "adult-friendly" places (Aronson, 2000; Breggin, 2000). Although the juvenile homicide rate has declined significantly and many studies have indicated that school violence is quite rare, mass media's spin on the current state of affairs still depicts schools as relatively unsafe places (Rimer, 2004; Selekman, 2002; Aronson, 2000).

Growing Up in a Culture of Fear

Several times a day, adolescents are assaulted by violent images and sensationalized stories in the media that produce tremendous fear and anxiety in them. All around them they read and hear about "terrorist alerts being ratcheted up," "Osama Bin Laden and Al Qaeda planning new strikes in the United States," "Saddam Hussein's weapons of mass destruction," "mad cow disease in America," "clergy who are sexual predators," "nuclear threats from North Korea," "the bird flu," and so forth. Recently, one of my self-harming clients shared with me her pronouncement that "Armageddon is near" and why should she stop cutting herself because she was going to be "killed by terrorists anyway." For her, cutting herself helped to relieve her anxiety and worries. Similarly, as with this adolescent, other youth I have worked with do not believe they will live long enough to make it to adulthood or have great difficulty in even imagining a future for themselves.

In an interview with Michael Moore about the irresponsible and damaging ways our media spins stories, shock rocker Marilyn Manson had the following to say:

> "The more fear instilled by the media, the more we consume. A lot of people are making money and careers from fear. The media spins events and turns it into fear; pumped for fear it becomes a campaign of fear and consumption. Keep everyone afraid and they will consume." (in Moore, 2002)

To a certain degree, most adolescents experience some form of *teen angst* and uncertainty about their future. However, the violent images and messages that TV news stations and other forms of the media are exposing youth to in an effort to increase their ratings are further intensifying teenagers' anxieties. Glassner (1999) has found in his research that, even as the national violent crime rates have gone down, the media often report that violent crimes are on the rise. Unfortunately, in America, violence sells! For more emotionally vulnerable youth, the combination of media-triggered anxieties and other stressors in their lives can lead to self-harming, substance-abusing, and eating-distressed behaviors as an attempt to soothe themselves.

The Seduction of "Quick-Fix" Solutions

Similar to how the media spins the news to instill fear and foster consumption by the public, advertisers have developed psychologically powerful and masterful strategies for seducing youth to purchase their products. Through expensive, artistic, and clever advertisements, companies have persuaded youth into believing that if they purchase their products they will be "cooler," "more beautiful," "more sexy," or "much better off" in ways that they could "never imagine" (Kilbourne, 1999). The trouble is that there are far too many material items to choose from. Schwartz (2004) has found in his research that the more we try to consume the *best* possible products on the market, the more insatiable our hunger becomes, the more we set ourselves up for failure, and the more anxiety and depressed feelings we are apt to experience. He refers to such consumers as "maximizers."

For these individuals, consuming becomes a recurrent problem rather than a solution, or comfort.

Parents nowadays, even more so than in the past, are turning to consumer goods as a quick-fix solution for pacifying their children. This attempted solution helps relieve them of their guilt and anxiety for not being fully available for emotional connection and support. They also don't like to see their kids experiencing emotional distress and believe that this shortcut to happiness will provide their sons and daughters with immediate relief. Once this pattern of overindulgence is set in motion, teenagers become the main decision makers in their families in terms of the selection of the commodities, including whatever big-ticketed items might raise their status with their peers. Some parents also believe that making their teenagers as attractive-looking as possible will help raise their family's status in the community (Milner, 2004).

Adolescents have also been taught by our mass media and by observing their parents, other key adults in their lives, and their medicated peer friends that if you take a pill it might well be the answer to your personal difficulties. Today, as never before, pharmaceutical companies are purchasing more advertising time and space to showcase their wonder drugs that can quickly alleviate anxiety and depression, and control symptoms for a variety of disorders. Drugs are commonly portrayed in the media as "magic bullets." In a similar fashion, alcoholic beverages are frequently portrayed as the answer to being more popular, landing dates, and for making yourself more "sexy," "funny," "confident," and "tough-looking"—qualities that many adolescents would like to possess. Some adolescents regularly observe their parents mismanaging work and other personal stressors in their lives through chain smoking, excessive drinking, and abusing illicit drugs. However, the message they are frequently given by their parents and other key caretakers in their lives is "Do as I *say*, not as I *do*." They learn that the best and quickest way to resolve personal difficulties and cope with stress is to anesthetize one's feelings with chemical substances. Adolescents who engage in self-harming behavior may have deduced that "cutting" and "burning" themselves can produce fast-acting endorphins, which can numb some of the emotional distress that they are experiencing.

"Fitting In"

One of the most important developmental tasks that adolescents need to master is being able to establish and sustain relationships with their peers. Being "dissed" (devalued, or put down) by powerful and popular peers is the equivalent of social death for many adolescents. In some cases, the only way an adolescent can get into a popular peer group's clique is to engage in such behaviors as self-harming, abusing drugs, self-starving or engaging in bulimic-like behavior to "fit into tight jeans," or committing a crime in order to join "the crew" (Selekman, 2002, 2004). Many of my clients have reported that peer group pressure is the number-one stressor in their lives. It is difficult to keep up because clothing trends, musical preferences, hair styles, language, and rituals change at a rapid pace. Research indicates that the pressure to have fashionable clothes and other "cool" possessions is one of the factors that have contributed to the high rate of shoplifting among teens (Milner, 2004; Cox, Cox, & Moschis, 1990).

In studying the hidden aggression of female adolescents, Simmons (2002) found that going underground through the use of Internet chat rooms and web-based bulletin boards was a common strategy used by girls to scapegoat peers they did not like, to lower their status in the social hierarchy, or as a powerful way to expel them as members of their peer group. Behind the scenes they would carefully plot the best way to scapegoat or reject a targeted peer. This often would entail spreading a nasty rumor that may have been sent to a large number of fellow students via Instant Messenger, e-mails, or by posting it on a website. The web-based bulletin board strategy provides near permanent slander and makes the rumor or bad press about the targeted peer available to large audiences (Milner, 2004). The next day at school, the targeted peer has no clue why her peers are giving her the cold shoulder, laughing at her, or treating her in a nasty way. In my practice, I have treated a number of young women who were victims of underground lynch mobs, which was so emotionally devastating for them that they became clinically depressed and engaged in a lot of self-destructive behaviors as a result of this mass humiliation or rejection process.

Growing Up Too Fast

Adolescents today have to cope with unhealthy and excessively high levels of stress more so than ever before. They are overscheduled, have excessive homework loads, and in some cases are overburdened by adult responsibilities (Taffel, 2003; Selekman, 2002). Some of the self-harming and eating-distressed clients I have worked with were overscheduled by their parents in far too many extracurricular activities and were constantly being pressured by them to get A grades so they could get into the finest colleges. For these clients, they felt so out of control that they turned to self-harm and bulimia as powerful and effective ways to regain control and comfort themselves. In some cases, adolescents have to assume junior parenting responsibilities with siblings and sacrifice their social life to help out their single parent who is working long hours to support the family financially. Overburdened and frustrated, the adolescent may become depressed, aggressive toward his or her siblings or parents, and in some cases engage in self-harming, eating-distressed, or substance-abusing behaviors to cope.

In a national survey conducted by the *New York Times* and CBS News, a large sample of teenagers were asked to compare their teenaged lives with those of their parents. Forty-three percent of the participants said they were having a harder time than their parents did; 50% of the teenagers who came from affluent families said their lives were a lot harder; and teenagers from low-income families felt that their lives were easier. When the investigators explored with the youth from affluent families why they felt this way, they noted that both their parents' and their own expectations were too high. The youth talked about "too-muchness": too many activities, too many consumer choices, and too much to learn. One commentator put it best: "Children fear the pressure . . . to be sure they don't slide back. Everything's about going forward. . . . Falling back is the American nightmare" (Schwartz, 2004, p. 185).

Another powerful way youth are hurried along into adulthood is through popular TV shows and movies that are jam-packed with adult themes. Many of these TV shows and movies feature teenaged or young adult actors and actresses who are struggling with issues that younger or older adults typically must confront. In addition, the young men and women in these TV shows and movies are portrayed in traditional—sometimes even highly stereotyped—gender roles. For example, some may perpetuate sexist attitudes that men should treat women as objects for their pleasure or that women should be subservient to men and should strive to look like fashion models, "be nice and polite," and, above all, "please your man." These powerful messages and images convey to young people that this is how they should think and conduct themselves in their relationships with their peers. For more emotionally vulnerable young women, failure to "live up to" or "look like" their idealized actress role models can lead to eating-distressed, self-harming, and substance-abusing behaviors.

Emotional Disconnection and Invalidation

Many of the adolescents who have been referred to me and described as "difficult," "resistant," "defensive," "anti-authority," and called "borderlines" have reported feeling emotionally disconnected from their parents, other key caretakers in their lives, and in some cases their peers. These youth often feel they are not listened to or respected by their parents and others. Research indicates that the more emotionally disconnected that adolescents are from their parents or key caretakers, the more extreme their acting-out behaviors or symptoms will be (Reimer, Overton, Steidl, Rosenstein, & Horowitz, 1996; Papini & Roggman, 1992). Seligman (2003) contends that emotional disconnection and the breakdown of the family have played a major role in why the mean age to develop clinical depression has lowered to 15 years old.

Unfortunately, when these youth feel emotionally disconnected and insignificant in their families, they have a tendency to gravitate toward a *second family* in their communities, which is often an unsavory group of peers that is even more troubled (Selekman, 2002; Taffel & Blau, 2001). Most of the gang-involved adolescents I have worked with found that the gang met a lot of their personal needs, especially providing a strong sense of belonging.

Another factor that has contributed to the erosion of family relationships consists of media screens (Taffel, 2003; Selekman, 2002). In our high-tech, media-driven, consumerist society, screens are replacing the need for human contact and are bending and shaping young people's minds. Computer screens do not necessarily foster connection building or teach adolescents how to strengthen their relationships with their parents, siblings, or peers. Playing popular computer games and spending endless hours in chat rooms have become a more inviting and valued pastime for youth today than spending time with their families or having face-to-face contact with their peers. Often, parents do not provide any or enough firm guidelines for their adolescents' time spent on the computer or watching TV, further fostering the process of disconnection.

TREATMENT SYSTEM-RELATED AGGRAVATING FACTORS

Over the past two decades, I have treated and consulted on numerous adolescent cases that have been given some of the worst DSM-IV (American Psychiatric Association, 1994) labels by former therapists and referral sources. Often described as "resistant," or "borderline," these adolescents typically have families that are described as "enmeshed," "chaotic," "crazy," "chemically dependent," "rejecting," and "multiproblem." Many of these youth and their families have experienced multiple treatment failures in a variety of treatment settings. In the stories of these adolescents and their families about their experiences with former therapists, treatment programs, and involved helping professionals from larger systems, two common themes emerged: (1) the labels given to the adolescents and their families had a stigmatizing effect and made their situations much worse, and (2) the treatment experiences were "more of the same" in terms of treatment variety, which further exacerbated the clients' presenting problems. I will now elaborate on how these two critical aggravating factors contribute to the development and perpetuation of the adolescents' and their families' continued involvement with mental health and addiction professionals and representatives from larger systems.

Labels Create a Therapeutic "Black Hole"

In thinking about the various oppressive and stigmatizing labels difficult adolescent clients tend to be given by the mental health and chemical dependency treatment delivery systems, I am reminded of the poignant words of family therapy pioneer Harry Goolishian. He had the following to say about the "deficiency language" that mental health professionals have used with clients over the past century:

> The deficiency language has created a world of description that understands only through what is wrong, broken, absent, or insufficient. This deficiency language has created a world of mental health that can be compared to a black hole out of which there is little hope to escape, whether we are a clinician, theoretician, or researcher. In using the metaphor of the black hole, I am trying to capture the essence of a system of meaning whose forces are so strong that it is impossible to escape out of the system and into other realities. (1991, pp. 1–2)

One powerful written work that has perpetuated the mental health "black hole" labeling problem is the fourth edition of the *Diagnostic and Statistical Manual of Mental Disorders* (DSM-IV; American Psychiatric Association, 1994). Although this manual has become "the Bible" for most therapists and insurance purposes, it does not provide clinicians with any practical treatment guidelines for the disorders presented within it, and it makes no mention of client strengths. Maddux (2002) contends that there are four *faulty* assumptions about the DSM: (1) the categories of disorders are facts about the world; (2) we have the ability to accurately distinguish between normal and abnormal behaviors; (3) the categories of disorders facilitate clinical judgment; and (4) the categories of disorders help facilitate the treatment planning process. As Maddux (2002) points out, we do not have a higher hold on "the truth" about the various categories of disorders described in the DSM. We lack the ultimate scientific method for accurately determining if an individual is normal or abnormal. The DSM does not take into consideration that it is impossible for clinicians to be totally objective and bias-free when it comes to selecting a diagnostic label for their clients. What we see (through our theoretical lens) is what we will get (e.g., a borderline personality disorder). Finally, the DSM provides absolutely no practical guidance for treatment planning.

In 1991, Wolin (1991) had recommended that this volume should contain a listing of client strengths as long and as technical as the diseases and disorders described within it. In response to growing concerns like Wolin's and Maddux's about the DSM's main emphasis on client pathologies, lack of guidance with treatment planning, and other limitations, positive psychologists Christopher Peterson and Martin Seligman have written a manual called *Character Strengths and Virtues: A Handbook and Classification*. In their groundbreaking volume, the authors present a classification system that consists of the following six virtues: *wisdom and knowledge*, *transcendence*, *temperance*, *justice*, *love*, and *courage*. In addition, there are 24 strengths that fall under the six virtues categorized as *cognitive strengths*, *strengths of will in the face of opposition*, *interpersonal strengths*, *civic strengths*, *strengths that protect against excess*, and *strengths that forge connections to meaning* (Seligman, 2003). Not only does Peterson and Seligman's book identify client strengths and virtues, but also it offers practical guidelines on how to increase clients' awareness of their key signature strengths, accentuate them, and deploy them more in all areas of their lives (Peterson & Seligman, 2004; Seligman, 2003). Clearly, their volume is about client empowerment. Unlike the DSM-IV, the *Character Strengths and Virtues* manual provides therapists with guidelines for treatment planning, is empirically based, and can help in reducing clients' length of stay in treatment because of its strong strengths-based orientation and emphasis on client empowerment.

The popular "recovery movement," which is based on the philosophy of Alcoholics Anonymous (AA) and the disease model of addiction, has extended its deficiency language to every possible human behavior, such as eating, sex, work, and exercise (Peele, 1989). Disease model proponents tend to believe that the majority of youths living with an alcoholic or substance-abusing parent will most likely become "emotional cripples" for life (Wolin, 1991). Their only hope of recovery is through their active participation in Alateen or children of alcoholics'/substance abusers' groups. The recovery movement literature fails to identify children of alcoholics'/substance abusers' strengths, resiliency protective factors, and specific competency areas (Wolin, 1991; Selekman & Todd, 1991). What tend to be in the literature—which are quite alarming to parents—are all of the negative traits that children of alcoholics or substance abusers are supposed to have, particularly being at high risk for developing alcohol or other substance-abuse problems themselves (Katz & Liu, 1991). Selekman and Todd (1991) have worked with numerous adolescent cases in which parental indoctrination to the recovery movement lifestyle and constant preoccupation with their adolescent's future use of alcohol or other substances end up creating negative self-fulfilling prophecies.

Once an adolescent is identified as having a substance abuse problem, he or she will most likely be referred to an outpatient chemical dependency program through a local hospital, agency, or community mental health clinic whose treatment philosophy is based on the Twelve Steps of AA and the disease model. There the adolescent will be prompted to admit to being an "alcoholic" or a "drug addict." If the adolescent refuses to admit to being one or the other, the treatment team will confront him or her on his or her "denial." Many of these chemical dependency programs provide "assembly line" treatment, which usually takes the form of total abstinence treatment goals, self-help groups, education, and family supportive counseling (Selekman & Todd, 1991). Perceived choice is not encouraged in a system where adolescents are coerced to take a particular course of action or in programs where a relatively standard treatment is provided for all clients (Orford & Hawker, 1974). Three major reasons why this heavy-handed treatment strategy does not work with substance-abusing adolescents are: (1) adolescent drug users rarely accept being labeled as an "addict," "alcoholic," or "drug addict" (Glassner & Loughlin, 1987); (2) adolescent drug users tend to view their substance use as a normal social behavior that they will outgrow in adulthood (Glassner & Loughlin, 1987); and (3) research indicates that when alcohol abusers are subjected to a confrontational therapy approach, they show much higher levels of resistance and negative treatment outcomes (Miller & Rollnick, 2003; Miller & Sovereign, 1989; Patterson & Forgatch, 1985). Moreover, follow-up studies with adolescent substance abusers that received both inpatient and outpatient traditional Twelve Step and disease model treatments have indicated that relapse rates were as high as 85% (Dembo, 1992).

Despite my qualms about the recovery movement and the use of the disease model with adolescents, I do believe strongly in utilizing self-help groups when clients are looking for further support outside of therapy sessions. I view their prior and concurrent involvement in Al-Anon or Alateen as a sign of their resourcefulness. I do not, however, adopt a coercive approach regarding family members' immediate participation in self-help groups at the beginning of treatment, including the toddler in Alatot! Similarly, I do not demand immediate abstinence from alcohol or other substance use with adolescents before I work with them. With regular and heavy substance abusers, cutting back has proven to be a much more palatable initial treatment goal (Selekman & Todd, 1991). MacMaster (2004) contends that facilitating some change in the client's pattern of drug use can reduce the negative consequences of this behavior and is better than not facilitating any change. Harm-reduction treatment approaches have shown good clinical results with substance-abusing clients not seeking immediate abstinence (Dimeff, Baer, Kivlahan, & Marlatt, 1998; Kivlahan, Marlatt, Fromme, Coppel, & Brand, 1990).

I will, however, attempt to pursue total abstinence treatment goals with adolescents that are experiencing severe physical complications from their heavy alcohol or substance abuse and are concurrently cutting themselves. Periodic use of outpatient or inpatient detoxification can also be useful for disrupting self-destructive cycles of heavy substance abuse.

"More of the Same" Treatment Variety

The average "difficult" adolescent case has been through two or more past treatment experiences that usually took the form of "more of the same" type of therapy (Watzlawick, Weakland, & Fisch, 1974). As the treatment failures pile up, the adolescent's symptoms or problem behaviors become more entrenched and chronic, which may trigger vicious guilt/blame cycles of interaction within the family. Frequently, difficult adolescent clients and their families have shared with me that they had very little input in their past treatment experiences, in terms of defining their goals for treatment, expressing their treatment expectations, preferences, theories of change, choice of treatment modalities that best suited their needs, and with the overall treatment planning process. The past therapists' treatment goals were often highly unrealistic, too vague, and driving the clients' treatment process. Another common theme in difficult adolescent clients' treatment experiences was the therapists' mismatching of interventions with their and family members' unique stages of readiness to change (Prochaska, Norcross, & DiClemente, 1994). Some difficult adolescents and their parents complained about previous therapists' and treatment program staffs' lack of sensitivity to their cultural values. With some residential and inpatient psychiatric treatment experiences, former adolescent clients reported that the treatment team failed to effect any significant changes with their families. Even when family therapy was utilized, some difficult adolescent clients told me that most of the therapeutic emphasis was on what parents wanted, and the adolescents' individual goals and expectations were not addressed. Finally, another common theme with most difficult adolescent cases was the previous therapists' and treatment program staffs' failure to actively collaborate with all of the involved helping professionals from larger systems.

Difficult adolescents and their families do not have to be hard to treat if there is a conscious effort to do the following:

1. Avoid the use of labeling, or, if necessary because of insurance purposes, involve clients in selecting the DSM label they think best fits the adolescent's situation.
2. Avoid at all costs repeating unsuccessful attempted solutions by former therapists and treatment program staffs by finding out what did not work or what clients found the most upsetting from these experiences.
3. Invite the clients to take the lead in defining their treatment goals and sharing their preferences, expectations, and theories of change.
4. Expect that all clients have the strengths and resources to change.

5. Give the adolescent individual session time to develop a therapeutic alliance and attend to his or her goals, expectations, and desired privileges to negotiate with the parents.
6. Carefully match therapeutic experiments designed and selected with the unique stages of readiness for change of each family member.
7. Beginning at intake and throughout the course of treatment, actively collaborate with the referring person and all involved helping professionals from larger systems.
8. Each session, elicit from family members feedback on the quality of your therapeutic relationship with them and their satisfaction or concerns with the treatment they are receiving with you.
9. Be therapeutically flexible and improvise when necessary.

By following these practical guidelines, therapists will be able to foster collaborative and meaningful therapeutic relationships with even the toughest of adolescent clients and their families. Over the past two decades of working with challenging adolescents and their families that had experienced multiple treatment failures—fork-lifted treatment file folders and all—they have taught me to honor their long problem-saturated stories, to be a better listener, to be patient, to be respectful of their pain and frustration, to be in awe of their persistence and resiliency, and to empower them to take the lead voice with goal setting and treatment planning.

SOLUTION-ORIENTED BRIEF FAMILY THERAPY: FURTHER EXPANSION OF THE MODEL

In 1993, I first presented the original solution-oriented brief family therapy model, which was an expansion of the solution-oriented brief therapy approach developed by William H. O'Hanlon and Michele Weiner-Davis (O'Hanlon, 1987; O'Hanlon & Weiner-Davis, 1989; Weiner-Davis, 1992). Their model is heavily based on the therapeutic ideas of the brilliant hypnotist Milton H. Erickson (Erickson, 1964, 1965, 1980a,1980b; Erickson & Rossi, 1983; Erickson, Rossi, & Rossi, 1976), but it also incorporates ideas from the solution-focused brief therapy approach developed by Steve de Shazer and his colleagues (de Shazer, 1982, 1984, 1985, 1988, 1991; de Shazer et al., 1986; Gingerich & de Shazer, 1991; Gingerich et al., 1988; Lipchik, 1988; Lipchik & de Shazer, 1986; Weiner-Davis, de Shazer, & Gingerich, 1987) and the brief problem-focused therapy approach of the Mental Research Institute (MRI) theorists (Fisch, Weakland, & Segal, 1982; Watzlawick, Weakland, & Fisch, 1974). As with all therapy models, no one model is a panacea for every type of adolescent presenting problem, particularly more complex case situations. In an effort to expand the base solution-oriented brief therapy approaches of O'Hanlon & Weiner-Davis (1989) and de Shazer (1988, 1991), and build in more therapeutic flexibility and adopt a multisystemic focus to handle more challenging adolescent case situations, I added the following treatment components: more emphasis on the therapist's use of self in the therapeutic process, integrating ideas from the narrative therapy approach (White & Epston, 1990; White, 1988b; Epston, 1998; Durrant & Coles, 1991), integrating postmodern family therapy ideas from the Houston–Galveston team (Anderson & Goolishian, 1988a, 1988b, 1991a, 1991b) and Tom Andersen (Friedman, 1995; Andersen, 1991; Lussardi & Miller, 1991), and emphasizing the importance of actively collaborating from the start of treatment with involved helping professionals from larger systems.

Over the past 12 years, I have observed in my clinical practice and through consulting with mental health professionals in this country and abroad some important new trends that have compelled me to further expand the solution-oriented brief family therapy approach to make it even more flexible, comprehensive, and capable of respectfully and adequately meeting the needs of challenging adolescents and their families. Some of these trends are:

- Today's adolescent presenting problems and family difficulties appear to be much more extreme, complex, and chronic than in the past.
- Family disconnection and breakdown continue to be growing problems, and we have to serve as the catalysts for connection building across social contexts.
- There is a need to extend our collaboration efforts beyond larger systems to actively involve key members of adolescents' social networks in the treatment process.
- We need to be much more sensitive to social injustice, cultural and gender issues, and societal aggravating factors in the lives of the adolescents and families we service.
- Many adolescents are complaining about (more so than ever before), their inability to cope with excessive levels of stress in all areas of their lives.

I now discuss several different ways I have expanded the solution-oriented brief family therapy model to address these important trends and treatment challenges.

Contributions from the Positive Psychology Movement

The positive psychology movement was launched primarily by four cutting-edge psychology theorists and researchers: Martin Seligman, Christopher

Peterson, Mihaly Csikszentmihalyi, and Donald Clifton. These pioneering researchers felt that the field of psychology needed to move its primary focus off of studying psychopathological conditions in humans and how to fix them to being equally interested and concerned about studying people's strengths and virtues, focusing on individuals who are already flourishing, and developing effective methods for empowering people to build productive and fulfilling lives (Peterson & Seligman, 2004; Seligman, 2002, 2003; Keyes & Haidt, 2003; Csikszentmihalyi, 1990, 1997, 2003; Fredrickson, 2002, 2003; Snyder & Lopez, 2002; Clifton & Nelson, 1992).

Seligman, the father of the learned helplessness and optimism frameworks (1998, 2002, 2003; Seligman et al., 1995), has lately been concentrating his efforts on studying how people can achieve happiness and fulfilled lives. He has identified three pathways to happiness: *the pleasant life*, *the good life*, and *the meaningful life*. The pleasant life consists of teaching people tools for increasing their positive emotion about the past, the present, and the future (Seligman, 2002, 2003). One great exercise that Seligman developed to help change a person's emotions about his or her past is *the gratitude letter and visit* (Seligman, 2002, 2003). I like to use this experiment with adolescents that have experienced traumatic or very difficult past life situations that appear to be affecting them in the here and now. They are to pick a mentor, an inspirational other, or significant person from their past that they would like to write a letter of gratitude to. In the letter, they are to indicate the various positive and meaningful experiences, words of wisdom, and skills their selected special other had provided for them in the past. After they write the letter, they are to try and schedule a meeting with their selected person and read the letter to him or her. Often, this powerful emotional experience produces big smiles, tears, and hugs.

Marci, a white 15-year-old depressed and bulimic adolescent, had experienced a lot of painful losses in her past that she was "having a hard time stomaching." Her parents divorced when she was 10 years old and her maternal grandmother, whom she was very close to, had died shortly after the divorce. Marci's father had remarried, and, aside from regularly paying child support, he had "checked out of" her life physically. Apparently, her father would only make himself available to her around major holidays, despite her phone calls to him. For Marci, her past was a "very dark place." Since Marci liked to write and was a gifted poet, in an effort to inject more positive emotion into her past memories and help enhance her present mood, I had recommended the gratitude letter and visit (Seligman, 2003) experiment to try. I asked her if she could identify an important inspirational other from her past that meant a lot to her and whose wisdom and support continued to be of help to her in the present day. Marci felt that her English teacher in eighth grade, Ms. Jackson, was her inspirational other. Apparently, Ms. Jackson exposed her to a lot of "famous poets' works" and taught her how "to write poetry well." It brought a big smile to Marci's face when I had proposed to her the idea of writing a gratitude letter to Ms. Jackson and setting up a meeting to read it to her. In Marci's gratitude letter, she thanked Ms. Jackson for teaching her how to "write poetry well," explained to her how writing poetry has helped her to cope with her problems and brings her great pleasure to do, and how she was "one of" her "all-time most favorite teachers." Marci set up a meeting with Ms. Jackson at her former middle school. According to Marci, Ms. Jackson was so emotionally moved by her gratitude letter that it "brought tears" to her eyes. Ms. Jackson offered to make herself available to Marci for added support and encouraged her to bring in some of her poetry the next time they got together. This powerful experiment helped paved the way to Marci's becoming more hopeful about her situation and being "less of a prisoner" of her painful past.

Another powerful and important coping strategy that we can teach adolescents for promoting positive emotion is *disputation skills* (Seligman, 1998, 2002, 2003; Seligman, Reivich, Jaycox, & Gillham, 1995). Adolescents can become master disputers of their pessimistic and self-defeating thoughts by learning how to do the following: playing detective and searching for clues or hard evidence to support their thoughts, generating as many alternative explanations as possible for upsetting events that occur, and asking themselves when bad things happen to them, "What is the usefulness of my dwelling on this particular event?" "Do I get more down or angry the more I think about it?" Seligman and his colleagues have found that learning how to become a master disputer can help protect children and adolescents from falling prey to depression (Seligman, 1995, 1998, 2003; Seligman et al., 1995). I find disputation techniques to be particularly useful in family therapy sessions when family members cling to negative, rigid, and pessimistic explanations for interactions that occur in and outside of their relationships.

"The good life" consists of having clients identify their top five *signature strengths* and how to deploy them in all areas of their lives (Seligman, 2002, 2003). As mentioned earlier, Peterson and Seligman (2004) have identified from their research 6 major virtues and 24 strengths that can be harnessed and used to empower our clients. In addition, Seligman (2003) contends that we should help our clients develop and utilize their other 19 nonsignature strengths. This raises some important questions: Do people have to have deficits or psychopathological conditions? Could it be that they are not aware of, have not utilized, or have not further developed their nonsignature strengths? Finally, Peterson and Seligman (2004) have found in their research that life satisfaction is strongly correlated with individuals whose top signature strengths are curiosity, zest for life, gratitude (a happy connection with his or her past), optimism, and the ability to love and be loved by others. Of these key signature strengths, they believe that therapists should target their interventions at developing and strengthening clients' optimism, gratitude, and relationship skill strength areas as an important dimension of the treatment process, which can greatly increase their life satisfaction levels.

By "the meaningful life," Seligman (2002, 2003) is referring to how individuals can utilize their signature strengths in the service of something larger than themselves. This would include encouraging adolescents to get involved in teen leadership programs, mentoring a younger child, volunteering in a nursing home (or soup kitchen serving the homeless), or getting involved in a community social action project. As an alternative to typical parental consequences for their adolescents' rule violations or misbehavior, I have had parents arrange as a positive consequence having their kids work in a soup kitchen or nursing home on a time-limited basis. Although most adolescents balk at this idea initially, some have responded by finding these experiences so meaningful and rewarding that they wanted to continue to serve as a volunteer beyond the parents' consequence periods or even try to land regular paid positions at these places.

Csikszentmihalyi's (1990, 1997, 2003) innovative work on *flow* is also an important dimension to establishing a meaningful and fulfilled life. He has found in his research that when we immerse ourselves in some activity that we are passionate about or that we find quite meaningful, time stops and everything else happening around us seems to disappear or become insignificant. This is what Csikszentmihalyi (1990, 2003) refers to as "flow." When beginning family therapy with a new adolescent client, I explore with him or her which specific healthy leisure activities he or she derives the most pleasure, joy, and meaning from engaging in. After I secure this valuable information, I encourage the adolescent to increase his or her involvement in flow-inducing activities to better cope with the stressors in his or her life.

Fredrickson's (2002, 2003) groundbreaking research on positive emotion provides empirical support for our trying to create therapeutic climates in our offices and in clients' homes that are positive, hopeful, and emotionally uplifting. Through numerous studies, she has demonstrated that, by inducing positive emotion in her subjects, the following can occur: individuals' problem-solving and creative capacities are greatly enhanced; our natural protective factors and coping abilities are strengthened; and positive emotions can help loosen the grip of negative emotions connected to past unpleasant experiences, build enduring personal resources (physical, psychological, intellectual, social), and over time produce upward spirals of personal growth (Fredrickson, 2002, 2003; Seligman, 2002, 2003).

Use of the Multiple Intelligences Framework in Family Therapy

Howard Gardner, an educational psychologist at Harvard University, developed the *multiple intelligences framework* in response to his concerns with our traditional educational system, where the major emphasis is on a student's ability to read, write, and do math. According to Gardner (1993, 1999, 2004), children and adolescents should be assessed in terms of 10 distinct intelligence areas rather than be judged solely by their verbal and academic scores on an IQ test. The 10 intelligence areas are *linguistic, logical–mathematical, musical, visual–spatial, bodily–kinesthetic, interpersonal, intrapersonal, naturalist, existential,* and *spiritual*. He believes that all humans possess these intelligence areas; however, each person has a unique style of learning and will learn best when the teaching methods used are matched with his or her unique gifts and talents in his or her key intelligence areas.

Gardner's innovative multiple intelligences framework is readily applicable to our clinical work with adolescents and their families. I like to use Gardner's ideas in two areas: in my therapeutic conversations, and in experiment design and selection. In the therapeutic conversation, it can greatly enhance the engagement process, create a positive emotional climate, and help build a cooperative relationship with adolescents and their parents when therapists take a strong interest in family members' key intelligence areas and converse in the metaphors and language that fit these areas. The following case example illustrates how to utilize a youth's key intelligence area to foster a cooperative relationship and design an on-target therapeutic experiment that empowers him to resolve his own difficulties.

Cedric, a 16-year-old African American adolescent, was passionate about playing football and starred on his high school football team. I asked him about the position he played on his team, why he liked to play that position, details about how he performed with excellence in that position, and details about some of his best games. Our conversations about his talents as a running back and my use of such football metaphors and lingo as "spinning off of would-be tacklers" and "seeking daylight" sparked positive emotions in him, reduced his defensiveness, and moved us away from dwelling on the negative behaviors that brought him into family therapy. Since Cedric clearly excelled in the bodily–kinesthetic intelligence area (Gardner, 1993, 1999), I collaborated with him and his parents on a therapeutic ritual in which he would have the opportunity to use his talents to "score touchdowns" with his parents over the next week. The parents came up with specific things their son could do to score those touchdowns with them, such as "no phone calls from the school" for being disruptive in class, talking to them in "a respectful way," and "doing his chores without reminders." In our next family session, Cedric enthusiastically and proudly reported that he had scored three touchdowns with his parents. According to my client, he had found "a lot of daylight" and "spun off his parents' attempts to tackle" him in the game. The parents were not only pleased with their son's progress, but they found him to be "too quick to handle on the playing field." Since we had had such success with this ritual on the home front, the family, the concerned school staff, and I decided to implement the same "game plan" at school to empower Cedric to resolve his disruptive behavioral difficulties there.

Figure 1.1 provides practical guidelines for matching eight of the major intelligence areas with therapeutic experiment design and selection. I describe the preferences for and key skills of each intelligence area and offer some specific examples of therapeutic experiments and rituals that match well with the intelligence areas of the client. These guidelines can also be used when designing and selecting experiments for parents as well.

The Adolescent's Social Network: Involving Key Resource People in Family Therapy

Surprisingly, many therapists fail to consider the involvement of the adolescent's concerned peers and adult inspirational others in their individual and family therapy sessions. For over a decade, I have been successfully involving my adolescent clients' peers in their treatment (Selekman, 1991, 1995, 2002, 2004). Not only have they generated very creative and high-quality solutions in our sessions, but also they have helped the clients stay on track outside the office. The concerned peers' involvement in family sessions can accomplish the following:

1. Help rebuild trust between the adolescent and his or her parents.
2. Provide the adolescent's parents with "newsworthy" information regarding his or her improvement in multiple social contexts outside the home.
3. The peers can share their wisdom and expertise regarding how they resolved similar difficulties with their parents.
4. They can participate and share their expertise in family–multiple helper collaborative meetings.
5. They can greatly aid in the relapse prevention and goal-maintenance process.
6. They can pair up with the adolescent's inspirational others and serve as a solid support system for him or her in the various social contexts in which he or she is experiencing difficulties.

Eight Major Intelligence Areas	Linguistic	Logical–Mathematical	Visual–Spatial	Bodily–Kinesthetic	Musical	Interpersonal	Intrapersonal	Naturalist
Preferences and Key Skills	Likes reading, writing, speaking, and listening to stories and speakers; speaks and writes effectively.	Likes to find patterns, make calculations, forming and testing hypotheses; skilled with numbers and inductive and deductive reasoning.	Likes to express self through drawing, painting, collaging, and sculpting; strong imagination powers and skilled at creating through visual means.	Expresses self best through dance, athletics, and drama. Prides self on his/her strength, balance, grace, speed, flexibility, and great physical coordination.	Likes to express self best by singing, writing, and playing music; skilled at creating and analyzing music.	Possesses strong social skills; likes to work with people and help them identify and overcome their problems.	Strong in the area of self-awareness, introspection, setting goals, self-regulation, and good at monitoring his or her thoughts.	Loves nature, animals, hiking, climbing, and camping out; concerned about environmental causes.
Therapeutic Experiments That Fit with the Key Intelligence Areas of the Client	Journaling, expressing oneself through creative writing and poetry; therapeutic use of storytelling and metaphor; responding to narrative therapy-informed questions and experiments; involvement in teen leadership programs.	Observing and graphing patterns of behavior; playing detective and searching for clues or evidence to support his or her beliefs; keeping logs on specific behaviors; and therapeutic use of scaling and percentage questions, and the invisible family inventions experiment.	Therapeutic use of visualization, the imaginary time machine, the imaginary feelings x-ray machine, pretend the miracle happened, interviewing the problem, family sculpting and choreography, my family story mural and other art therapy experiments, and the famous guest consultant experiment.	Therapeutic use of dance, sports and theatrical metaphors with questions and designed experiments, family sculpting and choreography, pretend the miracle happened, and habit control ritual.	Have client bring in music that will tell you more about him or her as a person; have client write a song about his or her situation; have the client perform for you or have a jam session in your office together.	Therapeutic use of family sculpting and choreography, the famous guest consultant experiment, habit control ritual, experiments designed to foster connection building, and involvement in teen leadership programs doing prevention work or serving as a mentor.	Enjoys learning mindfulness meditation, visualization, journaling about his or her feelings, A-B-C cognitive therapy framework, creating self-talk tapes, and may respond well to the imaginary feelings x-ray machine experiment.	Therapeutic use of nature metaphors, experiments designed to study patterns in nature and reflect on his or her experience, and the use of visualizing special experiences out in nature as a coping strategy; have client bring into office his or her favorite pet, or help client get involved with animal rights and environmental causes in his or her community.

FIGURE 1.1. Guidelines for matching therapeutic experiments with key client intelligence areas.

With adolescents that are affiliated with unsavory negative peer groups, I will introduce the idea of bringing in former adolescent clients that used to have similar difficulties to serve as a temporary peer support group for them until they can make some new friends. These alumni experts have valuable wisdom and suggestions they can offer these adolescents to help them turn their lives around.

After the adolescent and his or her parents agree to the idea of bringing in the concerned peers, I secure written consent both from the clients and the peers' parents to involve them in the treatment process. The rules of confidentiality are discussed and included on the consent form.

The adolescents' inspirational others (Selekman, 2002; Anthony, 1984, 1987) can also be valuable resource people to engage in the treatment process. The inspirational other can be a teacher, a coach, a close friend of the family, a clergyman, a community leader, a camp counselor, a neighbor, and so forth. These inspirational others have made themselves available with support, have offered valuable words of wisdom, and have served as advocates for the adolescents. Research indicates that the involvement of inspirational others with at-risk children and adolescents serves a resiliency protective function (Anthony, 1984, 1987). As mentioned above, once involved in treatment the inspirational other and concerned friends of the adolescent can join forces and establish a tight-knit support system for him or her in a social context that he or she continues to experience difficulties in, such as at school.

In case situations where the adolescents do not have inspirational others and they have highly strained or emotionally disconnected relationships with their parents, I have recruited former adolescent clients' inspirational others to play these supportive roles in their lives. Fostering this meaningful connection with caring and committed adults outside the home has helped many of my clients to cope better with specific stressors in their lives and resolve their difficulties. Before involving inspirational others in the treatment process, I get written consent from the adolescent and his or her parents to involve the inspirational other in our sessions. The inspirational others also agree to protect the adolescent's confidentiality and sign a special significant other consent form that I have developed.

Les, a 15-year-old white adolescent, had a long history of inpatient and outpatient treatment for depression, anxiety, and self-harming behavior. He was rejected and bullied a lot by his school peers. However, he had two concerned members of his social network in the school: Jennie, a close peer friend, and his computer graphics teacher, Mr. Robertson. According to Les, Jennie was the "best friend" he had ever had. Mr. Robertson was Les's favorite teacher, because he was "always caring" and taught him some "cool stuff" on the computer. Les identified Mr. Robertson as his main inspirational other. As a way to stabilize Les's "emotional meltdowns" and self-harming episodes at school, I actively collaborated with Mr. Robertson and Jennie to create a supportive crisis intervention plan for helping Les quickly get out of harm's way when he was in a bad place. Since the school social worker and Les's dean were at a loss about how to manage his "emotional meltdowns" and "cutting" episodes, they were completely supportive of my idea. The plan Jennie, Mr. Robertson, and I came up with consisted of making themselves available to Les for impromptu meetings with the two of them or individually, and providing Les "chill-out time" on the computer to externalize his disturbing thoughts and feelings into the creation of new graphic designs. Both of these strategies completely eliminated his "emotional meltdowns" and "cutting" episodes at school.

The Mind As Ally: Mindfulness Meditation Training for Adolescents

According to Mipham (2003), our *bewildered mind* is like "a wild horse." He says:

> It runs away when we try to find it, shies when we try to approach it. If we find a way to ride it, it takes off with a bit in its teeth and finally throws us right into the mud. We think that the only way to steady it is to give it what it wants. We spend so much of our energy trying to satisfy and entertain this wild horse of a mind. (pp. 18–19)

Many of the adolescents referred to me that are presenting with serious problems with anger management, depression, anxiety, and eating-distressed, self-harming, and substance-abusing difficulties have described their thoughts and emotional patterns as being like "wild horses" in their heads. When faced with major stressors in their lives, they often report being oppressed by repetitive, self-defeating thoughts and waves of unpleasant emotions, which often lead to their adopting a position of helplessness or engaging in behaviors designed to numb away the emotional distress. Goleman (2003) has found in his research that some individuals have a sped-up amygdale (the emotions center of the brain), which makes them highly susceptible to overwhelming *emotional hijacking* experiences. This takes the form of being flooded by waves of intense and unpleasant emotions. Some of the adolescents I have worked with turn to the use of food, the razor, or their drug of choice to combat their emotional hijacking episodes. Unfortunately, these attempted solutions to secure quick emotional relief become habitual and lead to serious physical, psychological, and social consequences for them.

Once I have developed a relationship with an adolescent experiencing emotional hijacking and self-soothing difficulties, I introduce him or her to *mindfulness meditation* (Hanh, 2001, 2003a, 2003b; Goleman, 2003; Bennett-Goleman, 2001; Bennett-Goleman & Goleman, 2001; Kabat-Zinn, 1990, 1995). I explain to the adolescent the following:

> "When one is truly mindful, he or she is totally focused on a specific object, bodily sensation, or mantra. A mantra consists of a word or line maybe from one of your favorite tunes that you select to say to yourself to help you to chill out when stressed. However, being mindful also means embracing all that occurs in the moment, including self-defeating 'stinkin thinking' thoughts and unpleasant emotions. These thoughts and feelings are like welcomed guests and labeled by us ('There goes a depressed thought'), and can visit our minds for as long as they wish, as we continue to focus our attention on a specific object, bodily sensation, or our mantra. By adopting a mindfulness way of living, life stressors affect us less and self-defeating 'stinkin thinking' thoughts and negative emotions that enter our minds can be quickly neutralized."

Most adolescents I have exposed to Buddhist principles and mindfulness meditation have thought this was a "cool thing to learn." There are a number of different types of mindfulness meditations. After demonstrating and having the adolescent practice in my office a variety of mindfulness meditations, he or she can choose which one or couple of meditations he or she would like to practice using at home. In order to become a skilled meditator, I like to have the adolescent practice twice a day for 10–15 minutes each time, depending on the mindfulness meditation used. The first practice session should occur right after getting up in the morning to "chill" him or her out for the school day. The second practice session should be before he or she goes to bed. This can help to soothe the adolescent and calm his or her mind before going to sleep. Some examples of mindfulness meditations I like to teach adolescents are as follows:

1. *The food meditation.* This consists of nestling a raisin in the left palm of the adolescent. The youth is to carefully study the raisin by looking closely at its shape, crevices, varying shades of brown coloring, and the shadowing around it. Next, the youth is to pick up the raisin with his or her other hand and roll it around in his or her fingertips, feeling its indentations and describing in his or her mind the sensations he or she experiences while doing this step. The next step is to slowly place the raisin in his or her mouth, but he or she is not allowed to bite down on it yet. He or she is only to pay attention to the salivation effect that occurs in his or her mouth and to slowly roll the raisin around with his or her tongue and teeth. After a few minutes, he or she is to bite down on the raisin and experience its sweet

or tart flavor and slowly chew it up without swallowing it. Next, he or she is to swallow the raisin and play close attention to the sensations he or she experiences in his or her esophagus. Finally, once the raisin enters his or her stomach, he or she is to pay close attention to the sensations he or she experiences as the raisin is being digested. Each step needs to be done slowly for approximately 2–3 minutes. The meditation takes about 12 minutes to do (Bennett-Goleman & Goleman, 2001).

2. *The sound meditation.* This consists of having the adolescent adopt a comfortable position on a couch, chair, or lying down on the floor. He or she is to close his or her eyes and carefully tune in to the various types of sounds he or she hears around him or her. The adolescent is not to get too attached to any one sound but just label the sounds in his or her mind. This meditation should be 10–12 minutes in duration (Bennett-Goleman & Goleman, 2001).

3. *Mindful breathing.* This meditation increases our awareness of our breathing patterns and puts us more in touch with ourselves and the world around us. Hanh (2003a, p. 19) recommends that we say the following sentences to ourselves while breathing consciously and doing this meditation:

- "Breathing in, I am aware only of my in breath. Breathing out, I am aware only of my out breath . . . In, out."
- "Breathing in, I am aware that my in breath grows deep. Breathing out, I am aware that my out breath grows deep . . . Deep, deep."
- "Breathing in, I am aware that my in breath goes slowly. Breathing out, I am aware that my out breath goes slowly . . . Slow, slow."

I have adolescents try this meditation for 12–15 minutes.

As Hanh (2003a, 2003b) contends, we would have a lot less violent world if everybody practiced loving kindness, compassion, and mindfulness meditation on a daily basis. He calls this type of community a "Sun God Community." In family therapy sessions and in my parenting groups, I like to teach parents how to use loving kindness and compassion with their adolescents and expose them to the benefits of mindfulness meditation to help them better cope with their stressful and challenging parental roles. Hanh (2003b) has demonstrated in a retreat format how the combination of teaching loving kindness, compassion, and mindfulness meditation can foster meaningful connections and peace between warring peoples. He recently demonstrated this with groups of Palestinians and Israelis.

Research indicates that once one becomes quite skilled in mindfulness meditation, the following physiological changes can occur: our breathing, heart rates, and blood pressure are considerably lowered, we are less emotionally reactive to environmental stressors because our amygdale have been cooled and slowed down, and our concentration, self-awareness, problem-solving, and creative capacities are strengthened (Bennett-Goleman & Goleman, 2001; Goleman, 2003). With the help of mindfulness meditation, adolescents learn how to use their minds as allies in helping them better cope with the multitude of stressors in their lives.

Doing *What Works:* Integrating Empirically Validated Findings from Psychotherapy and Family Therapy Outcome Research into Our Clinical Practices

Another important way I have expanded the solution-oriented brief family therapy model is integrating key treatment findings from 40 years of psychotherapy outcome studies (Beutler & Harwood, 2000; Beutler, Moliero, & Taleb; 2002; Norcross, 2002; Snyder, Rand, & Sigmon, 2002; Snyder, Michael, & Cheavens, 1999; McDermott & Snyder, 1999; Duncan & Miller, 2000; Hubble et al., 1999; Lambert, 2003; Lambert & Barley, 2002; Asay & Lambert, 1999; Bohart & Tallman, 1999; Prochaska & Norcross, 2002; Prochaska, 1999; Prochaska, Norcross, & Diclemente, 1994; Frank & Frank, 1991) and empirically validated family therapy outcome research with adolescents with serious emotional and behavioral problems over the past decade (Henggeler, Schoenwald, Rowland, & Cunningham, 1998, 2002; Henggeler & Sheidow, 2002; Liddle, 2002; Rowe & Liddle, 2002; Sexton & Alexander, 2002; Alexander, Pugh, & Parsons, 1998; Szapocznik & Williams, 2000). I now elaborate on some of the key findings from these two important bodies of research and how they can inform our clinical practices and help us be more effective in treating challenging adolescents and their families. This is followed by a case example to help illustrate how to utilize these key research findings in identifying major client strengths to capitalize on and with multisystems level treatment planning.

The Common Factors: Four Key Elements of Positive Treatment Outcomes

There are four major factors that have been found in rigorous psychotherapy outcome studies to be the core elements that contribute to treatment success, they are *extratherapeutic factors*, *relationship factors*, *hope and expectancy factors*, and *models and techniques*.

Extratherapeutic Factors. These have to do solely with what clients bring to us, such as their strengths and resources, resiliency protective factors, theories of change, their treatment preferences and expectations, stages of readiness for change, random events that helped improve their situations, and client-generated pretreatment changes (Beutler, Harwood, et al., 2002; Duncan & Miller, 2000; Hubble et al., 1999; Prochaska & Norcross, 2002). This common factor counts for 40% of positive treatment outcomes (Hubble et al., 1999). Interestingly enough, research indicates that it is the client that is the most important variable when it comes to positive treatment outcomes. Therefore, the therapist's expertise should be in eliciting the client's expertise.

Relationship Factors. These have a lot to with the therapist's ability to create a therapeutic climate ripe for change, such as having good listening skills, validating the client's thoughts and feelings, use of empathy, warmth, being genuine, conveying concern, and caring behavior (Norcross, 2002; Lambert, 2003; Lambert & Barley, 2002). The therapist's *structuring skills* have been rated as important by clients (Sexton & Alexander, 2002; Alexander et al, 1998). This important set of relationship skills has to do with the therapist's having the ability to take charge in sessions when necessary, displaying competence, and timing with changing the session format, such as working with subsystems. Relationship factors count for 30% of positive treatment outcomes (Hubble et al., 1999).

Hope and Expectancy Factors. This common factor area has to do with the client's belief in the therapist's abilities and procedures to be of help to him or her (Snyder et al., 1999, 2002; Frank & Frank, 1991). The therapist has successfully engendered hope by conveying his or her expectancy that the client *will* change and it is only a matter of *when*. This common factor counts for 15% of positive treatment outcomes (Hubble et al., 1999).

Models and Techniques. Surprisingly, only 15% of what counts for positive treatment outcomes has to do with the choice therapy models and techniques that therapists like to use in their clinical practices. Some clients will report in treatment outcome studies specific aspects or techniques employed by their therapists that they found to be most beneficial in helping them. However, for the most part, clients tend to offer much more feedback on therapeutic relationship variables than anything else (Hubble et al., 1999). Technically skilled therapists are more likely to accurately match their therapeutic experiments and other therapeutic actions with family members' theories of change, stages of readiness to change, problem explanations, and unique learning styles, which can help to foster cooperative relationships and promote change with them (Hubble et al.,

1999; Prochaska, 1999; Conoley, Ivey, Conoley, Schmeel, & Bishop, 1992; Reimers, Wacker, Cooper, & De Raad, 1992; Gardner, 1993).

Key Findings from Empirically Validated Family Therapy Outcome Studies

Four major federally funded, empirically validated, family-based ecological treatment approaches have been identified as "best-practice" models for adolescents with serious conduct, delinquency, and substance abuse difficulties. They are *multisystemic therapy* (Henggeler & Sheidow, 2002; Henggeler et al., 1998, 2002), *functional family therapy* (Sexton & Alexander, 2002; Alexander et al., 1998), *multidimensional family therapy* (Liddle, 2002; Rowe & Liddle, 2002) and *brief strategic family therapy* (Szapocznik & Williams, 2000). All four of these empirically validated family therapy models are integrative and theoretically operate from the core assumptions that severe adolescent behavioral difficulties are multidetermined and that therapists using these approaches need to intervene on multiple levels of the youth's social ecology. For the sake of brevity, I now will summarize some of the major treatment outcome findings from these empirically validated family therapy approaches that can inform our clinical practices with challenging adolescents and their families:

1. The therapist needs to be highly active and have strong relationship and structuring skills.
2. A careful multisystemic family assessment needs to be conducted with the family to determine at what systems levels the therapist needs to target his or her interventions in the adolescent's social ecology.
3. It is important to be sensitive to adolescent developmental and family life cycle issues.
4. When therapists are successful at strengthening the emotional connections between the adolescent and his or her parents or caretakers, he or she will be least likely to initiate involvement with a negative peer group or discontinue his or her affiliation with it.
5. Therapists need to be sensitive to their clients' social injustice, cultural, and gender issues and the role they play in maintaining the youth's and families' difficulties.
6. Therapists need to actively collaborate with involved helping professionals from larger systems and concerned others from the clients' social networks.

By being sensitive to and incorporating the important psychotherapy and empirically validated family therapy research findings mentioned above into our clinical practices, not only can the engagement and ongoing therapeutic process go more smoothly with our clients, but also it can help us maximize better treatment outcomes in our collaborative work with them. The case example below illustrates how these important research findings can inform our clinical thinking, use of self, and the strategies and techniques we choose to employ in the therapeutic process.

Ernie, a 14-year-old African American youth, was referred to me by his school social worker for "aggressive and threatening behaviors," "fighting with his peers," and "poor grades" in some of his major subjects. Ernie and his mother, Sandra, had been referred to me as "an alternative to Ernie's being suspended for fighting" and "intimidating" one of his teachers by "tearing up a workbook" in front of her "when angry." Ernie's parents had been divorced since he was 7 years old, and his father had completely dropped out of the picture until recently. Apparently, the father had resurfaced and had had some visitation time with Ernie. Although Sandra had some concerns about this, she felt that it was important that Ernie have a relationship with his father. The family used to live in an African American inner-city community before moving into Ernie's present school district. I explored with them if they had experienced any difficulties moving into a mostly white community. Both Sandra and Ernie shared that they felt like it was "tough to make friends." Ernie pointed out that in the former "'hood" (neighborhood) where he lived fighting was commonplace, particularly if someone "dissed you" (put you down). Ernie further added, "If you didn't fight, you got your butt kicked!" He shared how things were very different in his present school and "'hood." Sandra reported that "Ernie had a mouth on him" and in the past used to "physically push" her around. She reported that Ernie had been in counseling twice before for the "same problems." I asked the family how they felt about working with a white therapist. Neither Sandra nor Ernie had voiced any concerns about this. Sandra thanked me for asking her about this. I wanted to check this out with them, since their former therapists were also white.

In an attempt to establish an initial treatment goal with Sandra and Ernie, I asked the miracle question (de Shazer, 1988). Sandra reported a recent miracle-like occurrence where Ernie went a whole evening without once "snapping at" her, treated her in a "respectful way," and they "enjoyed" each other's company. In fact, Sandra was so pleased and encouraged by Ernie's positive behavior that she wrote a whole page in her journal about it. I asked her if she wrote her entry in the journal in gold, and she indicated that she put "a big star next to it in the margin." I asked Ernie if he was aware of how he and his mother got along so well the night before, and he pointed out that she was not nagging him about anything. In response to the miracle question, Ernie went off on a long monologe about how he and his father would be "doing a lot of fun things together" and he would "get to better know" his paternal aunts and uncles. Sandra was almost in a trance listening intently to Ernie's discussion about his relationship with his father and where he wanted to see it go in the future. This was a newsworthy experience for Sandra, in that Ernie never said a word to her about his father or how his visits went with him. When I asked the two of them "How will you know that you really succeeded in counseling?" Sandra replied that it was "already happening" and Ernie had taken "a big step" in that direction in our meeting and the night before. Ernie and his mother left the session very encouraged and hopeful about the new direction they were taking in their lives.

In reflecting on this initial family session, there were two important *extratherapeutic* factors that I capitalized on: client self-generated pretreatment changes and the mother's use of journaling. Through eliciting all the details about the pretreatment changes, I was able to find out what works best in the mother–son relationship and have them increase these solution-building patterns. Once I learned about Sandra's use of journaling as a coping strategy, I had her bring in her journal to the next session to see what other parenting treasures it contained. I was delighted to discover that her journal was loaded with lots of valuable nuggets of wisdom about what she did that seemed to work with Ernie, and she had documented several times in the prior 2 weeks encouraging and responsible things she saw her son do. Sandra agreed to experiment more with some of the "parenting moves" described in her journal that promoted more compliant and responsible behaviors. I used the relationship skills of humor, validation, warmth, and empathy to help create a climate ripe for change (relationship factors). The common factor of *hope and expectancy* also was present in this first session. Both Sandra and Ernie were very hopeful that their situation would continue to improve.

In regard to intervening in Ernie's social ecology, I secured a written consent from the family to begin actively collaborating with his principal, school social worker, and teachers to help improve their relationships with him and improve his school functioning. Sandra was totally supportive of my doing sessions with Ernie and his father and the paternal aunts and uncles. Ernie voiced a strong desire to strengthen his connections with his father and "get to better know" his adult siblings. It was clear in our first session that Ernie was longing to have his father more present in his life. Ernie also made a commitment to learn how to better manage his anger. I taught him mindfulness meditation (Hanh, 2001) and disputation skills (Seligman et al., 1995; Seligman, 2003) to help him "chill out" when he was angry or frustrated. In addition, I wanted to explore with the family whether they had encountered any form of racism at the school or in their community. The family did not report any concerns about experiencing any racist people at this time. It was interesting to note how fighting was about survival on the streets in Ernie's former "'hood." When collaborating with the school staff, I wanted them to be aware of this important cultural dimension to Ernie's aggressive reactions and fighting behavior. By intervening on all of these systems levels throughout the course of treatment, we collectively were able to effectuate dramatic improvement in Ernie's behavior both at home and at school.

SUMMARY

In this chapter, I have discussed the various ways I have further expanded my solution-oriented brief family therapy model to create possibilities with complicated and complex adolescent case situations. I have stressed the importance of keeping a strong emphasis on client strengths and adopting a multisystemic focus on determining at what systems levels to intervene in the adolescent's social ecology. In other chapters I go into more detail about the engagement process regarding challenging adolescents and their families, the therapist's use of self, various therapeutic experiments and team strategies, and how to establish successful collaborative relationships with key members of the adolescents' social networks and involved larger systems professionals.

Two

Guiding Assumptions with an Eye on Solutions

> We must look for the opportunity in every difficulty, instead of being paralyzed at the thought of the difficulty in every opportunity.
>
> —WALTER E. COLE

In this chapter I present 10 useful solution-oriented assumptions. The assumptions are highly pragmatic and offer therapists a new lens for viewing the difficult adolescent case. Each of the guiding assumptions provides a wellness perspective on adolescent problems, families, and brief therapy.

ASSUMPTION 1: Resistance is not a useful concept.

The traditional psychotherapeutic concept of *resistance* is an unhelpful idea that has handicapped therapists (de Shazer, 1984). It implies that the client does not want to change and the therapist is separate from the client system he or she is treating. De Shazer (1982, 1984) has argued convincingly for therapists to approach each new client case from a position of therapist–client cooperation rather than focusing on resistance, power, and control. Operating from a similar perspective, Prochaska and his colleagues (1994) have empirically demonstrated that by carefully matching what we do therapeutically with the unique stage of readiness for change that the client is presently in helps to foster a cooperative relationship very rapidly. As therapists, we are always observing ourselves in relation to the client systems we are treating. We can never find an outside place from which to observe our clients (Hoffman, 1988). According to de Shazer (1982):

> Each family (individual or couple) shows a unique way of attempting to cooperate and the therapist's job becomes, first, to describe that particular manner to himself that the family shows and, then, to cooperate with the family's way and, thus, to promote change. (pp. 9–10)

Like Columbo, the TV detective, we need to listen and observe carefully to find clues that help identify our clients' unique cooperative response patterns. These clues take the form of how family members respond to our questions verbally and nonverbally as well as how they manage proposed therapeutic experiments between sessions. Once important clues have been discovered, the therapist should continue to match his or her questions and therapeutic experiments with family members' unique ways of cooperating. For example, if a parent is highly pessimistic about a daughter's delinquent behavior ever changing, the therapist should assume an equally pessimistic stance, particularly if previous attempts to have the mother identify nonproblem patterns of behavior (exceptions) or hypothetical future solutions proved to be futile. The therapist could ask the following questions: "How come things are not worse with your daughter?" "What steps are you taking to prevent things from getting much worse?" If family members are given a therapeutic experiment and they modify it, this helpful clue tells the therapist that future experiments need to be modifiable for this particular family. Our clients want to cooperate with us; however, we have to be careful not to be resistant therapists!

Erickson (Gordon & Meyers-Anderson, 1981) shared a wonderful story with his hypnotherapy trainees that captures the essence of the cooperation principle:

> I was returning from high school one day and a runaway horse with his bridle on sped past a group of us into a farmer's yard, looking for a drink of water. I hopped on the horse's back. . . . Since he had a bridle on, I managed to take hold of the thick rein and said "Giddy up!" . . . headed for the highway. I knew the horse would turn in the right direction. . . . I didn't know what the right direction was. And the horse trotted and galloped along. Now and then he would forget he was on the highway and start into a field. So I would pull on him a bit and call his attention to the fact the highway was where he was supposed to be. And finally, about four miles from where I boarded him, he turned into a farm yard and the farmer said, "So that's how that critter came back! Where did you find him?" I said, "About four miles from here." "How did you know you should come here?" I said, "I didn't know, the horse knew . . . all I did was keep his attention on the road." (p. 166)

For Erickson, the horse story served as a great metaphor for how therapists should conduct therapy. Young Erickson's experience teaches us that it is easier to ride the horse in the direction that it wants to go.

ASSUMPTION 2: Cooperation is inevitable.

Besides carefully matching our questions and therapeutic experiments with our clients' unique cooperative response patterns and stages of readiness to change, there are several important rapport-building tools that therapists can utilize to further enhance the cooperation process. Therapists can first and foremost utilize whatever their clients bring to therapy—their strengths and resources, key client words and belief system material, their theories of change, their stages of readiness to change, as well as their metaphors and family themes (Prochaska, 1999; Hubble et al., 1999; Gordon & Meyers-Anderson, 1981; de Shazer, 1985). The following case example demonstrates the efficacy of the utilization strategy.

Joe, a single parent, brought his two adolescent children for therapy due to their stealing, lying, and failure to follow his "household rules." Joe had grown up in an "alcoholic family," and the children's mother was an "alcoholic." Joe and his ex-wife had been divorced for 5 years. Joe attended "seven Al-Anon meetings every week" and demanded that his two children also "work their own recovery programs" by regularly attending Alateen. The more Joe would force his children to go to Alateen, the more they would resist, steal, lie, and not follow his rules. In an attempt to disrupt this repetitive pattern of interaction, I shared with Joe that I had recently heard about a study at a big-name university that actually demonstrated that it is possible to "enable" your children to engage in "children of alcoholics" behaviors like "stealing and lying," and what he needed to do is "detach with love." Once Joe began detaching from his children regarding demanding their involvement in Alateen, the children not only stopped acting out, but they would spontaneously surprise him by occasionally asking to be taken to Alateen meetings.

With Joe's case, I had successfully utilized key client language and belief material from Joe's many years of involvement in Al-Anon to co-create a new construction of Joe's problem situation, a frame that was more acceptable to his worldview. Once Joe's thinking changed about how he viewed the problem, his parental behavior dramatically changed as well.

Tools for Fostering Cooperation

Positive relabeling is another useful therapeutic tool that can foster a cooperative climate and reduce client defensiveness (Barton & Alexander, 1981). An angry parent's behavior can be positively relabeled by the therapist as demonstrating a high level of concern and commitment toward resolving the presenting problem. A withdrawn adolescent can be positively relabeled as being a thoughtful adolescent.

Other useful rapport-building tools for fostering therapist–client cooperation are purposive use of self-disclosure, the use of humor, normalizing, demonstrating cultural and gender sensitivity, and therapeutic compliments. Mark Twain once said, "Against the assault of laughter nothing can stand." Humor can help create a relaxed atmosphere, distance the client from his or her concerns, and heal those in pain. Madanes (1984) contends that "what makes change possible is the therapist's ability to be optimistic and to see what is funny or appealing in a grim situation" (p. 137).

Family life-cycle changes and normative crises can contribute to the development of adolescent and family difficulties. By normalizing these difficulties, family members can be put at ease and begin to entertain new ways of looking at their problem situation. For example, I frequently normalize for parents the adolescent's rebellious behavior, drug experimentation, or other acting-out behaviors that may follow a parental divorce.

Finally, I like to compliment each family member on the various coping strategies and productive steps they have taken toward resolving the presenting problem. Therapeutic compliments and cheerleading (de Shazer, 1985, 1988) empower clients by providing them with positive reinforcement for their creative problem-solving efforts. Each compliment is carefully interspersed with key client words, belief system material, metaphors, or positively relabeled negative behavior. Both the compliments and the interventions designed or selected for a particular family grow out of the interviewing process. Typically, the compliments are constructed by the therapist during his or her intersession break 10–15 minutes before the conclusion of the therapy session. However, I also like to give spontaneous in-session compliments to family members as well. These in-session compliments may take the form of "high fives" or handshakes for adolescents who have taken responsible steps prior to entering treatment or during the course of therapy. With parents, I may give handshakes to further reinforce their productive problem-solving efforts as well. The "high fives" and handshakes are useful in conjunction with other cheerleading responses by the therapist. The therapist can respond to client exceptions with: "What did you tell yourself to pull that off?!" "Wow! Are you aware of how you did that!?" "How did you come up with that creative idea!?" "How" questions have clients compliment themselves on their resourcefulness.

During the therapist consultation break, the clients, while waiting in the lobby area, are often anticipating a "doom and gloom" presentation by the therapist. Parents who have already experienced failure in therapy typically assume that they will be blamed for their adolescents' problems. The adolescent clients may anticipate that they will be blamed for the family problems or that an argument will erupt when the session is reconvened. Much to family members' surprise, the therapist delivers an empowering message of hope and encouragement to them, which heightens their motivation levels and commitment to the therapeutic process. Well-constructed compliments can produce head nods or "yes-set" hypnotic responses (de Shazer, 1985) from family members. These nonverbal hypnotic responses indicate that the compliments are either acceptable to or come close to fitting family members' beliefs about their situation and will most likely lead to the family's compliance with the assigned therapeutic task. For example, the therapist compliments a mother for bringing her first-time court-involved son to therapy in an effort to take "preventative measures," thereby preventing his legal difficulties from escalating into a future incarceration. The son in this case would be complimented for "showing up" for the session and being "responsible."

ASSUMPTION 3: Change is inevitable.

Buddhists have professed for centuries that change is a continuous process and that stability is an illusion (Mitchell, 1988). If you expect that change will occur with your clients, your expectancy of change will influence their behavior. The therapist's belief in the client's ability to change can be a significant determinant of treatment outcome (Leake & King, 1977). Motivational researchers have found that one of the most important factors with motivated subjects is their self-perception that they are in fact doing well with task assignments (Peters & Waterman, 1982). Jones (1977) studied two groups of adults that were given the same 10 puzzles to solve. After having the subjects turn in their puzzles for scoring, half of the subjects were told that they did well on the puzzles, whereas the other half of the subjects were told they did poorly. The subjects were then given another 10 puzzles to solve. The half of the subjects that were told that they had fared well on the first set of puzzles ended up doing much better on the second set than did the other group. Similar studies have been conducted in the school context. One study demonstrated that when teachers believed that their students would do well on an IQ test, those students scored 25 points higher on their tests than other students with different teachers (Bennis, 1976).

In the context of brief therapy, it is helpful to think *when* change will occur with our clients rather than *if* it will happen. We need to co-create positive self-fulfilling prophecies with our clients. Gingerich and his colleagues (1988) have demonstrated in their interviewing research that there is a direct relationship between therapist "change talk" and positive treatment outcomes. The "change talk" therapists in the study used presuppositional language such as "when" and "will" rather than "if" and "would," and they spent the majority of their session time having clients talk about past, present, and future successes. The "problem talk" therapists, on the other hand, were lost in a sea of information about past and present problems. The "problem talk" cases tended to have negative treatment outcomes. There is sound empirical support for the deleterious effects of having clients work through their "bad" feelings in therapy. Snyder and White (1982) demonstrated in their study that depressed subjects tended to get more depressed when asked to talk about painful past events and encouraged to try to better understand their depression. The Milan Associates, in their clinical research with schizophrenics and their families, have observed that change cannot occur under a negative connotation (Boscolo, Cecchin, Hoffman, & Penn, 1987). Recently, Fredrickson (2002, 2003) has provided some solid empirical support for providing a positive therapeutic climate for clients. She has repeatedly demonstrated that, by creating a positive emotional climate in her laboratory with her experimental groups, they not only outperformed their control group counterparts in problem-solving tasks but also tended to be more optimistic when faced with adverse stressors in their lives.

Another important way therapists can co-create a context for change with families is through the use of humor and playfulness. Getting family members to laugh in one another's company can help them experience themselves together in a new way, which can open up the door for change.

ASSUMPTION 4: Only a small change is necessary.

Erickson believed that small changes will snowball into bigger changes (Gordon & Meyers-Anderson, 1981). Once clients are encouraged to value minimal changes, they are more likely to expect to make further changes. The Buddhist Lao-tzu believed strongly in this approach to problem solving, and he wrote: "Act without doing; work without effort. Think of the small as large and the few as many. Confront the difficult while it is still easy; accomplish the great task by a series of small acts" (in Mitchell, 1988, p. 63).

All parts of a family system are interconnected in such a way that a small change in one part of the system can ripple on and cause changes in the other parts. Szapocznik and his colleagues (Szapocznik & Williams, 2000; Szapocznik, Kurtines, Foote, Perez-Vidal, & Hervis, 1983, 1986), in their study for the National Institute on Drug Abuse, provided some empirical grounding for the idea that small changes can lead to systemwide changes in the family. The researchers had two groups of subjects; one group consisted only of the adolescent drug abusers, whereas the other group consisted of the drug abusers and their families. Both groups received a brief strategic family therapy treatment. Szapocznik and his colleagues found that the one-person group fared equally well on all treatment measures up to 3 years follow-up. Two important findings came out of this study: (1) it is possible to change an entire family system through one individual family member, and (2) it is not necessary to engage all family members for treatment in order to change the identified client. The latter finding challenges the longstanding family therapy rubric that all family members living under the same roof need to be engaged for treatment in order to change the identified client. Along these same lines, I have found it helpful to keep things simple and begin treatment with the nucleus of family members that present themselves for therapy. This is also another way to foster therapist–client cooperation.

Approximately 100 years ago, the Italian economist Vilfredo Pareto discovered the 80/20 principle, which provides further support for the importance of encouraging our clients to go for small changes and to simplify their efforts. Pareto found that a minority of the causes, inputs, or efforts usually lead to the majority of the results, outputs, or rewards (Koch, 1998). The case example below illustrates the 80/20 principle in action.

Jill, a single parent, discovered the power and effectiveness of the 80/20 principle once she moved away from unproductive yelling, lecturing, and imposing lengthy grounding periods on her underachieving and irresponsible son. Minimizing her efforts as a new tack, she decided to mimic her son's ways of responding to her, which typically took the form of being nonchalant and forgetful when it came to doing homework, chores, and sharing details regarding his whereabouts and actions outside the home. After she made this parental adjustment, not only did the son become more responsible for completing his homework and doing his chores, but he was much more forthcoming about important details regarding future school assignments and his social life outside the home. According to Jill, the son was experiencing grave difficulty coping with her new nonchalant and forgetful parenting style, particularly when it came to her forgetting that she had given him permission to participate in important activities with his friends!

ASSUMPTION 5: Clients have the strengths and resources to change.

American Health magazine once conducted a large, nationwide Gallup poll that surveyed how people best solve their problems. The vast majority of the people interviewed indicated that they were 10 times more likely to change on their own without the help of doctors, therapists, and self-help groups. Of the individuals surveyed, 30% reported that positive feelings, desires, and simply the recognition that the time has come for a big change were the motivating forces for them to give up such tenacious habits as cigarette smoking, overeating, and excessive drinking (Gurin, 1990). One of the most surprising findings was that only 3% of the time did doctors help these people change, whereas psychologists, psychiatrists, and self-help groups got even less credit for personal changes. Family members and close friends were ranked as providing the most support in helping with change (Gurin, 1990).

As the *American Health* survey demonstrates, all clients have strengths and resources that therapists can capitalize on in the co-construction of solutions. Any past successes that clients have had can serve as models for present and future successes. Clients are more likely to cooperate and change in a therapeutic context that accentuates their strengths and resourcefulness rather than one that focuses on problems and pathology. Beavers and Hampson (1990) found in their family therapy research that therapies that emphasize the power of families to possess the strengths and resources to solve their own problems tend to produce better outcome results than other therapies.

DeFrain and Stinnett (1992) and Stinnett and O'Donnell (1996) have developed a family wellness therapy approach based on their 20 years of researching what they call "strong families." These researchers elicited the subjects' expertise by asking such questions as "What are the strengths of your family?" and "What are areas of potential growth?" Based on the answers to such questions, they discovered six major qualities that these families possessed: (1) commitment, (2) appreciation and affection, (3) positive communication, (4) time together, (5) spiritual well-being, and (6) the ability to cope with stress and crisis. According to DeFrain and Stinnett (1992), "strong families are optimistic in the face of adversity and tend to view a crisis situation as being both a challenge and an opportunity for growth" (p. 22). Recently, these researchers demonstrated that their family wellness approach can be quite effective in improving family functioning with child abuse and domestic violence cases.

Wolin (1991) has also empirically demonstrated that individuals growing up in high-stress family environments can be "emboldened by adversity." Over a 20-year period, Wolin and his colleagues studied a large group of children of alcoholics. Of the sample, 85% grew up to become well-functioning adults. Wolin (1991) attributes the subjects' success to personal resilience and pride. Groundbreaking research such as Wolin's helps challenge the popular belief that children of alcoholics will grow up to become emotionally flawed adults.

More recently, Peterson and Seligman (2004) have identified in their research 24 character strengths and six virtues in individuals that we can educate our clients about, have them identify their top five signature strengths, and figure out together how they can deploy these strengths in areas of their lives where they may be experiencing difficulties. Furthermore, they recommend helping clients develop some of their 19 nonsignature strengths to enable them be more resilient in the face of life's demands and stressors, and create more fulfilled and meaningful lives.

With difficult adolescent clients, I have found it quite useful to place the adolescent in the position of an expert by asking him or her the following questions: "If I were to work with other teenagers just like you, what advice would you give me to help them out?" "What should I *not* do with them?" "What kinds of things should I avoid doing with them as a counselor?" "What kinds of things should I ask them about?" These types of open-ended questions can elicit the adolescent's strengths and expertise, help foster a cooperative relationship, and offer the therapist invaluable wisdom about helpful strategies for engaging and treating adolescents.

Another useful therapeutic strategy for capitalizing on the adolescent's expertise is to channel his or her strengths into the problem area. The following case example (Selekman, 1989a) best exemplifies this therapeutic strategy.

Robert and his mother pursued family therapy with the author because the former was heavily abusing alcohol. The mother was convinced that her son was an "alcoholic just like his father and grandfather." In the first interview, I discovered that Robert was a former "state wrestling champion" for his high school. I took a strong interest in Robert's wrestling abilities and inquired about his past "training regime." Throughout the interview, both the mother and Robert boasted about the latter's past illustrious wrestling career. However, the mother was quite worried that "the death grip of alcoholism was trying to claim Robert's life." Alcoholism was being described by the family as a three-generational oppressive monster! I decided to externalize (White & Epston, 1990) the alcoholism problem into the "alcohol monster." Sensing the family's love for wrestling and desire to conquer the alcohol monster, I developed a wrestling ritual using the wrestling scoring system: one point was an escape; two points was a reversal; and three points was a near pin. The family came up with their own scoring criterion—that is, Robert would receive three points from his coach (mother) if he would drink a soda rather than a beer with friends. At the end of each day, Robert was to report to his mother how well he scored in standing up to the alcohol monster. After three therapy sessions over a 2-month period, Robert and his mother had successfully pinned the alcohol monster. In fact, Robert rejoined his school wrestling team for his senior year and sported a 16–4 record.

Carl Hammerschlag, in his book *The Dancing Healers: A Doctor's Journey of Healing with Native Americans* (1988), shares with readers a valuable and humbling learning experience he had had as a psychiatrist while treating a Pueblo priest and clan chief named Santiago. Santiago had been admitted into Hammerschlag's hospital, dying from congestive heart failure. Upon meeting Santiago for the first time, Hammerschlag was asked by the priest, "Where did you learn to heal?" Hammerschlag quickly reeled off all of his many academic credentials. Santiago then asked, "Do you know how to dance?" Hammerschlag began to dance by Santiago's bedside. Santiago started laughing, got out of bed, and showed Hammerschlag how to dance. Santiago then said, "You must be able to dance if you are to heal people." Hammerschlag then asked, "And will you teach me your steps?" Santiago replied, "Yes, I can teach you my steps, but you will have to hear your own music" (pp. 9–10).

ASSUMPTION 6: Problems are unsuccessful attempts to resolve difficulties.

The Mental Research Institute theorists (Watzlawick et al., 1974) built their brief problem-focused therapy approach around the assumption that it is the client's attempted solution that is the problem. Family members are stuck viewing the problem in one particular way and engaging in the same repetitive patterns of interactions around the identified client. I like to share with parents that problems are like quicksand: the more they worry about them and frantically try to do something about them, the more they get swallowed up by them. To help increase parents' awareness of their part in inadvertently reinforcing the very troublesome behaviors they want resolved with their adolescents, I like to map out on a flip chart or sheet of paper how they and their kids get stuck doing *more of the same* when there are difficulties. This exercise can be an insightful experience for the parents in that they can visually see how the more superresponsible they are in relationship to their adolescent, the more superirresponsible he or she behaves. According to the MRI theorists (Watzlawick et al., 1974), there are three common ways clients mishandle their difficulties:

1. Action is necessary but is not taken.
2. Action is taken when it should not be.
3. Action is taken at the wrong logical level.

The first way of mishandling a problem is to behave as if it does not exist. By denying or minimizing the problem, any attempted solution to remedy the situation is perceived as being unnecessary. Thus, the problem becomes greatly compounded by the "problems" created through its mishandling (Watzlawick et al., 1974). The second type of mishandling has as its central theme the refusal to accept any proposed solution other than one based on a utopian belief that things "should be" a certain way, thus making the idea of going for small therapeutic changes an impossibility

(Bodin, 1981). The utopian extremist approach can frequently be seen with parents placing their rebellious acting-out adolescents in an inpatient psychiatric facility. Finally, the third type of mishandling takes the form of a "be spontaneous!" paradox (Watzlawick et al., 1974). For example, the more a father demands that his 16-year-old son be more affectionate toward his mother, the more the son fails because affection is a spontaneous behavior and cannot be forced.

The more restrained or stuck a family is in viewing their problem situation, the harder it is for new information to get into the system in order to alter outmoded beliefs and to change behavior. With chronic adolescent cases, the exceptions or nonproblem patterns of behavior often go unnoticed by family members and therapists, because they do not fit with the *dominant story* (White & Epston, 1990). In their problem-saturated stories, *the problem is the problem*, that is, the adolescent, the family members, and involved larger systems professionals have been brainwashed or coached by *the problem* to serve as its life support system.

With families that have had multiple past treatment experiences, it is important to inquire as to what family members liked and disliked about former therapists. I once worked with a 16-year-old chronic runaway who had had 16 therapy experiences in every type of treatment setting. This case exemplifies the importance of exploring past therapists' attempted solutions with a family.

Bonnie had been heavily abusing drugs and running away from state to state for 5 years. She had graduated from juvenile probation to adult parole status. Her mother was a recovering alcoholic and drug addict. The mother had been married five times and was quite happy with her fifth husband. In the first interview, I asked the family members what they did not like with their former therapists. The mother disclosed a recent negative experience she had had with a structural family therapist. The therapist had apparently balked at the mother's suggestion about having the stepfather serve as an active disciplinarian with her in a team effort. Bonnie shared with me that she gets "real mad" when therapists "side up" with her parents "against" her. This information proved to be quite useful to me in that I needed to operate differently as a therapist with Bonnie's family. For instance, I encouraged parental team work and gave Bonnie individual session time in the context of the family therapy sessions.

Avoiding "More of the Same"

Besides exploring past attempted parental and therapist solutions, the therapist needs to be cognizant of what he or she might be doing in treatment with a current case that might be *more of the same* (Watzlawick et al.,

1974). Often, when a therapist is feeling stuck, he or she might be asking questions and giving therapeutic tasks that may have already proved to be futile in earlier sessions or are too similar to what the parents have already tried in the past. When I'm feeling stuck with a particular family case, this is a signal to me that therapeutic improvisation is necessary. Therapeutic improvisation may take the form of storytelling, using humor, utilizing a therapeutic technique or task from a different therapy model, doing something dramatic, or changing the therapy context in some way, such as adding a reflecting team when working solo, changing the appointment time or day, or rearranging the office.

Outside of the therapy room, the therapist has to work collaboratively with the referring person and other involved helpers to negotiate realistic treatment goals for cases and maximize opportunities for them to notice changes in the identified client. In Chapter 8, I discuss this strategy in more detail.

Einstein believed that it is impossible to solve a problem with the same kind of thinking that created the problem. Solutions require a type of thinking and action outside the original problem explanations and problem-solving efforts.

ASSUMPTION 7: You do not need to know a great deal about the problem in order to solve it.

No problem happens all of the time; there may be hours, days, sometimes weeks when the identified client and his or her family are not being pushed around by the problem. With the analytic attention of a Sherlock Holmes, the therapist needs to investigate in great detail with each family member what he or she is doing differently during these nonproblem times.

In fact, often clients are well on their way to solving their problems before entering the therapy arena. McKeel (1999) and Allgood, Parham, Salts, and Smith (1995) have found in their research that not only are client self-generated pretreatment changes quite common but also when therapists amplify, consolidate, and build on their clients' pretreatment gains they are less likely to drop out of treatment until their goals are successfully achieved. Weiner-Davis and her colleagues (Weiner-Davis et al., 1987) found in their research that two-thirds of their sample had already taken some helpful steps toward resolving their presenting problems between the time of the phone call to the agency and the first session. I have conducted a similar study in my clinic in which each caller at intake was given a modified version of de Shazer's "formula first session task" (de Shazer, 1985). The intake specialist would give the calling parent the following pretreatment experiment to do on the telephone prior to the initial therapy session:

> "In order to better assist your therapist with knowing what your family strengths are, we would like you to notice what is happening in your relationship with your son/daughter that you would like to continue to have happen. Please write your observations down and bring your list to your first appointment with your therapist."

The exploratory study produced some interesting clinical results. In some cases, parents would cancel their initial therapy session appointments and leave such messages as: "I realized that things aren't that bad"; "I have a good relationship with my son"; "I want to hold off for a while." The majority of the cases involved with the research project ended up being one, two, or three session therapies. Many of the clients brought in long lists of "good things" that were already happening in their families. The therapists' main job with these cases was simply to capitalize on what was already working for the families by amplifying and consolidating pretreatment gains.

When exploring with family members about their exceptions, I not only ask questions about useful things they are doing and new ways of feeling about their situation but also inquire about helpful self-talk. Self-talk consists of useful tapes that family members play in their heads to help them to stand up to the problem. For example, I may ask an adolescent with anger management problems "What do you tell yourself to avoid allowing the anger to get the best of you?" or "What tape do you play in your head to help you stand up to the anger and not allow it to push you around?" The audio tape metaphor is particularly useful with adolescents.

Once important exception sequences of behavior and useful client self-talk have been identified, the therapist's job is to amplify this material through cheerleading, highlighting differences, and moving the clients into the future with presuppositional questions (O'Hanlon & Weiner-Davis, 1989). With some cases, I may bring out my trusty imaginary crystal ball and have family members discuss in great detail what further family changes they foresee 2–3 weeks down the road, through the crystal ball. The exceptions elicited by the therapist can serve as building blocks toward co-constructing solutions with clients. When the exception descriptions are placed next to the clients' problem-saturated construction of their situation, this will lead to clients making new discoveries about themselves and to what Bateson (1972) referred to as "news of a difference that makes a difference." Because there is a recursive relationship between meaning and action, a change in the client's view of the situation may lead to a change in his or her behavior.

On a cautionary note, with youth and families who have experienced a great deal of trauma in the past, are demoralized by their chronic difficulties, or have had multiple negative treatment experiences, we need to make sure we respectfully give these clients plenty of room to share their problem concerns and stories before we start inquiring about pretreatment changes and exceptions. Otherwise, these clients may feel slighted or invalidated, which will surely get in the way of fostering a cooperative therapeutic relationship.

ASSUMPTION 8: Clients define the goals for treatment.

If you do not know where you are going with your clients, you will end up somewhere else (O'Hanlon & Weiner-Davis, 1989). When stuck or frustrated with a particular case, the therapist may be lost in a sea of information about problems, he or she may not know what the client's treatment goal is, or the treatment goal may be too monolithic. Our job as therapists is to negotiate solvable problems and realistic treatment goals. We cannot change a "borderline" adolescent, but we can alter one of the presenting symptoms, such as self-mutilative behavior. As therapists, we need to point out to families that goals are the start of something new, not the end of something. We can see behaviors and observe behavioral changes over the course of treatment. It is important for the therapist to elicit from clients a videotaped description of how things will look when the presenting problem is solved (O'Hanlon & Weiner-Davis, 1989). Ideally, the client's videotaped description will contain the "who," "what," "when," and "how" of goal attainment. The more detailed the client's videotaped description is, including color and motion, the more likely we will be able to co-create with him or her a positive self-fulfilling prophecy.

When clients present for therapy, they often reel off a long laundry list of problems that they want to see resolved. The main task of the therapist is to have the family identify the problem it wants to see changed first. Once a problem is selected by the family as its initial focus of attention for treatment, the therapist needs to break down the treatment goal into something concrete, small, and changeable. For example, I once worked with a family case where the high priority for the parents was to have their substance-abusing son clean his entire bedroom in 1 week's time. The bedroom allegedly had looked "like a pigsty" for the past 5 years. The parents in this case had found petrified peanut butter and jelly sandwiches under their son's bed. Because the parent's goal was too monolithic, I encouraged them to negotiate with their son on one part of the bedroom that he would be willing to clean up in 1 week's time.

Research indicates the need for client self-determination in the therapeutic process. When clients think they have even modest personal control over their destinies, they will persist at mastering tasks, do better at managing them, and become more committed to the change process. There is empirical evidence that when clients themselves choose a course of action from among alternatives, they are more likely to adhere to it and succeed (Miller & Rollnick, 2002; Miller, 1985). Several studies in the addiction field have demonstrated that when clients are given a choice regarding treatment goals and the type of treatment they want to receive, they will be more motivated and have more favorable treatment outcomes (Miller & Rollnick, 2002; Kissen, Platz, & Su, 1971; Parker, Winstead, & Willi, 1979). Insistence on a particular treatment goal, despite the client's perceptions and wishes, can compromise motivation and treatment outcome (Sanchez-Craig & Lei, 1986; Thornton, Gottheil, Gellens, & Alterman, 1977).

ASSUMPTION 9: Reality is observer-defined, and the therapist participates in co-creating the therapy system's reality.

Bateson (1972) wrote that the beliefs a person has "about what sort of world it is, will determine how he sees it and acts within it, and his ways of perceiving and acting will determine his beliefs about its nature" (p. 314). As members of the new therapist–client observing system, our constructions of the client's presenting problem will be based primarily on our own theoretical maps and personal experiences in the world (Efran & Lukens, 1985; von Foerster, 1981; Maturana & Varela, 1988). Einstein believed that it is our theories that determine what we can observe. If you are a structural family therapist, most likely you will see pathological family structures like "enmeshment" or "disengagement" (Minuchin, 1974). If you are a psychodynamically oriented therapist, you probably will see unresolved conflicts and psychic deficits. What you will see is what you will get. Therapists "cannot not have a theory" (Anderson & Goolishian, 1991b).

There is no such thing as a "God's eye" view; we can never find an objective outside place from which to look at our clients (Hoffman, 1988). The therapist and supervisor/therapeutic team are members of the new therapist–client observing problem system. We are consulting coauthors in helping our clients rewrite their problem-saturated stories. In our conversational discourse with clients, we need to interact in a way that introduces meaningful differences that can challenge outmoded beliefs and alter behavior patterns. According to Andersen (1991), there are three types of therapeutic constructions that occur in conversations with clients: (1) constructions that are "too similar" to how the clients already view their problem; (2) constructions that are perceived by the clients as being "too unusual" and are rejected or disregarded; and (3) constructions that are neither too similar nor too unusual, and that can lead to a change in the client's original perceptions of his or her problem. The last category of therapeutic constructions can only be generated when the therapist is "staying close" to the client in the therapeutic process. By "staying close," I mean carefully utilizing key client words and belief material, and embedding the client's presuppositional language in therapeutic questions and prescribed tasks. This can lead to the coauthoring of a solution-determined story with the family (de Shazer, 1991).

ASSUMPTION 10: There are many ways to look at a situation, none more "correct" than others.

For every event that occurs in the world, there are at least two or more explanations of that event. Bateson (1980) referred to this form of description as "double or multiple comparison" (p. 97). There are no final explanations of reality. The great surrealist artist René Magritte liked to play upon the human urge to make sense of, or give definitive explanations for, the images in his paintings. He once said, "Our gaze always wants to penetrate further so as to see at last the object, the reason for our existence" (in Whitfield, 1992, p. 62). Many of the images found in Magritte's paintings are metaphors for the different ways in which truth and meaning remain *concealed*.

As therapists, we need to be careful not to become too wedded to our therapy models of choice. Emile Chartier, the French existentialist philosopher, once said, "Nothing is more dangerous than an idea when it is the only one you have." Therapeutic flexibility is essential with difficult adolescent cases. Solution-oriented brief family therapy is not a panacea for every adolescent case. When clinically necessary, I integrate ideas from other therapy approaches or abandon the solution-oriented brief family therapy approach and try a completely different therapeutic approach.

SUMMARY

In this chapter, I have presented 10 guiding assumptions that are the theoretical underpinnings of the solution-oriented brief family therapy approach. The assumptions offer therapists a highly pragmatic and optimistic lens for viewing adolescent and family difficulties and for doing therapy. Therapists will find that these guiding assumptions will help them to be more therapeutically flexible, utilize their clients' strengths in presenting problem areas more, and negotiate small and realistic behavioral goals with them.

Three

The Improvisational Therapist

Staying Alive and Creating Possibilities Outside the Comfort Zone with Challenging Families

> The theme that you play at the start of a number is the territory, and what comes after, which may have very little to do with it, is the adventure!
>
> —ORNETTE COLEMAN

Unlike the innovative and adventurous music of Ornette Coleman, which has the immediate effect of quickly propelling us into novel and creative musical realities, the brief therapy literature and many of the seminars we have attended place little emphasis on creative ways therapists can tap their unique strengths, talents, and inventiveness to create possibilities. By remaining in the comfort zone of our favorite therapy models, therapists rob themselves of the opportunity to take risks and stretch their imaginations, and limit themselves in terms of their therapeutic options when struggling and feeling stuck with their most challenging client families. Some of us succumb to complacency with "one-size-fits-all" thinking with our beloved therapy models and the notion that "therapy is serious business!" Another factor that may keep us stuck in the comfort zone with our more challenging families is the intimidating and chronic nature of their presenting problems. This can evoke fear and confusion in us and lead to therapeutic paralysis.

In an effort to help liberate therapists from the shackles of complacency and the fear of taking risks, I will attempt to provide answers to some key questions we can ask ourselves in the therapeutic process regarding our use of self with challenging families, such as:

- "What elements are operating in the therapeutic relationships with our clients that empower us to take risks?"

- "In what ways does this family or their stories inspire me to take risks with them?"
- "What methods of construction or use of self are more likely to foster a cooperative relationship with this challenging family?"
- "How specifically can we conduct ourselves in the therapeutic process with our more challenging clients in order to stimulate ideas that will make positive changes possible?"
- "Which of my personal strengths, areas of expertise, or life experiences can I draw upon to help us get unstuck?"
- "What constructions or storylines about the problem situation appear to be the most aesthetically pleasing to me and this family?"
- "What associations does the family's problem story trigger for me?"
- "What am I saying or doing that may be silencing particular family members' voices?"
- "If I were in the heads of these family members, how would they perceive what I am asking and doing with them?"
- "What have I said or done with similar families that proved to be quite useful to them?"
- "What insights would a third party with no previous involvement with this family and me have for us about what is keeping us stuck?"
- "What if I knew I could not possibly fail with this challenging family?"

I also present in this chapter a systemic framework for the improvisational use of self in brief therapy and several practice guidelines for staying alive and creating possibilities outside the comfort zone with challenging families.

THE IMPROVISATIONAL USE OF SELF SYSTEMIC FRAMEWORK

When we begin a new therapeutic encounter, a circular interactive process is set in motion. The client's problem story, family themes, and metaphors emotionally resonate with us and often trigger in our minds various associations: certain thoughts and feelings from our own professional or personal life experiences; images of TV, movie, and literary characters or historical figures; memories of former clients with similar difficulties; or even creative ideas for using the family members' key strengths and specific areas of expertise to help them resolve their difficulties. The nature of the clients' presenting problems, theories of change, key strengths, and goals will dictate which therapeutic approaches or combination of strategies and techniques we may be drawn toward in an attempt to find the right *fit*. In addition, improvisational therapists will entertain in their minds how to utilize their own key strengths, areas of expertise, past successful experiences helping similar clients, and powers of imagination to co-create with the clients new workable realities. Schon (1983) refers to this process as *reflection-in-action*. By taking risks, we can share with our clients new constructions of their problem stories and test out novel therapeutic experiments in the session, and then observe and carefully listen to how family members respond. Most importantly, the ideas and experiments we offer the family need to come close to fitting how they view their problem situations, albeit with a twist of novelty. What we may say or try to do in the therapeutic process may be sparked by a gut reaction or derived from an action script (a past successful change strategy used with a similar family) triggered by the client's problem story or themes. Family members' nonverbal and verbal feedback will determine what our next therapeutic moves will be or what adjustments we will need to make to find a better fit. Throughout this whole process, the therapist needs to critically meta-observe—that is, step outside oneself and watch oneself in relationship to each family member. How well are we connecting? Are we cooperating in such a way with our clients that we better understand their problem stories, and are our constructions and actions producing the kinds of results the family desires (see Figure 3.1)? Schon (1983) refers to this type of critical self-reflecting as *reflection-on-action*. Finally, we need to critically examine our own assumptions and beliefs and be open to discarding our misguided or unhelpful views that may be blocking the generation of new ideas and the kinds of changes the clients would like to make.

THE IMPROVISATIONAL THERAPIST: PRACTICE GUIDELINES FOR THE SYSTEMIC USE OF SELF

In any given session, there are numerous ways we can improvise, tap our inventiveness and intuition, and utilize our key strengths to create possibilities with our clients. The therapist's use of self is not just a facet of what we do with our clients, but equally as important, it is a philosophy about why we choose to do what we do. Deissler (1989) suggests we should think about and ask ourselves the following questions: "How do we construct what we construct?" or "How do we invent what we invent?" He argues that by asking ourselves these questions we are no longer tied to the limits of our perceptions and free to apply our creativity, inventiveness, and collaborative solution building with our clients. The following practice guidelines for the improvisational therapist's use of self are based on years of clinical-practice

Family's Problem Story
- Listen carefully for central family themes, metaphors, key words, and beliefs.
- Elicit from family members their theories of change, preferences, expectations, and best outcome hopes.
- Find out about family members' key intelligence and skill areas, and passions.

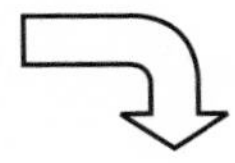

Reflection-in-Action
Triggers associations in us:
- Self-reflect on what was most inspiring or aesthetically pleasing about the family story.
- Look for pattern recognition and typicality.
- Draw upon past road maps for action with similar families.
- Think about therapeutic approach and fit with unique client characteristics.
- Imagine how family members or their stories resemble TV, movie, historic figures, popular book characters or stories.

Taking Risks outside the Comfort Zone
- Use humor and playfulness.
- Offer an alternative construction of family's story.
- Ask questions that capture family members' curiosity, imagination, and expertise.
- Test out a therapeutic experiment that taps family members' key intelligence and skill areas and is in line with their goals.

Reflection-on-Action
- Closely assess client nonverbal and verbal feedback.
- Determine if found fit or not.

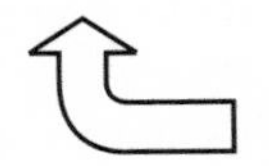

Improvising-in-Action
If no fit, you as the therapist can:
- Tap your inventiveness, imagination powers, and key personal intelligence skill areas to generate something new to offer the family outside choice therapy model.
- Try integrating other ideas with your therapeutic approach.
- Be less predictable and inject more surprises and novelty intro your sessions.

Reflection-on-Action
- Closely assess client nonverbal and verbal feedback.
- Determine if found fit or not.

FIGURE 3.1. Improvisational use of self systemic framework.

wisdom gained from influential theorists and trainers (Seligman, 2002, 2003; Gilligan, 2002; Hoffman, 1988, 2002; O'Hanlon & Weiner-Davis, 1989; Goolishian & Anderson, 1988; O'Hanlon, 1987; Minuchin, 1986; Minuchin & Fishman, 1981; Keith & Whitaker, 1981; Erickson, 1964, 1965; Whitaker, 1975) and from many years of working with difficult adolescents and their families. The improvisational therapist:

- Views the family's presenting problem as a gift.
- Is adventurous, full of surprises, and feels quite at home taking risks.
- Is genuinely and deeply curious about the second, third, and fourth possible explanations for the family's presenting difficulty.
- Carefully listens and reads the verbal and nonverbal feedback family members provide to determine the next therapeutic question or experiment, or what adjustments he or she needs to make in relationship to them.
- Is passionate, enthusiastic, and like an inspirational coach.
- Maintains his or her optimism when faced with adversity.
- Honors every moment and is transparent in his or her thoughts and feelings.
- Maintains an authentic presence and oneness with each family member.
- Believes the therapist's expertise is in eliciting family members' expertise.
- Uses poetic language, metaphors, and enticing and thought-provoking visuals in the therapeutic conversation.
- Avoids at all costs being a slave to any particular therapy model.
- Trusts his or her intuition to recognize important cues, patterns, or past successful action scripts.
- Uses lots of humor, absurdity, and playfulness.
- Actively seeks family members' assistance when feeling incompetent, confused, or stuck.
- Regularly taps his or her key strengths, inventiveness, and areas of expertise to empower the family.

REFLECTIONS ON THE PRACTICE GUIDELINES

I discuss each one of the practice guidelines and offer examples of how these ideas can be applied in specific clinical situations. In any one family session, we may need to use a variety of these practice strategies, depending on what a family's unique needs are at the time and what we may think might work in the therapeutic process.

Views the family's presenting problem as a gift.

What happens when we begin to view our clients' *problems* as gifts rather than as the enemy we need to rid them of? Most importantly, we begin to appreciate their positive qualities and how helpful they have been to our clients as resources and, in some cases, solutions for their life difficulties. Psychotherapist Stanley Siegel, author of the informative book *The Patient Who Cured His Therapist and Other Stories of Unconventional Therapy* (1999), put it best in saying:

> A patient's "problem" may not be a problem, but instead, a solution waiting to be discovered and put to use. Problems provide stability, respite, continuity, or even security to the patients who cling to them. The more we explore what is "right" rather than wrong about their problems, the more creativity we can discover, and the more we will see how the human spirit is way ahead of the human mind in its genius for adaptation. (p. xiii)

Like warm and gracious hosts, we can welcome clients' problems into our offices as friends or allies who are visiting us, rather than viewing them as intimidating or threatening foes that will try to thwart our efforts to be helpful to our clients. The case example below of 15-year-old Sylvia, who was chronically cutting herself, illustrates how to embrace the client's presenting problem as an ally that can offer us valuable wisdom regarding how best to establish a therapeutic alliance with a challenging client that has had multiple treatment experiences.

In my first session with Sylvia, I asked her to share with me how her cutting had been helpful to her. Sylvia shared with me how it kept her "company" when she "felt alone" with emotionally unmanageable peer and family stressors. She further added, "It was a friend that I could count on." When I inquired with Sylvia about her five former therapists' and her parents' unproductive attempted solutions at trying to stop the cutting behavior, she quickly pointed out how both the therapists and her parents "lectured too much," how she felt "blamed by them" and "not listened to." With her parents, they had a tendency toward emotional withdrawal when frustrated with their inability to stop the cutting behavior and often threatened to send her off to a residential treatment center. According to Sylvia, neither the past therapists nor her parents attempted to understand why she was cutting and how it was helping her; instead, "they were just trying to take it away from me." By taking the time to elicit this critical information from Sylvia, I was able to come to appreciate the importance of cutting in her life and strived to create a relaxed and nonthreatening therapeutic climate where she felt supported and was more receptive to exploring alternative coping strategies.

We can begin to appreciate the aesthetically pleasing aspects of our clients' problems once we enter their worlds and get to know them. The idea of viewing clients' problems as gifts is not new. The great hypnotist Milton H. Erickson believed that clients' problems or symptoms were unique presences that could, under the proper conditions, be the basis for new learning and personal growth (Gilligan, 2002; Havens, 1985; Erickson, 1965, 1980a, 1980b).

One way to learn more about how our clients' problems have served as gifts and resources for them is to ask the clients the following playful questions:

- "Imagine that your problem came to see you for counseling; what questions would you ask it?"
- "What would we learn about it, you, and your situation?"
- "In what ways will it tell us it has been a friend to you?"
- "What aspects of it would it recommend that you keep?"
- "If the problem were to totally leave your life, what would you miss the most about it?"
- "What wisdom have you gained from the problem?"

By asking these playful questions and eliciting the expertise of our clients about their difficulties, we can learn what aspects of their problem they wish to keep and continue to use as resources. Some of the ways clients may be employing certain aspects of their problem as resources are as follows: benefiting from its mood-elevating effects, its soothing qualities, effectiveness at disrupting oppressive thought patterns, how it empowers them in relationship situations, and so forth. Once we have a solid relationship with our clients, we can begin to introduce them to a wide range of therapeutic tools they can use to achieve the same effects through more adaptive and healthy means.

Is adventurous, full of surprises, and feels quite at home taking risks.

Difficult adolescents and their families often come to us after repeated experiences with clinicians practicing "more of the same" kind of therapy (Watzlawick et al., 1974). They may feel highly demoralized and stuck. We can empower these families by liberating them from their restrained and fixed problem-saturated views and patterns of interaction by injecting novelty and playfulness into our therapeutic conversations with them and by channeling their strengths and resources into their identified problem areas. Like skilled jazz musicians, we can achieve this by being adventurous with our improvisational moves, full of surprises with the way we share our associations and bring in different ideas or strategies from other therapy approaches, to make the process even more captivating for our clients. And yet, we need to be able to bring our playing back to the original melody as a tribute and respect for what is familiar to them, their problem stories. In order for meaningful changes to occur for our clients, we need to combine elements from their problem-saturated, straight-ahead-played standards with our new, improvised, and upbeat renditions of their standards, so that we can co-create something novel and special together.

Kurt Hahn, the father of the Outward Bound movement, once said about the importance of risk taking in challenging life situations: "We are all better than we know; if only we can be brought to realize this, we might never settle for anything less" (Curtis, 1995, p. 74). What Hahn found from his teaching experiences, and what happens a lot with many therapists when faced with tough situations, is that they are far too cautious and retreat into complacency or they are paralyzed by fear when leadership and risk taking are called for. I agree with Hahn that we should not ignore our natural leadership abilities, and we should put "right action before expediency" (Khan, 2001, p. 43).

Is genuinely and deeply curious about the second, third, and fourth possible explanations for the family's presenting problem.

Harry Goolishian, the brilliant family therapy pioneer, believed that "knowledge is always on the way" (Goolishian & Anderson, 1988). These valuable words of wisdom have resonated with me for years and are always in the back of my mind when I enter a therapeutic conversation with a new family, particularly a therapy-veteran family. They have a long story to tell about their problem-saturated situations and negative and frustrating treatment experiences (Goolishian, personal communication, March 7, 1988). Our questions need to be asked from a position of "not knowing" and we have to be curious about the second, third, fourth, and fifth possible explanations for how a therapy-veteran family became plagued with difficulties and have not responded well in past treatment experiences. It is imperative that we constantly remind ourselves that what we currently know often gets in the way of what we need to know about the family's story. "Not knowing" is a gift. It allows us to open ourselves up to be compassionate and can spark in us a strong desire to learn more about the family's story. Like a deeply curious anthropologist wanting to learn more about a particular tribe's culture, we need to invite the family to be the privileged experts of their own experiences and help us understand their cultural world. In addition, we need to employ *generous listening*, by resisting the impulse to jump in too quickly with goal setting, potential solution identification, and structuring or steering the session too sharply in one direction (Hoffman, 2002). Lyotard (1996), in discussing language games and the importance of being a respectful listener in conversations, argues that "such a game is the game of the just" (p. 71). Being a respectful and deeply curious listener will help create a sacred conversational space by aiding in opening up doors for the therapist and the family to co-construct new ideas and meanings.

Is passionate, enthusiastic, and like an inspirational coach.

With some challenging families, their entrenched difficulties and low family morale levels are similar to those in football teams that are plagued by recurrent bad slumps. They are desperately in need of a charismatic new coach who is passionate, enthusiastic, and inspirational. Before Vince Lombardi became their head coach, the Green Bay Packers had historically done poorly in the standings and never had made a playoff appearance. Under Lombardi's leadership the Packers won three NFL championships and two Super Bowl games. What was it about Lombardi's leadership abilities that made the Packers one of the all-time greatest NFL football teams? Lombardi inspired each player and got to know him personally. With great confidence and in the pursuit of excellence, he relentlessly empowered his players to keep trying and to go beyond themselves until they performed at their highest levels. Finally, Lombardi regularly invited his players to evaluate how he was performing as their coach and welcomed their input about adjustments they needed to make as a team (Maraniss, 1999).

Like Lombardi, we can passionately empower our clients to shift into more preferred realities by confidently conveying to them our expectation that they will succeed in resolving their difficulties. In addition, as coaches we can share inspiring stories of how other families with similar difficulties successfully conquered their problems, use our optimism and enthusiasm to spark family members' courage, passion, and excitement about facing and tackling their difficulties, and strategically lead them to victory through our on-target and timely play calling.

Maintains his or her optimism when faced with adversity.

Some of our tougher clients—such as those families that are crisis-prone or whose problem-maintaining patterns of interactions appear to be impervious to the various therapeutic experiments we had thus far offered them—can trigger in us feelings of pessimism and incompetence. At all costs, we must avoid adopting a pessimistic mindset, which can further disempower the clients. Instead, we need to model for the family the importance of maintaining an optimistic stance even when the going gets rough. As Seligman and his colleagues (Seligman et al., 1995, 2003) have demonstrated through rigorous research, when teachers and parents maintain an optimistic explanatory style with children and adolescents, this insulates them from falling prey to difficulties with depression and anxiety. He contends that one of the best life skills we can teach children and adolescents is *disputation skills* (Seligman, 2003). We can invite family members to begin to challenge their own narrow or rigid beliefs or unproductive attempted solutions, which may be contributing to why their situation is remaining the same or getting worse. For example, the therapist can ask the following questions:

- "In what ways does that explanation for your son's behavior offer us any other road maps for action other than medication?"
- "In the long run, do you think yelling at your daughter will empower her to continue to make better or worse choices in the future?"
- "Can you [the parents] think of two or three other possible explanations for why your daughter is cutting herself?"
- [The therapist can shed doubt by asking] "How do you know that?"
- "How has thinking that way taken its toll on you?"

Our confidence in a family's ability to change can greatly influence their behavior (Hubble et al., 1999). Inviting family members to talk about the times when things are presently going well for them, their past successes at overcoming adversity, and having them gaze into an imaginary crystal ball into a future place where they have achieved their goals can instill hope and optimism. I often invite parents in our family sessions to share with their adolescents their personal stories of resiliency and how they overcame adversity when faced with similar difficulties that their kids are presently struggling with.

Another pathway we can pursue when faced with adversity or feeling stuck in the therapeutic process is to shift gears and *go back to basics* with the clients and explore the following areas with them: possible mismatching with the therapeutic experiments that had been offered and the stages of readiness for change of family members (Prochaska, 1999) and misunderstanding their theories of change (Hubble et al., 1999) and treatment expectations and preferences. In addition, the treatment goal may still be too big or unrealistic and need to be renegotiated. Once these adjustments are made, optimism can be sparked in both the clients and the therapist, and the change process can be set in motion.

Honors every moment and is transparent in his or her thoughts and feelings.

As therapists, we need to honor and be mindful of the miraculous moment with our clients. Our ability to stay close to our clients, accurately pick up on changes in their nonverbal behavior and vocal tone when discussing certain subjects, and use ourselves as emotional barometers and be transparent in reflecting our thoughts and feelings in the interviewing process will help us to establish strong and meaningful therapeutic relationships with them. Some examples of being transparent and reflecting one's thoughts and feelings with clients are as follows:

- "It feels so heavy in the room, like there are gray clouds over our heads, almost like we are at a funeral home together. Is anybody else thinking and feeling like that?"
- "You know, there was a famous comedian named Rodney Dangerfield, and his most famous line was, 'I don't get no respect!' Do you feel like that [*asking the adolescent client*] with your parents—that your parents need to get their act together?!"
- "Sometimes my clients will say certain things, and it will suddenly trigger in my mind a lot of different ideas, some of which might be really off-the-wall or maybe helpful to them. Can I present them to you, and you let me know if they sound really far-fetched or if any of them sound useful to you?"
- "How did you come to be such a mystery man in your family?"

Maintains an authentic presence and oneness with each family member.

We need to maintain an authentic presence and a sense of oneness with each family member. A therapist who is authentically present with families captivates them with his or her goodness, caring, and fearless giving of support and wisdom. The therapist sees and feels family members' experiences from the heart with compassion and generosity. The hope that we instill in our clients rises up from our hearts and is the gift that we give to them. The therapist's mind needs to be "free from subconscious gossip, hesitation, and disbelief" (Trungpa, 1988, p. 114) in order to be authentically present with his or her clients.

The pioneering physicist David Bohm believed that "we are all one." He refers to this as the *implicate order*, that is, everything in the universe enfolds into everything else because they are part of the same unbroken whole (Bohm, 1980). According to Bohm (1980), as humans we have a tendency toward fragmentation and see others as separate from us. When we allow the barriers to dissolve in our relationships with others, we become one mind and constructively move in relationship with one another. Once we have established a strong connection or sense of oneness with each family member, the *undiscussables*, or unspoken chapters of their stories that had been lingering below the surface, will be accessible for important heart-to-heart meaning-making conversations.

Believes the therapist's expertise is in eliciting family members' expertise.

When we begin working with a new family, it is critical that we spend ample time inviting each family member to teach us about his or her key strengths, areas of expertise, and what he or she is most passionate about. While carefully listening to what their jewels are and what they are most passionate about, we can use the metaphors and key language connected to family members' strengths and talents in our conversations and with the therapeutic experiments we offer them. Simply having clients talk about their goodness and how they shine in life can trigger positive emotion and help us co-create with them a therapeutic climate ripe for change. For example, inviting a gang-involved adolescent who is a highly passionate and talented basketball player talk about how he shines on the court, his best shots and dribbling moves, and other secrets for success will make this young man feel good about his interests and skills. In addition, this type of conversation will be much more enjoyable to him than discussing why he was on probation or other difficulties he is supposed to have. Furthermore, inviting the adolescent to share his stories of success on the basketball court will help the therapist rapidly build a therapeutic alliance with him. If his best shots are fade-away jumpers or shots from the three-point range, we could discuss with the parents what specifically the boy could do over the next week to score two- and three-point baskets with them. The boy and his parents would need to determine a clear criterion of what constitutes baskets worth three versus two points. The parents can then establish a reward system for the son's efforts to try to score as many such points as possible in a single week. If this change strategy works for the clients, you want to have them continue it until they are satisfied with their progress.

Uses poetic language, metaphors, and enticing and thought-provoking visuals in the therapeutic conversation.

In carefully listening to our challenging clients share their problem stories of oppression and perseverance, we may empathize with their emotional pain and sense of hopelessness, be in awe of their amazing resilience, be touched by and curious to learn more about their stories, or find certain associations or images being triggered. These thoughts, feelings, and images spark in us a creative flow process and stimulate the development of inventive ideas, which can aid us in the construction of novel alternative stories or intriguing experiments we can offer to the family. Like weaving together a beautiful tapestry, we can share our metaphors, aesthetically appealing images, and new constructions that our clients' stories sparked in us and combine them with the clients' problem views and storylines of resourcefulness. As Allman (1982) has pointed out, "When we help the family see themselves as a system and teach them to play with their meanings, we open each member to his own poetry and creative twinkle" (p. 53).

The following case example of 14-year-old Charles and his family illustrates how the therapist's use of metaphor can spark the "creative twinkle" in family members and open the door for possibilities with a stuck case situation.

Charles was in a residential treatment setting for just over a year for his aggressive and violent behaviors. His parents had cut off all contact with him for approximately 6 weeks due to his aggressive behavior toward them on a recent weekend visit. The parents had felt that this extreme consequence would trigger guilt in Charles and teach him a lesson about taking responsibility for changing his aggressive behavior. The treatment team had supported the parents' position. In a consultant role, I encouraged the treatment team and the parents to break the silence and for us to begin having family sessions with Charles. Charles was longing to reconnect with his parents and had taken some constructive steps to better manage frustration and his aggressive behaviors. He also wanted another chance to redeem himself on a weekend visit. At first, the parents were quite resistant to the visit idea and appeared stuck in the past with their views of Charles as still being a danger to them. They also were putting a lot of pressure on him to express his thoughts and feelings about the disastrous weekend visit situation. While carefully listening to the parents' concerns and observing Charles's pleading with the parents to give him another chance, the image of Charles walking on a very high tightrope struggling to keep his balance with no people or protective mat below was triggered in my mind. I shared my dramatic image with the family. Charles became quite animated and shared with us that the tightrope metaphor did capture the current way he was feeling about his family situation. For the first time in the session, the parents, in an emotionally supportive way, rallied around Charles and shared with him that this was a team effort. Knowing that Charles and his father loved to play basketball together, the mother suggested to her husband that they buy team jerseys for the whole family. The remainder of the family session was upbeat, filled with laughter and playfulness, and the parents were receptive to trying another weekend visit with Charles.

When we are able to successfully weave our poetic language and stories with our client families' constructions, family members' self-healing capacities and inventiveness are stimulated, which in turn can lead them to generating their own novel solutions to their difficulties.

Avoids at all costs being a slave to any particular therapy model.

As therapists, we need to be careful not become too wedded to our beloved choice therapy models. The great hypnotist Milton H. Erickson had stressed, "Yes, therapy should always be designed to fit the patient and not the patient to fit the therapy" (Erickson & Rossi, 1983, p. 415). By adopting a kaleidoscopic viewing of our clients' problem stories and interactions and carefully tailoring what we do therapeutically to their unique theories of change, expectations, stages of readiness for change, and goals, we can better maximize our treatment success. Therapists will have many more avenues available to them for intervention when they can broaden their horizons by familiarizing themselves with and logically integrate ideas from a wide range of individual and family therapy approaches. Furthermore, research indicates that flexible and integrative family therapy approaches have produced the best treatment outcomes with challenging adolescent treatment populations (Henggeler, Schoenwald, Rowland, & Cunningham, 2002; Alexander et al., 1998; Lebow & Gurman, 1996).

Trusts his or her intuition to recognize important cues, patterns, or past successful action scripts.

Another important resource we can tap while in the midst of the interviewing process is our intuition, which for many of us has been like a trustworthy ally or friend when we had to think about our therapeutic options and make quick decisions on our feet in our family sessions. Gary Klein, a psychologist and researcher, has conducted groundbreaking research on the intuitive processes of firefighters, police officers, emergency room nurses and physicians, and professionals who work in control towers at airports. The most interesting finding that Klein and his colleagues discovered was that, across all of these professional disciplines, the majority of the participants in the study conducted mental simulations, or *premortems,* before taking action. To help safeguard against the potential weaknesses or flaws of their selected action or crisis intervention plans, these professionals would be observed mentally projecting themselves into the future after they had implemented their selected strategies and imagining a fiasco occurring. Next, they would generate a list of reasons why their selected action plans failed. This would be followed by closely evaluating the weaknesses of their plans and seeing whether they could be remedied or whether a new action plan should be selected or constructed that was more promising (Klein, 1998, 2002). Klein took his research investigation a step further and explored with his subjects other reasons why they chose certain actions in their problem-solving process, which eventually led to the development of his *recognition-primed decision-making model.* According to Klein (2002):

> When you notice a pattern you may have a sense of familiarity—yes, I've seen that before! As we work in any area, we accumulate experiences and build up a reservoir of recognized patterns. The more patterns we learn, the easier it is to match a new situation to one of the patterns in our reservoir. When a new situation occurs, we recognize the situation as familiar by matching it to a pattern we have encountered in the past. (p. 11)

For Klein, you don't choose a goal first and then take action. Instead, Klein contends that the goal arises when you see that an action can succeed. Furthermore, what triggers active problem solving is the ability to recognize when a goal is reachable (Klein, 1998, 2002).

Klein's ideas can be of great benefit to therapists when it comes to decision making with intervention selection and evaluating with our clients their concerns with and readiness to implement our proposed therapeutic experiments. Often, what we decide to do therapeutically while in action with our clients has a lot to do with recognizing familiar cues or patterns from our past experiences with other clients. Pattern recognition has been found by researchers to play a major role in effective problem solving, particularly for champion chess players (Klein, 1998, 2002; Simon, 1955, 1956). Although we may not always have the time to conduct thorough premortems with our clients, it is still worthwhile to trust our instincts and ask a particular question or test out a therapeutic experiment that had been useful to similar challenging families that we have worked with in the past.

Uses lots of humor, absurdity, and playfulness.

When I am referred a family that is deemed noncompliant and difficult, I always listen and observe carefully for humorous and absurd elements in their problem story and family interactions that can be positively exploited to create possibilities. Once we can help the family gain a meta-perspective on their problem situation, they can begin to recognize how absurd their attempted solutions and interactions are at times, playfully laugh at themselves, and discover how changing their situation can be similar to a fun and upbeat adventure. The therapist's use of humor, playfulness, off-the-wall free associations, and antics can take the sting out of the family's chronic difficulties and create a positive emotional climate that can strengthen their self-healing and problem-solving capacities.

Actively seeks family members' assistance when feeling incompetent, confused, or stuck.

Some challenging families are masters at making therapists feel highly incompetent and like royal bunglers. It becomes like a vicious circle: the more we try to ward off our feelings of incompetency, vulnerability, and confusion, the more we struggle and increase our incompetent behavior. Instead, we need to allow our incompetency to shine through and bungle to the hilt! In most cases, these families will eventually feel sorry for us and want to help us out. When I am feeling stuck or confused with a difficult family, I will share with them my frustration about not being more helpful to them, how I feel like I am letting them down, share with them my fears about failing with them, free-associate about other personal woes in my life, or put them in the expert position and have them inform me what I have missed with their situation or what ideas they have for me to help out a similar family. Some examples of the kinds of responses and questions I may pose to these challenging families are as follows:

- "I really feel like I am blowing it with you guys. This has been a really tough week for me with my clients. Lately, I have been seriously thinking about hanging up my counseling career and going to cooking school to become a chef. What do you guys think—should I take the plunge or hang in there with the counseling job?"
- "I really need to get my act together here in being more helpful to you. My fear is if we do not get some kind a change going soon my supervisor might decide to take me off of your case. For some reason he likes to put me on the plank with my clients. Believe me . . . I can almost feel those sharks hovering below my feet!"
- "Boy, this has been a rough week for me. My boss has been on my case about helping my clients achieve the kinds of outcomes they would like to have in shorter amounts of time. My wife has been on my case about my being real sloppy with the way I clean the house. The trouble is that I will never be a master cleaner like her. I am better in the kitchen. Do you have any advice for me about how I can be a better cleaner? What about what I could do differently with you to help you get to where you want to be in a shorter amount of time? Once you guide me with this, I can prove to my pessimistic boss that I am capable of doing this. I really would like to prove him wrong and get him off my back!"

- "I am working with another family just like you, and I am feeling really stuck. Do you have any advice for me about how I can best help them out?"

My experience has been that even the most challenging of families will find it tempting to try to rescue a bungling therapist, be forgiving, and help guide him or her in a more favorable therapeutic direction. For example, let's take the case of an alcohol-abusing parent requesting me to convince her 16-year-old daughter to stop abusing marijuana. I really allow my curiosity to run wild in these situations! It is helpful to play dumb in these situations and ask a lot of open-ended questions regarding the situation, such as:

- "When your daughter sees you drinking regularly, do you think she thinks it is not okay to get high—or it is an okay thing to do?"
- "I may be missing the boat here, but what do you think the biggest worry that your daughter may be harboring about you is that—if she shared it—she might be less likely to get high and take more responsibility?"
- "I am not asking you to do this or trying to imply that this is the right thing to do . . . but do you think if you instituted a no-drug or no-drinking policy in your household that your daughter might take you seriously and start to get her act together?"
- "I am really confused and feeling quite stuck right now. How do you think I can best convince your daughter not to get high and just not pay any attention to your drinking?"

This line of questioning can in a nonthreatening way invite the substance-abusing parent to begin to look at his or her troublesome behavior and see the effects of it on the adolescent's behavior. After raising the substance-abusing parent's awareness level that there is a problem here, the therapist will have more cooperation and openness on the parent's behalf to move from *contemplation* to the *preparation* stage of readiness to change (Prochaska, 1999). Once this occurs, the parent will be closer to taking responsibility for his or her substance-abuse difficulty and be more available to his or her adolescent as an authority figure.

Regularly taps his or her key strengths, inventiveness, and areas of expertise to empower the family.

One major resource we have available to us to tap in any given session is our own key strengths, passions, inventiveness, unique talents, and life experiences. Gardner (2004) contends that one of the major levers for changing people's minds and behaviors is sharing stories that the speaker embodies that emotionally resonate with his or her audience. In reflecting back on our past life experiences, there may be some emotionally powerful stories that were told to us by friends or family members or certain tough life experiences we had endured that may be similar to the client's situation that we had gained wisdom from that might be worth sharing with them.

At times, we become so paralyzed by and preoccupied with our clients' challenging behaviors and our own feelings of impotence that we totally forget about our inner plethora of strengths and resources that we can draw upon to create possibilities. Since I am passionate about jazz and blues music, gourmet cooking (see page 67), and modern art, I often use metaphors from or tap my expertise in these knowledge and skill areas to generate new ideas. Jung (1923) believed that "the creative mind plays with the objects it loves." When feeling stuck with our most difficult families, we can ask ourselves the following kinds of questions:

- "Which of my key strengths can I call upon to best assist me with this difficult family?"
- "If Miles Davis, Salvador Dalí, and Emeril Lagasse were to knock on my office door and call me out for an impromptu consultation, what advice would they have for me about what I need to do differently with this family?"
- "What valuable words of wisdom did my parents share with me when I was going through rough times as a teenager that may be worth sharing with my client's parents?"
- "How can I tap my expertise as a gourmet cook to spice this session up a bit?"
- "What inspires me the most about this family that empowers me not give up on them?"
- "Let's say a miracle happened during this intersession break. What will I be doing differently with this family when we reconvene that is more likely to work? When they respond more positively to what I try with them, how will that change my view of them? What will they be telling me that I said or did that they found to be the most helpful to them? In what ways will my new way of interacting with the family help the parents get along better with their daughter? What else will be better?"

The following case example with a depressed biracial 17-year-old named Chris illustrates how I used my music knowledge and personal experience singing a jazzy blues tune with my high school friend's garage band to energize the client and empower him to "get back in the groove" with playing his electric bass guitar.

Chris was brought in for counseling by his mother for "withdrawing from the family," "underachieving in school," and "not socializing with his peers anymore." Chris felt that his mother "nagged" him "too much." Both Chris and his mother were very pessimistic about the likelihood of being able to change their situation at home. The first two sessions I had with them, the atmosphere in the office was very heavy, and I felt like I was being sucked into the pessimistic void the family was experiencing, despite my efforts to better cooperate with their pessimism with my questioning. Knowing that Chris used to be passionate about playing his electric bass guitar and that he was strong in the musical intelligence area (Gardner, 1993), I spent most of the third session alone with him talking about music. Chris had an eclectic taste. Up to this point in the session, Chris's affect was still pretty flat, and I could still barely hear his voice. I decided to tap my own knowledge and personal experience with music and self-disclose one of my "15 minutes of fame" sparkling moments as a singer. I shared with Chris how my good friend had a garage band and had invited me to sing one of my favorite jazzy blues tunes called *Take Out the Dog and Bark the Cat*, which had been written and performed by Elliott Randall (who played rhythm guitar for the popular group, Steely Dan). While sharing my experience singing this song with my friend's band and picturing the scene in my head, I spontaneously began to sing some of the lyrics. For the first time, Chris became animated and smiled as I was performing for him. His vocal tone had become louder, and he began to talk about how he needed to "get back in the groove" with his electric bass playing again. I encouraged him to do this and to start jamming with his friends again. I asked him to bring in a demo CD so I could check all of them out. Our enjoyable conversation about music proved to be pivotal in helping us get unstuck, energized Chris, and opened the door for future possibilities.

SUMMARY

In this chapter, I have presented 15 practice guidelines that inform decision-making in the therapeutic process and can aid therapists when feeling stuck. Even when the going gets tough with our most challenging clients, we can always tap our own key strengths and inventiveness to resolve therapeutic impasses. By dreaming, daring, and living outside the comfort zone, the possibilities are boundless with how we can creatively use ourselves as the catalyst for change.

MATTHEW'S WILD MUSHROOM PASTA

1 yellow onion, finely chopped

4 cloves of garlic, finely chopped

2 ½ lbs. of mushrooms (combination of crimini, portobello, porcini, shiitake, and chanterelle; stems removed and caps chopped)

1–2 drops of white truffle oil

1 tsp. salt

1 tsp. freshly ground pepper

16 oz. sour cream

¼ C. white wine

1 stick butter or margarine

2–3 Tbsp. unbleached white flour

1 lb. fettuccine pasta

1. Melt the stick of butter in a nonstick large skillet and begin boiling 6 quarts of water in a pot for the pasta.
2. Sauté the chopped onion and garlic; add a little salt and pepper.
3. Add the mushrooms; stir the ingredients together and continue to sauté.
4. Add the wine, sour cream, and the truffle oil, and stir the mixture together.
5. Add the flour to thicken the sauce and more salt and pepper for taste.
6. Cook the pasta until it is *al dente*, drain, and place back in the pot.
7. Stir in the mushroom sauce, mix together well, and serve immediately.
8. Optional: Grate fresh parmigiano-reggiano cheese over the pasta or garnish with fresh Italian flat parsley leaves.

Serves 4 to 6.

Four

The First Family Interview

Co-Creating a Context for Change

> Whatever you can do, dream you can, begin it. Boldness has genius, power, and magic in it.
>
> —JOHANN VON GOETHE

CO-CREATING A THERAPEUTIC CLIMATE RIPE FOR CHANGE

When beginning with a new family, the therapist needs to strive to create a therapeutic atmosphere in which the family feels validated, that instills hope, is upbeat, and empowers family members to envision compelling future realities of success liberated from the shackles of their chronic difficulties. There are four important therapeutic activities that the therapist must engage in to co-create a climate for change with difficult adolescents and their families: (1) explaining the session format, (2) establishing a therapeutic alliance, (3) assessing customership and the stages of readiness to change, and (4) interviewing for possibilities. After discussing these four important therapeutic activities, I conclude the chapter with a brief overview of the mechanics of conducting the solution-oriented brief family therapy interview and offer helpful guidelines for therapeutic experiment matching and selection.

Explaining the Session Format

Before beginning the rapport-building process with new clients, I like to explain the session format and see if I can secure written consent to videotape the session and also have my therapist colleagues serve as a consultation team for collaboration purposes. When describing the session format, I explain to the family that I like to spend some time with the whole group together, meet with the parents alone, and give the adolescent individual session time as well. I also tell the family that we will be taking an intersession break, at which time my colleagues will come into the therapy room and we (the family and I) will go behind the one-way mirror to listen to their reflections about the interview thus far. I explain to the family that we will then switch rooms with the team again and that the family will be invited to reflect on the team's reflections. I also point out to the family that I might invite the team to briefly come in to join us later in the session so we can brainstorm some useful ideas and experiments to offer them that are in line with their goals. When working alone, I still take a mini-break to "meet with myself" to prepare my editorial reflection on the session, compliment family members on their resourcefulness and self-generated pretreatment changes, offer them some useful ideas and experiments to try, and invite them to provide feedback on how our meeting was for them.

With regard to my request to videotape our therapy sessions, I explain to my clients that the video camera acts as a second set of eyes and ears, and it often captures important things that I missed in the session that can help me help them better. I also explain to them that the videotapes can be used in our sessions to increase their awareness of *what works* in their interactions with one another. When presenting the idea of having my therapist colleagues observe and collaborate with us during our sessions, I point out to the family that "three heads are better than one" in terms of brainpower and creativity. Families have rarely turned me down about videotaping or having a consultation team observe our sessions. Sometimes a family will request that the consultation team join us in the same room, particularly when there has been a family history of abuse. My colleagues and I have no problem honoring this request.

Establishing a Therapeutic Alliance

After explaining the session format to the family, I begin the relationship-building process. I invite each family member, beginning with the parents, to share with me what they do best, their personal strengths, talents, hobbies, and the extracurricular activities they are most passionate about engaging in during their free time. This inquiry about their strengths and talents provides us with important information regarding their unique learning styles and key intelligence areas (Gardner, 1993). With parents, I am particularly interested in the type of work they do and detailed information about their strengths in their work roles. The parents' talents and skills in their work roles can be channeled into the presenting problem areas. The following case example illustrates how I utilized a parent's champion chess-playing ability to help him resolve his power struggle difficulties with his 16-year-old daughter.

During the first 10 minutes of the initial session with Bob and his daughter, Patricia, I discovered that the former was a world-class chess player. He had won numerous matches worldwide. While listening to Bob talk about his great chess-playing abilities, I explored with him what it was about his style of play that had made him a champion. Bob shared with me that it was "the first move" that makes the difference between winning and losing. I asked him more detailed questions about how he decides what the "first move" should be. According to Bob, he would "carefully think out different first moves" and his "opponent's countermoves" before doing anything. This strategy had consistently worked for Bob in his chess matches. With his daughter, Patricia, on the other hand, he would not carefully think through his "first move," but instead would overreact to her testy behavior by yelling and getting trapped in power struggles with her. I decided to channel Bob's chess-playing "first move" strategy into the problem area. I told Bob to reflect upon his "first move" chess strategy every time Patricia tried to push his buttons. Bob quickly discovered that thinking through his "first move" with Patricia led to a decrease in his yelling, and his daughter's behavior changed.

When meeting with adolescents, I like to know what grade they are in, what their favorite subjects are and why, whether they play any sports, what musical groups they like, what they like to do with their friends, and whether they have any special talents and hobbies. You don't have to like the adolescents' music, but if you know the names of the popular alternative, techno, and rap groups, the adolescents think you are "cool." With more streetwise youth, it is helpful to be familiar with the street lingo, particularly the street names of drugs of abuse and drug paraphernalia (Selekman, 1989b).

I also build rapport with difficult adolescents and their families by using a lot of humor, normalizing and positively relabeling negative family behaviors, utilizing key client words, metaphors, and belief system material in our therapeutic conversations, and improvising on central family themes. Throughout the first interview, I actively listen for humorous elements in the family's story that I can use to make the therapy session more playful and lively. I believe that humor can promote family healing and open up space for new possibilities. By using family members' key words and belief material in our therapeutic questions, we are "staying close" to the family, and thus our constructions of their problem situation are more likely to be acceptable to their worldview. During the therapy session, it is essential for the therapist to be able to demonstrate to the adolescent and parents that he or she can provide structure in the session, negotiate realistic goals, and disrupt unhelpful patterns of interaction occurring during the session. This type of therapeutic activity helps give the family confidence in the therapist's ability to effectuate change in their situation. When there is a great deal of arguing and blaming in the therapy room, the therapist needs to split up the parents and adolescent and meet with each subgroup separately. This is also a useful strategy when it is not possible to negotiate a mutual treatment goal between the parents and adolescent. The therapist can then negotiate separate goals with the parents and adolescent.

Assessing Customership and Stages of Readiness to Change

De Shazer (1988) has developed a highly practical and useful therapeutic guide for assessing who in the client system is most motivated to work with the therapist in resolving the presenting problem. He has identified the following three different therapist–family relationship patterns: visitors, complainants, and customers. These therapist–family relationship patterns are not fixed but rather change as the therapist develops *fit* (de Shazer, 1985) and a cooperative working relationship with the family. Prochaska and his colleagues (1994) have provided some solid empirical support for de Shazer's therapist–client relationship pattern framework. However, they refer to these relationship patterns as *stages of readiness to change*. There are six stages of readiness for change: *precontemplation*, *contemplation*, *preparation*, *action*, *maintenance*, and *termination*. Following a brief description of each of these therapist–client relationship patterns and stages of readiness for change, I provide case examples of a visitor and a complainant, and I offer guidelines for therapeutic experiment selection.

Visitors/Precontemplators

The "visiting" adolescent and his or her family are usually sent to therapy by some social control agent. Another common scenario in these cases is the youth who is dragged into therapy by concerned and frustrated parents. When asked why they think they were brought for counseling, they will often indicate it is their parents and the referring person who think they have a problem. As Prochaska and his colleagues (1994) have demonstrated in their research, there are some good reasons why precontemplators are not quick to identify a problem to work on or establish a treatment goal, such as: they are demoralized by their chronic difficulties or unsuccessful past treatment experiences; they have been mismanaged by previous therapists and treatment programs; or they have grown up in families where no one has conveyed the benefits of changing oneself or problem situations. Often, these youth or their parents are labeled "resistant," "noncompliant," "unmotivated," and "in denial" by previous therapists and treatment program personnel. Most difficult adolescent cases were referred for treatment by a probation officer, a school counselor or dean, or a child protective worker. Two useful questions to ask visiting families that help to clarify the referral process and maintain therapeutic maneuverability early on in the first interview are "What do you think gave [the referring person] the idea that you needed to go for counseling?" and "What do you think [the referring person] needs to see happen in counseling that would convince [him or her] that you wouldn't have to come here anymore?" Finally, it is helpful to put these youth and their parents in the expert position and ask: "You have seen a lot of therapists before me. What did they miss with your situation that is important for me to know?"

There are three therapeutic strategies that I have found to be useful with visitors/precontemplators. They are (1) empathizing with the adolescent and his or her family's dilemma about being coerced into therapy, (2) restraining from immediate change, and (3) accepting whatever goals they may have for themselves (de Shazer, 1988; Fisch et al., 1982). Restraining from immediate change consists of cautioning family members to go slowly with the change process. Some of these visiting adolescents have wanted to work on resolving relationship problems with their intimate partners, learning new ways to change their parents' behavior in relationship to them, learning new ways to change their parents' difficult behaviors, or getting the social control agents off of their backs. The therapist can set up a split between him- or herself and the social control agent by offering to get the latter off the client's back.

A final therapeutic strategy that I may use with a more challenging adolescent visitor is the "Columbo" approach. Some youth can make even the most seasoned of brief therapists feel very incompetent. The TV detective Columbo has taught me some valuable lessons on how to be strategic and use my confusion and feelings of incompetence with difficult adolescent visitors (see Chapters 5, 6, and 7 for more on the Columbo approach).

If none of the above strategies has produced a joint therapist–family work project or treatment goal, I simply compliment the clients on whatever they report doing for themselves that has been good for them, such as showing up for our first scheduled appointment, and I do not offer them a therapeutic task. I routinely compliment visiting adolescents for being responsible by coming in and "not blowing the session off!"

The following case example illustrates the utility of setting up a split between the probation officer and the therapist to help get him or her off the client's back.

Christopher had been referred to me by his probation officer after being caught at school with a "dime" ($10) bag of marijuana in his locker. The incident also prompted a 3-week school suspension. The parents were utterly shocked after finding out about the marijuana incident, for "Christopher had never been in trouble with the law before." Earlier in the first interview, the parents could not identify anything they wanted to see changed or any other problems happening in the family that could have led to Christopher's wanting to use or sell drugs. Christopher denied having a problem with drugs, but admitted that some of his friends abused them. He claimed that he was holding the dime bag for a friend who was being watched at school by the dean. Christopher took a risk in the session with his parents by telling them that he had experimented with marijuana and alcohol in the past. Because the parents were unable to identify any other treatment goal than helping Christopher stay out of further trouble with the law and the school authorities, I spent the majority of the session time eliciting their strengths and resources and discussing their strategies for preventing future legal or school difficulties. Christopher's main goal was for me to get the probation officer off his back. This was discussed during my individual session time with Christopher.

CHRISTOPHER: Mr. Williams [the probation officer] really pisses me off. He's constantly snooping around my school checking up on me. He thinks I'm a dealer or something. Honestly, I've only smoked weed [marijuana] three times. I actually like beer better, but I do that at parties. Look, I don't have a problem. I don't know why I have to come for counseling. There's nothing wrong with my head.

THERAPIST: It must be a real drag having a probation officer "snooping around" and "checking up" on you at school. How would you like me to get him off your back?

C: Well, that would be great if you could do that—but *how?*

T: Well, two ways. I know Mr. Williams well. We have worked together on other cases, so he pretty much allows me to call the shots with counseling—you know, how often we meet with your parents. So, although we have to meet throughout your 9-month probation period, we will not have to meet weekly. Another way for us to get Mr. Williams off your back is to prove him wrong—you know, show him that you are not a drug abuser or dealer, by taking responsible steps to turn this situation around. What are some positive steps you will take to prove Mr. Williams wrong about you at school?

C: Go to all of my classes, stay away from my friends that party . . . I don't know, I guess do my homework.

T: What about at home? What responsible steps will you take at home to convince your parents that you're not a drug abuser or dealer?

C: Come home on time on the weekends. Don't drink. Do my chores.

T: When you take all of these responsible steps, what will Mr. Williams tell you he was most impressed by that you did?

C: Going to my classes. He thinks I've been cutting classes to go party with my friends. Yeah, he will freak when he finds out from my teachers that I'm going to my classes and doing my work.

T: What about at home? Which responsible step will Mr. Williams be the most surprised with that you will take at home with your parents?

C: Coming home on time on the weekends. He probably thinks that I'm out drinking and partying with my friends all weekend. He doesn't know anything!

T: Let's prove him wrong together! *(We shook hands.)*

I ended up having a total of seven sessions with Christopher and his parents over 9 months. Two of these sessions were joint meetings with the parents, the probation officer, and involved school personnel. Christopher had not only successfully terminated his probation, but he took all of the "responsible steps" he had identified in the first interview to "get Mr. Williams off my back."

Complainants/Contemplators

The complainant/contemplator can be a parent, sometimes an adolescent, a school official, or some other social control agent. The parents and other involved adults are very concerned about some aspect of the identified adolescent client's behavior; however, they may feel stuck or do not include themselves as part of the solution construction process. In addition, they may think if they continue to persist with specific attempted solutions (yelling, lecturing, nagging, harsh discipline) that eventually the adolescent's problematic behaviors will change. Little do they know that in spite of their best efforts to resolve their kid's difficulties they are further exacerbating and maintaining them. With difficult adolescents, a common case scenario involves complaining parents who want the therapist to "fix" their son or daughter through individual therapy. These parents may also complain about not having time in their hectic work schedules to bring their son or daughter in for scheduled therapy sessions.

Because the complainant/contemplator has tremendous insight into the identified client's behavior, I compliment them on their insight into the situation and for being helpful to me in better understanding their concerns. I also compliment them on any other useful coping strategies they report engaging in around the identified client. Two highly effective therapeutic strategies to use with these parents are *observation tasks* (de Shazer,

1988) and *the decisional balancing scale* (Prochaska et al., 1994). The parents can be asked to carefully notice on a daily basis any encouraging or responsible steps they see their adolescent take in 1 week's time. The decisional balancing scale has parents list the advantages and disadvantages of continuing to employ their unproductive attempted solutions.

Lucy brought her 17-year-old son, Bob, in for therapy because she thought he had a "drinking problem," he was "not doing his homework," and he failed to keep his "bedroom floor clear of dirty clothes and paper scraps." The excerpt below is taken from the first interview, when I met alone with Lucy.

THERAPIST: You have given me a pretty good picture of all of the difficulties and concerns you have with Bob. However, in order for me to have a more complete picture of the home situation, I would like you to pull out your imaginary magnifying glass over the next week and look carefully for all of the times when Bob is not making you worry about him and he is doing the kinds of things you want him to do. Notice what positive steps he will be taking during those times and write those things down.

LUCY: I really do worry too much about him, but I really want to see him stop getting drunk on the weekends with his friends. And his bedroom looks like a pigsty.

T: You know, problems are like quicksand: the more we think about them or complain about them, the more we get swallowed up by them. We need to get out of the quicksand and notice what Bob is doing that we want to capitalize on.

L: Maybe you're right; I've been stuck in "quicksand" for a long time, and I'm sick of it!

T: So, over the next week I want you to grab your imaginary magnifying glass and notice what's happening with you and Bob when you're not "stuck in quicksand."

Lucy returned the following week with a one-page list of changes she observed in Bob's behavior. He did not "come home drunk on the weekend," and Lucy observed him twice "doing his homework." Lucy also came to the realization that it was "up to Bob to decide to be a pig" with his "messy bedroom" and that this would be "one less worry" for her.

Customers/Action-Stage Clients

The customer or client in the action stage is the client who presents for therapy wanting to work with the therapist to resolve a specific problem. It has been my clinical experience that customers are typically parents. However, some difficult adolescent clients will decide to become customers when the therapist has negotiated a good quid pro quo contract between the youth and his or her parents. For example, the mother will take her daughter out shopping later when she gets up on time to go to school at least two times over the next week. Ideally, having at least one customer in the family sessions is all it takes to resolve the presenting problem. Another useful way to assess the customer in the client system is to ask the following questions: "Who in your family is most concerned about this problem?" "Who else?" [*asking the identified client*] "On a scale from 1 to 10—10 being most concerned about you—what number would you give everybody in your family?" "What difference will it make to each person in the family when this problem is solved?"

On a cautionary note, Prochaska and his colleagues (1994) have pointed out that some clients may appear to be in the *action* stage but are really in the *preparation* stage. They are getting closer to wanting to take action but may report some anxiety about potential obstacles to achieving their goals, such as pessimistic or self-defeating thoughts, lack of family support, pessimistic involved helpers from larger systems, and so forth. Some adolescents or family members we work with may be in the *maintenance* stage, that is, they have already taken some important steps towards achieving their goals; however, they fear slipping back into old patterns and negative habits that previously got them into trouble. Besides underscoring and increasing what the client is already doing to stay on track, they also can be taught additional goal-maintenance and solution-enhancement tools to further increase their confidence levels (see Chapter 9). Finally, some adolescents and family members may come to us in the *termination* stage; that is, they are totally confident about not slipping back into old patterns or negative habits again. It is important to remember that with any given family each member may be in a different stage of readiness to change, and we have to carefully match our interventions with where each family member is in the change process.

Interviewing for Possibilities

The solution-oriented therapist asks questions in a purposeful manner by carefully assessing the family's cooperative response patterns and matching questions with those patterns (de Shazer, 1988, 1991; Lipchik, 1988; Lipchik & de Shazer, 1986; O'Hanlon & Weiner-Davis, 1989). For example, if the use of solution-building questions is generating important client exception material, then the therapist should continue using this category of questions and gradually move the family toward the future with presuppositional questions (O'Hanlon & Weiner-Davis, 1989). The purposeful interview is a recursive dance in which the family's verbal and nonverbal feedback guides the therapist about future question category selection. The purposeful systemic interviewing guidelines presented in Figure 4.1 outline the major choice points in selecting or changing question categories in the interviewing process. The various interventive questions discussed in this section can promote self-healing (Tomm, 1987) and liberate families from their oppressive problems by opening up space for new possibilities. I will now present several different categories of questions, offer guidelines for question category selection, and provide some case illustrations to demonstrate the utility of the various interventive questions in the interviewing process.

Pretreatment Change Questions

Weiner-Davis et al. (1987) have demonstrated that clients often proactively take steps to resolve their difficulties between the time of the first call to the agency or clinic and the first therapy session. This can frequently be seen with cases on the agency waiting list or where there has been some lag time between the initial call and the first interview. Based on this research and my strong belief that all clients have the strengths and resources to change, I like to begin a first interview with waiting list or lag-time cases with the question "So what have you noticed that's better since you first called our clinic?" Not only does this question convey the idea to clients that the therapist believes they have the strengths and resources to change, but also it presupposes that changes have already occurred, which can help set in motion the co-creation of a positive self-fulfilling prophecy for them.

The following case example demonstrates the utility of capitalizing on pretreatment changes with a lag-time case (2 weeks after initial call).

Randy, a white 16-year-old delinquent boy, had been referred to me for family therapy after having spent 1 month in the juvenile detention center. He was accompanied to the session by his mother, Mary.

THERAPIST: Since Randy got out of the "juvie" [Randy's language], what have you noticed that is better?

MARY: Everything has been great! He's been going to school and following my rules. He's not smoking that marijuana stuff. It's like he's another person.

T: Wow! How did you get him to do all of those "great" things!?

M: Well . . . I told him when I picked him up at the juvenile detention center that I'm not going to put up with his nonsense anymore, and from now on he's going to live by my rules or go to live with his alcoholic father.

BEGIN HERE

Pretreatment change sequence **NO** → (Option 2)
YES ↓
Problem idea dissolved
YES ↓
Consolidating questions
YES ↓
No goal
YES ↓
Terminate
NO ↓
Longer time interval

OPTION 2

Client problem defined **NO** → (Option 3)
YES ↓
Miracle question sequence
YES ↓
Pretreatment change/ solution-building questions
YES ↓
Scaling questions
YES ↓
Client goal defined

OPTION 3

Coping question sequence **NO** → (Option 4)
YES ↓
Solution-building questions
YES ↓
Scaling questions
YES ↓
Client goal defined

OPTION 4

Pessimistic sequence **NO** → (Option 5)
YES ↓
Solution-building questions
YES ↓
Scaling questions
YES ↓
Client goal defined

OPTION 5

Problem tracking
YES ↓
Scaling questions
YES ↓
Client goal defined

Future-oriented questions
YES ↓
Scaling questions
YES ↓
Client goal defined

Externalizing unique account/ redescription questions
YES ↓
Percentage questions
YES ↓
Client goal defined

Conversational questions
YES ↓
Making more room for problem storytelling/ undiscussables
YES ↓
"Right" problem defined
YES ↓
Scaling questions
YES ↓
Client goal defined

FIGURE 4.1. Guidelines for purposeful systemic interviewing in the first session.

After Mary reported some of Randy's changes, I utilized cheerleading and a "how" solution-building question. The cheerleading helps punctuate exceptions and make them "newsworthy." "How" questions help family members to compliment themselves on their resourcefulness. I spent the remainder of the first interview and subsequent sessions with Randy and his mother amplifying and consolidating the multitude of pretreatment changes. Other pretreatment change questions include "Is it different for him to do those things?" "What will you have to continue to do to get that [exception behavior] to happen more often?" "Are you aware of how you did that?"

"Why Now?" Questions

Solution-oriented therapists believe strongly that the therapeutic context is a place for change and not for endless "problem talk," which can trigger negative emotions and further disempower the family (Fredrickson, 2003; Gingerich et al., 1988). However, it is essential for us to elicit from our clients what specifically led to their pursuing therapy, as a preliminary step toward goal formulation. Therefore, it is helpful to begin an interview with clients who do not readily report pretreatment changes by asking "What brings you in now?" or "What would you like to change today?" rather than asking "What is the problem?" If parents reel off a long list of presenting problems, I ask them, "What would you like to change first?" Once we know what specifically the clients want to work on changing, we can break down the behavior of concern into bite-size pieces, and they can determine which piece of the problem they would like to resolve first.

Solution-Building Questions

With many difficult adolescent cases, it is not so easy early in the first interview to steer away from "problem talk" or negotiate solvable problems and goals. Therefore, the therapist needs to actively disrupt the clients' problem-talk interactive pattern and inquire about exceptions (de Shazer, 1988, 1991; Lipchik, 1988; O'Hanlon & Weiner-Davis, 1989). Exceptions take the form of useful patterns of behavior, thoughts, beliefs, and feelings that have helped the client not to be pushed around by the presenting problem. These exceptions when amplified by the therapist can serve as building blocks for solution construction. Some examples of solution-building questions are:

- "You have given me a fairly good picture of the problem you are concerned with, but in order to have a more complete picture about what needs to be done here, I now need to know: When this problem does not happen, what's happening instead?"

- "What are you [the parents] doing differently around Bill [the son]?"
- "Are you aware of how you did that?"
- "Was that different for you to do that?"
- "If Bill were sitting here today, what would he say he would want the two of you [the parents] to continue doing that was helping you get along better?"
- "What will have to happen for that [parental exception behavior] to happen more often?"
- "How will you know when the problem is really solved?"

Rebecca and her mother, Linda, were referred to me by their family physician. Linda was convinced that her 16-year-old daughter had "depression." Although there were no readily identifiable precipitants or familial history of depression, after reading a popular magazine article, Linda believed that Rebecca had all of the "symptoms of teenage depression," such as "isolating" from the family, being noncommunicative with Linda, some slight decline in her grades, "being moody," and so forth. Despite the mother's concerns, the family physician did not corroborate her diagnosis, but felt that a little therapy might be useful. Linda brought Rebecca to the first session.

THERAPIST: What brings you in now?

LINDA: Well, I think Rebecca has teenage depression.

T: How do you know that?

L: Well, she has all of the symptoms . . . I think of teenage depression . . .

T: I'm curious, Linda, what's different with Rebecca during the times when she's more up?

L: Well, she's playing her piano, she's helping me out in the kitchen, and I guess she's telling me good things about her boyfriend.

T: Did you give her boyfriend the "*Good Housekeeping* seal of approval," Linda?

L: *(laughing)* He's a good kid.

T: So, Rebecca's got good taste in young men?

L: Very good taste.

REBECCA: Yeah, my mom really likes Steven . . . Look, I really didn't think we needed to come here. I've been a little bummed about a friend of mine moving away . . .

L: Oh, you mean Helen? I didn't know the two of you were so close?

R: Yeah, after school I used to go over to her house a lot before you came home after work.

T: How can your mother be helpful to you at this time in dealing with the Helen situation?

R: Stop asking me 20 questions about being "depressed!" Sometimes my mom gets carried away with magazine articles.

T: Is there anything else she could do or has done in the past with you that has been helpful when you're "bummed?"

R: Talk about it . . . I guess we haven't gone out shopping together in a long time. *(Looks at her mother, smiling.)*

I saw Linda and Rebecca only one time. Besides utilizing exception-oriented questions, I introduced doubt in Linda's mind about Rebecca's having a "teenage depression" by asking the former "How do you know that?" Rebecca normalized her own behavior by describing it as her being "bummed" about the loss of a friend, which is a temporary and solvable difficulty. I then elicited Rebecca's expertise regarding more productive things her mother could do in relationship to her to help her feel less "bummed."

Unique Account and Redescription Questions

Unique account and redescription questions were developed by Michael White (1988b) to assist families in the coauthoring of new stories about themselves and their relationships that counter the dominant stories that have been oppressing them. Unique account questions invite family members to make sense of important exceptions by linking them to particular patterns of interaction or a series of events in time or place (White, 1988b; White & Epston, 1990). Two examples of unique account questions are "How did you manage to take that important step to turn things around?" and "What were you telling yourself to get ready for this big step?"

Unique redescription questions invite family members to ascribe significance and new meaning to the exceptions and unique accounts through the redescription of themselves, their family relationships, and significant others (White, 1988b, 1995; White & Epston, 1990). These questions empower family members "to operate in the domain of consciousness and to call forth alternative knowledges" (White, 1988b, p. 12). Two examples of unique redescription questions are "What does this tell you about yourself that is important to know?" and "How has this new picture of yourself changed how you view yourself as a person?"

The following excerpt is taken from my first interview with Randy and his mother, Mary. I utilize a unique account question with Randy to find out what he told himself in the juvenile detention center that made him decide to turn over a new leaf after getting out.

THERAPIST: What kinds of things did you tell yourself in the "juvie" that made you decide "I'm going to be a different person when I get out?"

RANDY: Well . . . I told myself, "I can do better than ending up in places like this"; "I have to stop smoking reefer"; "I need to stop cutting school"; "I gotta listen to my mom." Things like that, man.

T: Wow! It sounds like you were really doing some heavy soul searching in the juvie.

MARY: I've noticed that he's really trying this time.

T: Randy, what will be the next step you plan to take in your continued journey to pioneer a new direction in your life?

Throughout the first interview with Randy, I was truly amazed by how much he had changed during his month-long incarceration experience in the "juvie." I frequently made distinctions in the interview between the new responsible Randy versus the old "I don't care" Randy. The mother clearly noticed Randy's growth steps and was a key coauthor in helping her son rewrite his story as a responsible young man pioneering a new direction in life.

Presuppositional Questions

Presuppositional questions (O'Hanlon & Weiner-Davis, 1989) are powerful interventive questions that can be utilized to amplify pretreatment changes and exceptions, to convey the inevitability of change to clients, to elicit the client's outcome goal, and to co-create a future client reality without problems. Presuppositional questions can also produce significant changes in the client's perceptions and behaviors. Listening carefully to our clients' own presuppositions can give us clues as to where they are stuck and what directions to pursue with them. If family members appear to be stuck in the past with their perceptions about their present problem situation, it makes sense to move the therapeutic conversation into the future where there are many more possibilities for change. Some examples of presuppositional questions are:

- "How will you know when you would not have to come here anymore?"

- "If you were to show me a videotape of how things will look over the next week when Johnny has stopped breaking curfew, how will the three of you be getting along better?"
- "What will we see different happening?"
- "Johnny, what will we see you doing differently in relationship to your parents?"
- "If we were to gaze into my imaginary crystal ball after you have 'fixed' [client's language] your relationship with your dad, what kinds of things will we see you and him doing together, and how will you be talking to him differently?"
- "Suppose we were to run into one another in a month at a 7-Eleven store after we successfully completed counseling together, and you proceeded to tell me the steps you took to get out of counseling. What steps would you tell me you took?"
- "Imagine you are driving home from our session today and it had achieved what you were hoping for, what will have changed with your situation?"
- "What will a small sign of progress look like in the next week that will indicate to you that you are heading in the right direction?"
- "What are you going to do to get up to a 6 over the next week?"

Miracle Question Sequence

The miracle question was developed by de Shazer (1988, 1991) to rapidly move clients into a future reality without problems. This question is particularly useful for eliciting from clients their treatment goals and a detailed description of what an ideal outcome picture will look like to them when the problem is solved. I like to move quickly to the miracle question when my clients are negating my solution-building questions and are pessimistic about their problem situation. The miracle question sequence is as follows:

- "Suppose the three of you go home tonight, and while you are asleep a miracle happens and your problem is solved. How will you be able to tell the next day that a miracle must have happened?"
- "What will be different?"
- "How will you have done that?"
- "What else will be different between the three of you?"
- "Who will be the most surprised when you do that?"
- "Who next?"
- "If I were a fly on your living room wall watching the three of you after the miracle happened, what kinds of things will I see you doing together?"

- "If your sister were sitting here, what will she notice first and be the most surprised with that changed in your relationship with you and your mother after the miracle happened?"
- "How will that change make a difference for you [the daughter]?"
- "I'm curious: are any pieces of the miracle happening a little bit already?"

The key to getting the most mileage out of the miracle question is to expand the possibilities—that is, to have family members describe a detailed picture of what all of the miracle-produced changes will look like in every context they interface with and what the significant others in their lives will notice is different about them after the miracle.

The following case example demonstrates the utility of the miracle question for helping to co-create a context for change with a white 14-year-old depressed boy and his mother.

Robert had been referred to me by his school counselor for "depression," "school failure," and "poor peer relations." The excerpt below is taken from the first interview after Robert and his mother had negated my solution-building questions.

THERAPIST: Suppose the two of you were to go home tonight and while you are asleep, a miracle happened and your problem is solved. How would you be able to tell the next morning that a miracle happened? What will be different?

ROBERT: Well, I would wake up and get out of bed with a smile on my face and tell my dad: "It's time to go to school!"

T: So, you will "wake up with a smile" on your face; what else will you be doing differently at school?

R: I will be listening more, paying more attention in class, not asking as many questions, doing my work . . .

T: Which one of your teachers will be most surprised by the new Robert?

R: They will all probably faint!

T: Which one of your teachers will faint first!?

R: I'd probably have to say Mr. Johnson.

T: After you help revive Mr. Johnson, what will be the first thing he will comment to you that has changed about you?

R: "Robert, an A on your math test!?"

T: Who will be the next teacher to faint?

R: I would have to say Mrs. Williams.

T: After she wakes up, what will her first words be to you?

R: Good job, Robert!

T: What else will be different at school for you?

R: Well, I would have made a couple of friends.

T: Two friends?

R: Yeah. There's this one guy named Juan who I've seen in some of my classes.

T: Will you have approached him, or what will you have done with Juan?

R: I will have approached him and asked him if he would like to grab a taco at the El Toro restaurant after school.

T: He strikes you as someone who likes to eat tacos? How can you tell the difference between someone who likes to eat tacos and a non-taco-eater?

R: There's one thing . . . the color of the skin . . . he's Hispanic. *(laughter)*

T: Oh! What about on the home front? If your father were sitting here, what would he say has changed about you after the miracle happened?

I ended up spending close to 30 minutes on the miracle inquiry with Robert and his mother. Besides asking about the changes Robert's father and mother will notice in Robert and in their relationships, I brought into the miracle picture the maternal and paternal grandparents and other relatives. Because Robert and his mother were able to describe in great detail how things would look when the problems were solved, I simply had to prescribe that they engage in the solution behaviors they identified in the miracle picture.

Coping Sequence

With families that tend to be more pessimistic and do not respond well to the miracle question, I shift gears and mirror their pessimistic stance by asking them: "How come things aren't worse?"; "What are you and others doing to keep this situation from getting much worse?" Once the parents respond with some specific exceptions, I shift gears again and amplify these problem-solving strategies and ask: "Are you aware of how you did that?"; "What will you have to continue to do to get that to happen more often?"

In the following case example, I utilized the coping sequence (Berg & Miller, 1992; Berg & Gallagher, 1991) with June, an African American single parent who was quite pessimistic about her 16-year-old boy, Sid, ever changing.

Sid had longstanding problems with underachieving and being truant from school. Early in the first interview, I found myself stuck doing "more of the same" (Watzlawick et al., 1974) by asking solution-building questions that were being met with responses from June like "He's always been an underachiever," "He's not going to school," or "He's got a bad attitude." When I asked June the miracle question, she could envision neither Sid ever changing nor her being able to do anything differently to affect his behavior. Sid, on the other hand, was able to spell out numerous miracle behaviors he would be engaging in, two of which he was already doing—completing his homework assignments and going to school! However, June had not made any mention of these big changes on Sid's behalf earlier in the interview.

JUNE: You know, that's the thing I don't like about him . . . He's got a lot of anger inside him . . . I'm not even sure if he went to school yesterday . . . You know, he's your kid, and . . .

THERAPIST: I'm curious, how come things aren't worse?

J: Well . . . he's got a good home environment, you know, he's not had to grow up in the slums . . .

T: What else have you been doing to prevent things from getting worse?

J: Well, I make him watch those educational shows on TV . . . We talk a lot, joke and punch . . . He's just rebellious at times.

T: Yeah, teenagers can be real rebellious at times. What else are you doing to prevent things from getting worse? I mean he could be running away, doing drugs . . . he even came to our therapy session!

J: Yeah, that's a real miracle! I don't know . . . I guess I keep the lines of communication open.

T: How do you do that?

J: Well, I make myself available to him and let him know I am concerned and proud of him at times . . . In fact, just the other day, I complimented him. I had to go to the grocery store and had asked him to not go out until I returned home . . . and he waited for me!

T: Wow! How did you get him to do that!?

J: Yeah . . . I was so proud of him and he's even gone to school a few days this week . . .

T: Really! So you're already noticing that he's making a little progress? How did you get that to happen!?

J: I guess keeping the lines of communication open, you know, letting him know not to mess around with Mom. When Mom says something, she means it!

T: Yeah, don't "mess around with Mom!"

As readers can clearly see, we made a complete U-turn in the interviewing process. Through mirroring June's pessimism, I was able to move our therapeutic conversation in a positive direction that produced some important parental exceptions. I ended up giving June an observation task to continue to notice all the various things she did in relationship to Sid that further contributed to his turning things around at school and at home.

Scaling Questions

Scaling questions (de Shazer, 1985, 1991) are useful for securing a quantitative measurement of the family problem prior to treatment and presently, and of where they would like to be in 1 week's time. This category of questions is a valuable goal-setting tool and helps maintain a clear focus throughout the course of therapy. Once the family has identified and rated the problem situation on a scale of 1 to 10, the therapist's job is to negotiate with the parents and adolescent what each party will have to do to get at one point higher on the scale in 1 week's time. I like to use pluses and minuses when clients report their progress on the scale in second and future sessions. For example, if a parent returns to a second session reporting that she had scored a 5 or 6, I would ask her, "Would you rate the situation at a 6-minus or a 5-plus?" Scaling questions can be used to measure a client's confidence level regarding the possibility of resolving their presenting problem. I may ask a parent who has been frequently arguing with her son: "How confident are you on a scale from 1 to 10—10 being totally confident—that you will resolve this difficulty with your son?" Once the parent provides me with a number on the scale, I can ask what he will need to do as well as what adjustments she could make for him to gain a point higher on the scale. This will then become the initial goal for therapy. After utilizing the miracle question (de Shazer, 1988) sequence, scaling questions can be used to negotiate a well-formed and realistic treatment goal (de Shazer, 1991) with families (see Figure 4.2).

In case situations where the adolescent and her parents cannot agree on a mutual treatment goal, I establish separate goals and work projects. Another effective way to gain the adolescent's cooperation is to have her scale what she considers her parents' most annoying or upsetting behaviors to be. For example, the adolescent will rate on a scale from 1 to 10 her parents' "yelling" behavior a month prior to beginning therapy, presently, and what specifically would they need to do in 1 week's time to get a point higher on the scale as a sign of their efforts to reduce this behavior.

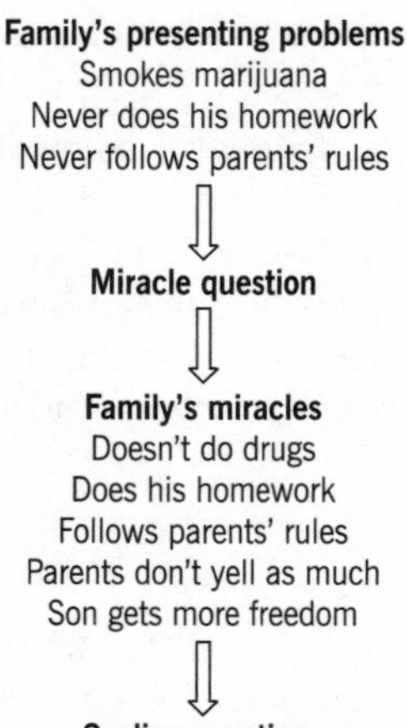

Scaling questions

Parents presently rate their son at a 3. He will make it to a 4 if he does his homework daily for 1 week.

Therapist negotiates a more realistic and smaller goal with the parents and adolescent.

Treatment goal

Son earns a 4 parental rating when he does his homework 2 days out of 5.

Privilege negotiated

Son will be able to come home 1 hour later Friday night when he achieves the goal established.

FIGURE 4.2. Establishing a well-formed treatment goal.

Josephina, a Latina 15-year-old, was referred to me for family therapy for "running away" and "family problems" by her school guidance counselor. Her mother had been identified as being an "alcoholic" by Josephina's counselor. Throughout the first interview, the mother was highly pessimistic and voiced her opinion that "counseling is not helpful" and "has not worked in the past." Once I asked the mother to scale Josephina's arguing behavior, the session became more focused and she was less negative. The mother identified two treatment goals for Josephina, to stop running away and for her daughter to stop arguing with her all of the time. Surprisingly, I was able to get the mother to agree to work on changing the arguing problem first, rather than trying to take on the monolithic goal of stopping the running away behavior.

THERAPIST: On a scale from 1 to 10—10 being the best, 1 the pits—how would you have rated Josephina's arguing with you 4 weeks ago?

MOTHER: She was probably at a 2, but the shit really hit the fan when she ran away the last time, and now she's grounded.

T: Where would you rate her today?

M: Well, she's been pretty good lately . . . Well, I'd have to give her a 6.

T: Wow! That's quite a leap for her. How did you get her to move up the scale from a 2 to a 6?

M: Well, I've grounded her and tried not to blow up as much as I used to.

T: What will Josephina have to do to make it to a 7?

M: Well, listen to me without putting up a fight. If she could go 2 days without arguing with me, I would give her a 7.

T: Is there anything you think you could do differently around Josephina over the next week that can help make that possible?

M: It's really up to her to change, but I suppose I can try to not blow up as much.

After meeting alone with the mother to further negotiate her treatment goal, I met with Josephina before the intersession break to see if she would accept her mother's goal and to explore with her if she had a separate goal or any privileges she wanted me to pursue for her with her mother. Josephina confidently said she could go for more than 2 days without arguing with her mother.

One week later, Josephina and her mother returned, with the latter reporting that her daughter had "scored a 9." Josephina had gone an "entire week without arguing" even once with her mother. I spent the whole second session amplifying all of the family changes.

Finally, with more chronic adolescent case situations that are riddled with past treatment failures and family members who are highly pessimistic, I may use a totally subzero scale, with –10 being the worst and the situation is hopeless and –1 being the problem situation has slightly improved. This question can dramatically increase the optimism and confidence levels of some of the most pessimistic clients, including suicidal clients.

Percentage Questions

Similar to scaling questions (de Shazer, 1985, 1991), percentage questions help provide a clear focus in treatment and a quantitative measurement of progress in the family's goal area across the course of therapy. Percentage questions also provide the family with a double description (White, 1986) of their problem situation, which can open up space for new possibilities for them. Some examples of percentage questions are: "What percentage of the time does Bill invite you [the parents] to take responsibility for him?" "What percentage of the time, Bill, do you take responsibility for yourself?" "What percentage of the time are you standing up to bulimia versus bulimia's getting the better of you?"

The following case example illustrates how percentage questions can be utilized to co-create a double description (White, 1986) of a parent's pathological label of her daughter's behavior, with each of the therapist's descriptions indicating more normal and solvable adolescent behaviors.

Marjorie sought therapy for help in dealing with her daughter's "behavior disordered" problem. Sarah, Marjorie's 16-year-old daughter, had been chronically "violating" the "rules," "constantly arguing" with Marjorie, and sometimes "ditching school." The excerpt below is taken from the first interview.

THERAPIST: What brings you in now?

MARJORIE: My daughter Sarah is "behavior disordered." She never listens to me, we're constantly arguing, she's always violating my rules, and there are days where I'm convinced she is ditching school . . . and . . .

T: How do you know she is "behavior disordered?"

M: Well . . . that's what her school counselor thinks . . . What do you think?

T: I'm curious: what percentage of Sarah's behavior would you consider to be normal teenage rebelliousness versus obnoxiousness?

M: Well . . . I . . . I never thought of it that way . . . but if I had to give you percentages . . . I would say she's probably 60% rebellious and 40% obnoxious.

T: Help me out; how were the percentages different 4 weeks ago?

M: Well, 4 weeks ago I would have given her a much higher ranking on the rebelliousness end of things.

T: What percentage number would you have given her back then?

M: Oh, I would have to say . . . she was really infuriating me back then . . . I would have given her 90% on the rebelliousness end of things!

T: Wow! How did you get her down to only 60% of the time being rebellious? What have you been doing differently?

M: Well, I'm not yelling as much. I have been going for walks.

T: What else have you been doing to help her be less rebellious?

I ended up spending the remainder of the session eliciting other important exceptions on Marjorie's behalf that had not only helped her better cope with Sarah's normal teenage behaviors but that also helped her have a more cooperative relationship with her daughter. After three sessions of therapy with

Marjorie, she was totally convinced that Sarah was a "normal teenager." Sarah's final percentages ended up being "50% rebellious" and "50% obnoxious" in our termination session.

Pessimistic Sequence

If a family continues to be pessimistic about the problem situation after I have utilized the coping sequence with them, I will shift gears and match their unique cooperative response pattern by utilizing the pessimistic sequence (Berg & Miller, 1992; Berg & Gallagher, 1991). Despite the therapist's best efforts to create hope and a context for change, highly pessimistic parents will insist that their adolescents' behaviors will continue to get worse and produce dire consequences. Therefore, it makes the most sense to join these parents on their own level. Often this line of questioning will enable family members to generate some useful problem-solving and coping strategies to better manage their difficult situation. Some examples of pessimistic questions are:

- "What do you think will happen if things don't get better?"
- "And then what?"
- "Who will suffer the most?"
- "Who will feel the worst?"
- "What do you suppose is the smallest thing you could do that might make a slight difference?"
- "And what could other family members do?"
- "How could you get that to happen a little bit now?"
- "Some parents in your situation would have thrown in the towel a long time ago with counseling. Why are you willing to give it another try?"
- "Some parents in your situation might have shipped their son off to a boarding or military school by now. What has stopped you from doing that?"
- "Since your daughter continues to persist with her daredevil ways, have the two of you ever wondered what life would be like without having her in the picture anymore?"

The pessimistic sequence may successfully elicit parents' affection for and willingness to not give up on their adolescent, even when the family situation is at its all-time worst. These questions can also successfully create emotional intensity with laissez-faire parents to get them more involved in the problem-solving efforts, particularly in situations where you feel like you are working harder than them to save their kids from serious consequences or tragic outcomes. The case example below demonstrates how the use of the pessimistic sequence can open the door for possibilities.

Darcy, a white 14-year-old, was brought in for a consultation with me after receiving a therapeutic pass from her doctor at the psychiatric hospital she presently was in. She was accompanied by her parents, Helen and Charlie, and the three involved outside therapists who had been seeing various members of the family. What led to this third psychiatric admission was Darcy's threatening her parents and sister with a butcher knife. Darcy had a long history of violent, self-harming, and oppositional behavior. She also had some past serious bouts with depression and would become suicidal at times. The conflict was so intense between Darcy and her parents that alternative living arrangements were being pursued, particularly residential treatment. The family was so highly pessimistic that it felt like we had just come from the funeral of someone significant they had lost. Much to my surprise, once I employed the pessimistic category of questions to better cooperate with their pessimism, a breakthrough occurred in the session. Up to this point in the session, the parents could not say one positive thing about Darcy nor envision her returning back home.

THERAPIST: Some parents in your situation—not that I think it is a good idea—would have tried to put their daughter in a group home, made their kid a ward of the state or, better yet, put their kid up for adoption! What has stopped you from doing that!?

HELEN: I could never do that! I love Darcy too much. (*Darcy leans forward in her chair and acknowledges nonverbally that she is pleased to hear this.*)

T: In what ways do you show Darcy that you really love her?

H: I hug her a lot and give her a kiss when she allows me to.

T: Throughout the session you alluded to how you would like Darcy to "get well." What would be some hard signs that will tell you that she is really "well?" What specifically does she need to do that will show you that she is well?

H: Well, she would not hurt herself when upset. She would talk about what was making her mad, what others did that upset her, how she responded, and what she could have done differently.

CHARLIE: She made some great strides in anger management!

H: Yeah, it was really big!

C: We went to the Red Lobster restaurant, and she was shaking the ketchup bottle, and suddenly she was coated—and she did it again. . . . Before this night we would have had a major nuclear meltdown! But she just laughed it off! I was trying to stop myself from laughing—not at Darcy but at the whole ketchup thing. I was very proud of how well she handled this embarrassing situation. (*Darcy looks up at Charlie and smiles.*)

T: Darcy, are you aware of how you handled that situation so well!? That's incredible! I would have gotten upset. Way to go!

Following this portion of the session, the atmosphere in the room dramatically shifted, and Darcy and her parents began to discuss how they were going to fix up her bedroom when she came back home from the psychiatric hospital.

Externalizing Questions

Externalizing the problem (White, 1984, 1985, 1986, 1987, 1988a, 1988b, 1995; White & Epston, 1990) is a useful therapeutic option with highly entrenched families that are not responding well to solution-oriented questions in the interviewing process. The family's presenting problem can be externalized into a problem lifestyle or career, a pattern, a DSM-IV label that has taken on a life of its own, or an objectified oppressive tyrant (Selekman, 1996, 2002). When externalizing the family's presenting problem, it is most important to carefully use family members' language and belief material about the problem. Otherwise, family members will interpret your new construction of their problem situation as being "too unusual" and will disregard it (Andersen, 1991). According to Michael White (White & Epston, 1990), externalizing the problem can therapeutically accomplish the following six things with entrenched families:

1. Decrease unproductive conflict between persons, including those disputes over who is responsible for the problem;
2. Undermine the sense of failure that has developed for many persons in response to the continuing existence of the problem despite their attempts to resolve it;
3. Pave the way for persons to cooperate with each other; to unite in a struggle against the problem and to escape its influence in their lives and relationships;
4. Open up new possibilities for persons to take action to retrieve their lives and relationships from the problem and its influence;
5. Free persons to take a lighter, more effective, and less stressed approach to "deadly serious" problems;
6. Present options for dialogue, rather than monologue, about the problem. (pp. 39–40)

The following case example illustrates the therapeutic utility of externalizing the problem in disrupting a longstanding blame–counterblame pattern of interaction in the family.

The Browns were a remarried family. Both Fred and Lisa had been married once before. Their previous marriages were reportedly quite stormy, and Sean, Lisa's only child from her first marriage, was being identified as the current family problem. Sean had longstanding problems with stealing, being disruptive in school, and not responding to Lisa's limits. Sean greatly disliked Fred and did not get along with the latter's two sons from his first marriage. Throughout the first interview, there was a great deal of blaming and arguing across family subgroups. My attempts to elicit exception material and utilize the miracle question were thwarted. However, both parents pointed out how "blaming" had riddled their previous marriages and was clearly a problem in the present family drama. I decided to capitalize on this oppressive past "blaming" pattern by externalizing it and moving the focus off of Sean as the problem.

THERAPIST: How long has this "blaming" pattern been pushing all of you around for?

FRED: Well, I was married to my first wife for 5 years, and Lisa and I have been together for the past 2 years.

LISA: I have been dealing with this blaming thing for about 9 years, and Sean's father and even Sean still blame me for everything now.

SEAN: Can I leave now? I'm sick of her [his mother's] bullshit! She's always jumping on my case all of the time!

T: Do you see how blaming got in between the two of you right there and made you lock horns with each other?

F: You know he's right. We need to stop dumping on one another and close the door on our pasts. This is our new family, and we have to make it work.

T: I'm curious, Lisa: have you noticed any times lately where this blaming thing was trying to make you "dump" on Sean, but you stood up to it and did something else?

L: In fact, yesterday I was tempted to "dump" on Sean about how he reminds me of his father when he leaves his things laying all over the house, but I asked him nicely to put his dirty clothes in the laundry basket.

S: Yeah, usually you're screaming at me about what a "pig" I am.

T: Sean, I think I'm going to give your mom a high-five for achieving that victory over blaming. *(Gives Lisa a high-five and, much to my surprise, Sean gives his mother one as well.)*

The remainder of the interview was more positive, and we focused our attention on the various things family members were doing to both accept invitations from the blaming pattern to "dump" on one another as well as discussing important things they were already doing to stand up to it. I gave them a task to keep track on a daily basis of the various things they did to achieve victories over the blaming pattern. They were also asked to keep track of blaming's victories over them. I recommended that they train as a family for their big battle with blaming, because "it will not die easily, for patterns are powerful things." Sean was placed in charge of developing a family exercise program because he was the "true athlete" in the family. Fred and Lisa were in charge of charting their daily victories and losses with blaming.

Future-Oriented Questions

For our clients, the future is fertile ground for change, because it has not happened yet. We can be co-architects with our clients in designing the kind of future realities they wish to have. Research indicates that those individuals who can envision a future of mastery and success at performing tasks will tend to outperform those subjects that anticipate hypothetical failure (Sherman, Skov, Hervitz, & Stock, 1981). Spanos and Radtke (1981) and Spanos (1990) have found in their hypnosis research that having subjects absorb themselves in imagining future events has a powerful hallucinatory effect. The subjects actually believed that their imaginings were a reality for them. These studies help provide some empirical support for the use of imagination and the imagined future in the therapeutic arena.

Future-oriented questions are particularly useful with "past-bound" (Tomm, 1987), chronic, and entrenched family cases. According to Penn (1985), future-oriented questions "promote the rehearsal of new solutions, suggest alternative actions, foster learning, discard ideas of redetermination, and address the system's specific change model" (p. 299). Some examples of future-oriented questions are:

- "When Johnny gets a job, who will be the most surprised in the family?"
- "If we were to gaze into my imaginary crystal ball after you got over your 'anger and bitterness' [client's words] toward your father, what will we observe happening that is different about your relationship?"
- "What else will be different?"
- "When I'm gazing into the crystal ball, what will I notice that is different about you that will surprise me the most?"
- "If you were to show me a videotape of your family after we successfully completed counseling together, what kinds of changes will we observe on the video?

- "What will your probation officer be saying on the videotape that he was the most pleased with that changed with your situation?"

Billy, a white 17-year-old, was court-ordered for 9 months of counseling after being arrested for dealing LSD, PCP ("angel dust"), and "magic mushrooms." Billy had a very stressful home situation. His mother had bipolar disorder, his father was always yelling at and criticizing him, and his sister was in residential treatment for severe behavioral difficulties. Surprisingly, Billy showed up to our first session alone. This transcript is during the goal-setting portion of the session. It illustrates the importance of matching our presuppositional and metaphorical language with the client's. I thought the use of the imaginary crystal ball would be quite fitting for Billy in that he loved to hallucinate!

THERAPIST: Let's say I handed you an imaginary crystal ball, and you gazed into it after you got over your "anger and bitterness." What will you see in there?

BILLY: Well, I will be looking at how I fixed my relationship with my father.

T: Okay, we are gazing into the crystal ball. What will you tell me you did to "fix" the relationship with him?

B: Well, I will be giving him the benefit of the doubt, listening to what he said, I would probably be talking to him differently, I guess . . .

T: By doing those things, how will it make a difference in your relationship with him?

B: Well, we would probably get along better. I could talk to him like the way you and I are hitting on right now.

Our imaginary crystal ball conversation went on for approximately 30 minutes. Billy systematically spelled out the steps he needed to take to "fix" his relationships with all family members. Initially, I prescribed for him to experiment with his self-generated solution strategies with his father. By the time that his father had come to a session with his son, their relationship had greatly improved, thanks to Billy's efforts. He also became drug-free as well.

Problem-Tracking Sequence

Once the brief therapist has exhausted the possibilities with the solution-oriented model, one good therapeutic option is to shift gears into more of an MRI brief problem-focused (Fisch et al., 1982; Watzlawick et al., 1974) therapeutic approach. The focus of therapy then becomes not only attempting to alter the family's perception of their problem situation but also actively disrupting the problem-maintaining sequences of interaction in the family. Problem-tracking questions (Palazzoli, Boscolo, Cecchin, & Prata, 1980) can elicit from family members a detailed videotape description of the circular patterns of interaction around the presenting problem. After securing this information, the brief therapist will then have several focal points at which to disrupt the circular problem-maintaining patterns (see Chapter 9 for pattern intervention strategies). Some examples of problem-tracking questions are:

- "If you were to show me a videotape of how things look when your brother comes home drunk, who confronts him first [asking a sibling of the identified client]—your mother or your father?"
- "After your mother confronts him, what does your brother do?"
- "How does your mother respond?"
- "Then what happens?"
- "What happens after that?"

Ideally, the therapist will secure a detailed picture from family members regarding the specific family patterns that have maintained the presenting problem. Pattern intervention (O'Hanlon & Weiner-Davis, 1989; O'Hanlon, 1987) can then be utilized to disrupt the problem-maintaining patterns.

Conversational Questions

Postmodern family therapy approaches (Anderson, 1997; Friedman, 1995; Andersen, 1991; Anderson & Goolishian, 1988a; Deissler, 1989; Lussardi & Miller, 1991) are becoming increasingly more popular today. They are particularly useful with families that are grappling with chronic difficulties and traumatized families that have had multiple treatment experiences. I have also found these collaborative and meaning-based approaches useful with cases where there appear to be family secrets and many helping professionals from larger systems involved. It has been my clinical experience that using only the solution-oriented brief therapy approach may disempower these families by editing the long stories they need to tell about their problem-saturated situations. Solution-oriented questions can shut down the therapeutic conversation by blocking family members from feeling free to share their painful and problem-saturated stories about their family drama. Conversational questions (Anderson, 1997; Anderson & Goolishian, 1988a, 1988b) are the therapist's primary tool for helping keep the therapeutic conversation going. These questions are opened-ended and are informed from a position of "not knowing" as opposed to "preknowing." By asking questions from a position of "not knowing," we place ourselves in the position of learning (Anderson, 1997; Anderson & Goolishian, 1988a). When family members feel free to tell and retell their stories, this can lead to the disclosure of the "not yet said" (Anderson & Goolishian, 1988b) and the generation of new meanings and possibilities for the family. Some examples of conversational questions are:

- "You have seen many therapists before me. What do you suppose they overlooked or missed with your situation?"
- "If I were to work with another family just like you, what advice would you give me to help that family out?"
- "Do you [the adolescent] have any advice for your parents about how they can argue less?"
- "Do you have any advice for your parents about how they can be less in charge of your motivation to do your homework?"
- "What's missing with your situation that, if provided, would make a difference?"
- "If there were one question you were hoping I would ask you during our work together, what would that be?"
- "Who in the family will have the most difficult time talking about this issue?"
- "If 'cutting' came to you for counseling, what questions would you really want to ask it?"
- "Before you came in here for the first time, was there anything that you told yourselves that you were not going to talk about in our family meetings together?"

The following case example illustrates the importance of therapeutic flexibility in the interviewing process.

I had begun my first interview with Sharon and her mother by using solution-oriented questions. Sharon, a white 16-year-old, had been brought to me for her chronic headache problem. After many years of extensive testing, the family physician and other headache specialists had not been able to find any physical signs for this problem. Sharon had been plagued by headaches since she was 12 years old. Solution-oriented questioning had failed to generate exceptions. At this point in the interview, I decided to abandon this type of questioning and asked conversational questions instead. The excerpt below is taken from the first interview.

THERAPIST: Who in your family gives you the biggest headache?

SHARON: My dad. He is so bigoted and conservative. He's always putting down gays, Jews, and so forth.

MOTHER: Yeah, he can be like that at times, but he's getting better.

Throughout the interview, Sharon appeared to get quite emotional when she talked about her father. I decided to meet alone with Sharon to give her more room to tell her story, particularly about her relationship with her father.

THERAPIST: If there were one issue in your family that has not been talked about yet, what would that be?

SHARON: *(Begins to shake and cry.)* Well . . . um, well *(crying and shaking)* I think I'm gay . . . and I'm so afraid if my dad finds out he'll never talk to me again. Please don't tell my mom *(crying and shaking)*.

T: I won't say a word until you are ready to talk about it. How long have you thought you were gay?

S: Since around sixth grade.

T: This has been a heavy load you have been carrying around in your head, hasn't it?

S: I'll say. The safest place for me to write down my thoughts about it is in my creative writing class assignments. I play all of the different characters in the stories. Sometimes I'm a man or a half-boy and half-girl.

Sharon and I continued to talk about her lifestyle choice in future sessions. Much to my surprise, in the second therapy session Sharon disclosed to her mother that she was gay. Initially her mother was quite shocked, but after three family sessions she came around to accepting it. This was a "newsworthy" experience for the mother in that it helped explain why Sharon was having her stress-related headaches and reacting so strongly to her father when he would criticize gays. The mother also successfully got Sharon's father to be a little more understanding with Sharon.

Consolidating Questions

Consolidating questions are useful for amplifying pretreatment changes and for reinforcing family changes that occur in second and subsequent sessions. At times, I may use my imaginary crystal ball (de Shazer, 1985) and videotape metaphor (O'Hanlon & Weiner-Davis, 1989) to invite clients to provide a visual description of how things will have further improved with their situation 2 weeks to 6 months down the road. Some examples of consolidating questions are:

- "What will you have to continue to do to keep these changes happening?"

- "Are you aware of how you got that to happen?!"
- "What would you have to do to go backwards?"
- "What would you have to do to prevent a major backslide?"
- "What did you learn from your slip on Tuesday that you will put to use the next time you're faced with a similar stressful situation?"
- "How were you able to stay on track on Wednesday?
- "If I was to invite you to my next parenting group to serve as guest speaker, what helpful advice and pointers would you give to those parents?"
- "Let's say this was our last counseling session together: what fun things will you be doing during this time?"
- "Let's say we got together 1 month from today to celebrate your successfully completing counseling. If each of you were to give speeches reflecting on the further changes you had made happen, what would each of you be eager to share with me?"

When conducting the purposeful systemic interview, the brief therapist needs to carefully read the family's nonverbal and verbal feedback as well as be prepared, at any given moment in the session, to shift from one question category to another. By "staying close" to the family, we are making room for the familiar and opening up space for new possibilities.

MECHANICS OF THE SOLUTION-ORIENTED BRIEF FAMILY THERAPY INTERVIEW

After establishing good rapport with each family member, I begin the interview by exploring what the trigger was that led the family to pursue therapy now, as well as inquire about pretreatment changes. As early as possible in the initial interview, I engage family members in change talk (Gingerich et al., 1988) and attempt to move them into the future with presuppositional questions (O'Hanlon & Weiner-Davis, 1989). When families are able to spend most of the session time reporting the present and future changes that they envision for themselves, that approach can dissolve the idea that they have a problem. I have experienced this with clients who present with significant pretreatment changes. If the parents identify a problem area they wish to see changed with their adolescent, I attempt to deconstruct the problem into a more solvable behavior and negotiate a smaller and more realistic treatment goal with the family. The miracle question (de Shazer, 1988) and scaling (de Shazer, 1985) or percentage questions are useful tools during the goal-setting process. However, if no goal can be negotiated between the parents and adolescent, the interactions in the therapy room are destructive; and if the use of the miracle, coping, pessimistic sequence questions (de Shazer, 1988; Berg & Miller, 1992) fails to produce exceptions or a treatment goal, I separate the family and meet with subsystems and establish separate treatment goals and work projects.

Brainstorming with the Parents

When meeting alone with the parents, I use the time to explore with them their past and present attempted solutions, negotiate a separate treatment goal with them, and address any expectations or concerns they may have. While exploring with the parents their attempted solutions, I ask: "Has there been anything that you have tried in the past with your son that worked with some other problem that we may want to use now?"; "Has there been something that you thought about trying out with your daughter, but for whatever reason you didn't think it would work?"; and "Has there been anything you tried in the past with your other kids when they were having similar difficulties in the past that seemed to work?" These questions capitalize on the parents' resourcefulness and creativity, as well as help to generate potential solutions. I punctuate the parents' resourcefulness and creativity through cheerleading, which helps make these potential solutions "newsworthy" to them. When I establish a separate treatment goal with the parents, it usually involves having them experiment with new behaviors they wish to pursue around their adolescent—for example, to go 2 out of 7 days without yelling at their son. At times, the parents cannot readily identify a treatment goal but want to do something about the son or daughter's problematic behavior. If they indicate a desire to experiment with some new parenting strategies, I may offer them an observation task (Molnar & de Shazer, 1987) or the "do something different" task (de Shazer, 1985), depending on their treatment goal, cooperative response patterns, and stages of readiness to change.

Empowering the Adolescent

I like to use individual session time with adolescents to increase rapport, establish a separate treatment goal, negotiate the parents' treatment goal, make room for them to tell their stories about their family situations, and find out what specifically they would like me to work on changing with their parents that annoys them the most and if there are any privileges they wish me to advocate for them with their parents. Because the majority of difficult adolescent clients are visitors/precontemplators (Prochaska, 1999; de Shazer, 1988), I accept whatever goals they identify for themselves, which may be completely unrelated to what brought them in for therapy. However, it has been my clinical experience that if the therapist joins well enough with the adolescent, the youth may be willing to do whatever the parents and the therapist request, particularly if a privilege could be earned as a reward. With adolescent cases, the therapist needs to be an intergenerational negotiator. Most adolescent clients tend to cooperate with therapists that pay attention to what *their* goals and expectations are, not just what the parents want. I like to ask my adolescent clients, "How can I be helpful to you?" This conversational question can open the door for the adolescent to identify his or her goals and expectations, share what privileges he or she wants, and tell his or her story about the family drama. In Chapter 6, I discuss 10 effective engagement strategies for difficult adolescents.

Approximately 40 minutes into the hour, I have the reflecting treatment team (Andersen, 1987, 1991; Lussardi & Miller, 1991), who have been observing the session from behind the one-way mirror, come into the therapy room, while the family and I go behind the mirror to listen to their reflections about the interview. One at a time, the reflecting team members reflect on significant family themes of resourcefulness and family strength, compliment family members on their past and present successes, offer new constructions of the family's problem situation, and reflect on the interviewing therapist's ability to cooperate with and assist the family in the change effort. According to Lussardi and Miller (1991), "it is the movement from one explanation to many, which allows information, new meanings, and the possibility for new behavior to occur" (p. 235). When giving reflections, team members should begin with such qualifiers as "I'm astonished by . . . ," "It seems to me . . . ," "I'm struck by . . . ," "Could it be . . . ," or "I wonder if . . . ." It is very important that the team members are careful not to bombard the family with too many ideas. The reflecting team members also need to "stay close" to the family by carefully utilizing the family members' language and belief system material in their reflections.

Another useful reflecting team format is to have two therapists in the therapy room: one therapist in the observing position and the other therapist interviewing the family. At the intersession break, the therapists will reflect in front of the family. This will be followed by the family's reflections on the therapists' conversation. This reflecting team format can be used with families that have requested having the team member present in the therapy room.

I have observed that families listening to the team's reflections behind the one-way mirror appear to be very absorbed in the reflecting team's conversation about them, and sometimes even in a trance. In fact, I frequently have observed head nods (yes-set hypnotic responses), parents smiling or shedding tears, and nonverbal gestures of affection exchanged between family members. Often the treatment team's reflections make family exceptions even more "newsworthy" to the family, alter family members' outmoded beliefs about their situation, and open up space for the "not yet said" or family secrets (Anderson & Goolishian, 1988b) to be disclosed by a family member. Once the reflecting team's conversation is over, we switch rooms again and the family and the interviewing therapist reflect on the team's reflections.

Because the reflecting team has such an empowering effect on the family, it is not always necessary for the therapist and team to offer the family a therapeutic task. After we discuss the reflecting team's conversation, if it appears that the team's reflections were not "newsworthy" to the family and there is still a strong concern on the family's behalf about a specific problem they want to actively do something about, I ask them if they would like a couple of ideas to experiment with over the next week. At this point, I have the team come into the room and brainstorm with them one or two therapeutic experiments that fit with family members' goals and cooperative response patterns. The team and I then present to the family the experiments we have selected or designed, and we give them a choice regarding which of the experiments they would like to try out. We also address any concerns they may have regarding the implementation of any of the experiments they have been offered. If need be, the experiments can be modified or better tailored to certain family members' liking.

When I am working solo, I still take a break and "meet with myself" to think about key family themes or stories, how I can positively relabel negative family members' behaviors, to construct compliments regarding family members' self-generated pretreatment changes and resourcefulness, and design or select appropriate therapeutic experiments for the family. After my minibreak, I share my compliments, offer some new constructions of the family's story, and present a menu of therapeutic experiments for family members to experiment with. With some families, if its members do not request a therapeutic experiment or if they present themselves as visitors, I only offer my reflections. I call this portion of the session "the editorial." At the conclusion of my editorial, I invite family members to reflect on how the meeting went for them and inquire what they liked about it, whether they learned anything new about their situation, and whether there is anything we did not cover that would be important to address in future sessions.

GUIDELINES FOR THERAPEUTIC EXPERIMENT DESIGN, SELECTION, AND IMPLEMENTATION

In this section I present useful guidelines for selecting and matching major solution-focused brief therapy experiments in first interviews with family members' treatment goals, unique cooperative response patterns, and stages of readiness for change (Prochaska, 1999). As a rule of thumb, all compliments, alternative constructions of the family's story, and therapeutic experiments evolve out of the interviewing process. De Shazer and his colleagues at the Brief Family Center in Milwaukee, Wisconsin, have developed a highly useful and accurate computer-based expert system called BRIEFER (de Shazer, 1988; Gingerich & de Shazer, 1991) that can aid therapists and trainees in clinically deciding which experiments to select for a particular case situation. I have found the BRIEFER II (Gingerich & de Shazer, 1991) flowchart to be quite useful when working with difficult adolescents and their families. However, if it appears that the clients are not responding well to my using a more pure solution-focused approach with them, I will opt for pursuing new therapeutic pathways with them to better foster a more cooperative relationship and promote change. I now present some practical guidelines for therapeutic experiment design and selection and provide case examples.

Formula First-Session Task

If a family presents with a vague or global complaint, Gingerich and de Shazer (1991) recommend the *formula first-session task*. Because this is a vague task, it will fit with the family's unique cooperative response pattern. De Shazer (1985) contends that this task is likely to work with these types of clients, because "the prophecy is that something worthwhile is going to be noticed between the first and second sessions, and the likelihood is that, indeed, that will be the case" (p. 139).

Eileen, a Latina 16-year-old, was referred to me by her probation officer for prostitution, running away from home, heavy substance abuse and drug dealing, and assault and battery charges. Her mother had been married 4 times to abusive alcoholic men, and there had been frequent family moves. Although Eileen's stepfather, Steve, displayed a lot of concern and investment in building a relationship with her, they argued a lot with each other. Efforts in the first session to help the family identify a small realistic treatment goal proved to be futile. The parents wanted to see the running away and substance abuse behaviors stop. Since during the majority of the session time the parents relentlessly complained about how awful Eileen's behavior was, they were offered the formula first-session task to experiment with providing a more complete picture of Eileen's behavior and the family situation. One week later, Eileen enthusiastically reported some positive events that had occurred with her parents and her. They went for "a long family drive," they went for "a long walk through the local forest preserve park," and Eileen and Steve did some "house repair work" alone without arguing. The parents were quite encouraged by Eileen's responsible behavior.

As mentioned earlier, with visitor families who cannot identify a goal or joint work project, Gingerich and de Shazer (1991) recommend that therapists simply compliment the family on anything they report having done that has been good for them, such as just showing up for the session. Therapeutic experiments should not be offered to them, because they are not customers or in the action stage of readiness for change, at least during the first interview (de Shazer, 1988; Prochaska, 1999).

Pretend the Miracle Happened

If the family is unable to identify any exceptions, Gingerich and de Shazer (1991) recommend that the brief therapist give the *pretend the miracle happened* task. In some case situations, I will have the parents pick 2 days over the week to pretend to engage in the miracle behaviors their adolescent would like to see occur with them, and while pretending, notice how their son or daughter responds. In a similar fashion, I have had the teacher the adolescent has had the most conflict with experiment with pretending to engage in miracle-like behaviors in relationship to the student when he or she knows what the latter wants from them in the ideal miracle scenario. The following case example illustrates the effectiveness of this experiment with a chronic acting-out adolescent and his family.

Paul, an African American 15-year-old, was referred to me for his "attention-deficit disorder" problem, and for chronically violating his parents' rules, "stealing money" from his parents, and hitting his teacher. My first session with Paul was right after he had been discharged from a local psychiatric hospital. Paul had been admitted to the hospital after striking his school teacher. In the earlier part of the interview, I attempted to elicit exceptions from the parents, but they negated my exception-oriented questions. After asking the miracle question (de Shazer, 1988), I was able to secure two important changes that the parents would notice with Paul: "Paul would not be swearing at us" and "He would not fight us when we say 'No!'" Paul reeled off a long list of changes that he envisioned occurring with himself and family members after the miracle happened. I decided to separate the family when the parents became negative again after the miracle inquiry. I met alone with Paul and asked him to pick 2 days to pretend to engage in his parents' miracle behaviors so we could "blow their minds!" Paul thought this was a "real neat" idea, particularly the idea of watching how his parents would react differently to him when he was pretending. One week later, the parents came back stating that "a miracle must have happened!" They reported at least eight significant exceptions on Paul's behalf. Most importantly, "Paul did not swear" or "fight" with his parents even once over the entire week. Future family sessions involved prescribing more of what works. Therapy was successfully completed by the fourth session.

Do Something Different

With case situations where the parent's goal is not related to the reported exceptions, Gingerich and de Shazer (1991) recommend the *do something different* task (de Shazer, 1988, 1991). This "skeleton key" intervention is particularly useful with overinvolved or highly reactive parents. I explain to parents that their son or daughter has "got their number"—he or she knows every move that they are going to make. After this short rationale for their need to be less predictable, the parents are given the following directive: "Between now and the next time we meet, I would like each of you to do something different—no matter how strange, weird, or off-the-wall what you do might seem, as long as it is different" (de Shazer, 1985, p. 123). With some case situations, I will have the adolescent or his or her teacher do this experiment to help disrupt negative interactions occurring in their relationships. The following case example shows how a parent's off-the-wall behavior can effectuate change in her son's longstanding behavioral difficulties.

Deborah and her 17-year-old son, Seth, were referred to me because the latter had been placed on probation for shoplifting, assault and battery charges, gang involvement, and school truancy. According to Deborah, Seth "ran the household" through "breaking things" when angry and "winning power struggles" with her. The more she would "yell at Seth" and attempt to place limits on him, the more he would act up. Deborah was at her wits' end and was ready to try anything with Seth. Because Seth boycotted our initial therapy session, I had to intervene through his mother. I gave Deborah the "do something different" task. One week later, Deborah came back reporting dramatic changes in Seth's behavior. What Deborah decided to do was that whenever Seth would push her buttons she would sing the children's song *Row, Row, Row Your Boat.* This totally disarmed Seth and led to such comments as: "Are you okay?" "What's wrong with you?" "Maybe you need to see the therapist more often." Apparently, the more Deborah engaged in her off-the-wall behavior, the more Seth's behavior changed. Seth became more respectful toward his mother and stayed out of further legal difficulties. The biggest surprise for me was having Seth show up at the third therapy session, wanting to help his "freaked-out mother."

Prediction Task

Gingerich and de Shazer (1991) recommend the *prediction* task for cases in which the reported exceptions occur spontaneously and are not deliberate. The prediction task can set in motion a positive self-fulfilling prophecy for the clients. In the following case example, both the parents and their bulimic 16-year-old daughter, Patricia, could not explain why at least 3 days per week the latter would not "binge and purge."

Patricia and her parents had been referred to me through an HMO. Patricia had been diagnosed as having bulimia nervosa by a psychiatrist she had seen for a year. Because "nothing had changed" with "Patricia's bulimia problem," the parents decided to pursue family therapy. Early in the first interview, I discovered that the binging and purging episodes were occurring on a random basis. However, neither the parents nor Patricia could identify the reasons for why the exceptions were happening. I decided to give the family the prediction task. Each night the parents and Patricia were separately to predict whether the latter would be "standing up to bulimia and not allowing it to push her around" that day; then, by the middle of the day following the day predicted, each was to explain what she did to be victorious. The next week, Patricia came in with her parents, happily reporting that "six days out of seven" they had "achieved victories" over bulimia. Both the parents and Patricia reported several exceptions that had contributed to the family's victories over bulimia. As constructive ways to stand up to bulimia and not let it push her around, Patricia used self-talk, "called a friend," listened to her favorite music, and sought her mother's support when she felt like she was caving into bulimia's hold on her. Since the prediction task had worked so well, I continued to use it in future sessions.

More of What Works

Finally, if family members readily report engaging in deliberate exception behaviors, Gingerich and de Shazer (1991) suggest that the therapist should *prescribe more of what works*. Observation tasks (de Shazer, 1988; Molnar & de Shazer, 1987) are particularly useful with these families to amplify their present exception patterns of behavior and to have them keep track of further changes they make.

If the family does not request a therapeutic experiment or all of its members are visitors/precontemplators, I will keep things simple and give compliments only. In addition, some difficult adolescents and their families may not be good candidates for the solution-focused brief therapy experiments discussed earlier and may respond better to interventions from other therapeutic approaches. They may require more time to share their long problem-saturated stories (Anderson, 1997) or may respond better to other pattern interventions (O'Hanlon, 1987) or narrative therapy experiments (Epston, 1998, 2000; White, 1995; White & Epston, 1990), family connection-building rituals (Selekman, 2002), or family play and art therapy activities (Selekman, 1997). I will discuss these therapeutic strategies further in Chapter 9.

When selecting and designing therapeutic experiments, it is important to remember that we need to match our experiments with family members' unique stages of readiness for change and cooperative response patterns, theories of change, goals, and key intelligence areas (Prochaska, 1999; Gingerich & de Shazer, 1991; Hubble et al., 1999; Gardner, 1993, 2004). To help increase the likelihood of family members' success and compliance with proposed experiments, it is helpful to write the experiments down for them, present the implementation steps in concrete and simple terms, and address any concerns they may have with the implementation process. Finally, I like to offer families a menu of therapeutic experiments to choose from, which is another effective way we can foster a cooperative relationship with them.

SUMMARY

In this chapter, I have provided a comprehensive roadmap for conducting first family interviews with difficult adolescents. Several categories of therapeutic questions were presented that elicit important information about family members' problem stories, key strengths, past successes, and ideal treatment outcome goals. Four major solution-focused therapeutic experiments were discussed as well. How we conduct first family interviews with difficult adolescents can either open the door for possibilities, get us off to a shaky start with them or worse yet, lead to a premature drop-out situation occurring. Therefore we need to strive to make meaningful connections with each family member, create a warm, respectful, and positive therapeutic climate, and carefully match our therapeutic questions and experiments with their stages of readiness to change and unique cooperative response patterns.

Five

Guidelines for Fostering Cooperative Relationships with Difficult Parents

> You can surmount the obstacles in your path if you are determined, courageous and hard-working. Never be fainthearted. Be resolute, but never bitter. . . . Permit no one to dissuade you from pursuing the goals you set for yourselves. Do not fear to pioneer, to venture down new paths of endeavor.
>
> —RALPH BUNCHE

At one time or another, throughout our professional careers, we have all been faced with difficult parents that have been extremely angry and hostile toward us, highly pessimistic, way too laissez-faire in providing limits for their seriously acting-out adolescents, and grappling with mental health or substance abuse issues that have not been addressed and may be contributing to the adolescent's behavioral difficulties. Some of these parents may place blame on their difficult adolescents, their partners, certain extended family members, former therapists, the school, and other larger systems professionals for their present untenable state of affairs. Many of these parents have experienced multiple treatment failures with their adolescents and have been mismanaged by former therapists, treatment program personnel, and representatives from larger systems. In some cases, these parents did not have a lead voice in their own treatment planning, were disempowered by the helping professionals involved who had adopted a privileged expert position with them, were misunderstood by these helpers in terms of their problem views, preferences, cultural differences in parenting practices, and the attempted solutions by the therapists and the treatment programs were "more of the same" variety of interventions, thus further exacerbating and compounding their problem situations.

In this chapter, I discuss how to establish strong therapeutic alliances with even the most difficult of parents and present useful therapeutic guidelines for co-creating possibilities with them. It is important to remember that some difficult parents will present with a combination of parenting styles and characteristics, and so being flexible therapeutically is a must.

RELATIONSHIP MATTERS

As research indicates, 30% of what counts for successful therapy outcomes has to do with *relationship factors* (Selekman, 2002; Hubble et al., 1999). When parents feel therapists have a thorough understanding of their difficulties with their adolescents, feel validated, and experience empathic attunement from their therapists, a therapeutic alliance will begin to develop. Furthermore, the therapist's use of *structuring skills*, that is, his or her ability to take charge in a session when it becomes chaotic or when destructive family interactions occur, demonstrating professional competence, conveying with confidence his or her ability to be helpful, and having good timing in deciding when to work with family subsystems and in proposing therapeutic experiments, have been found to contribute to positive treatment outcomes (Alexander, 1998; Alexander & Parsons, 1982). Finally, Lambert (2003) has found in his research that, by regularly eliciting feedback from clients regarding the quality of the therapeutic relationship, we can more accurately adjust our therapeutic stances to find a better *fit* with our clients' unique therapeutic needs and expectations, can help prevent premature dropout situations from occurring, and help maximize for treatment success. Difficult parents can be asked the following questions at the end of each family session:

- "What was the meeting like for you today?"
- "Did you learn anything new about your situation?"
- "What did you find to be most helpful?"
- "Was there anything we did not discuss or address that you think we need to talk about the next time we get together?"
- "How did our meeting feel different for you from other counseling sessions you have had in the past?"
- "Are there any adjustments you would like me to make that would make you feel more comfortable while we continue to work together?"

Other important ways to foster cooperative relationships with challenging parents is to utilize their *extratherapeutic factors* (Selekman, 2002;

Hubble et al., 1999)—that is, their language, metaphors, beliefs, and self-generated pretreatment change information—in our conversations with them. Invite the parents to share with you what their theories of change, treatment preferences and expectations, and resiliency protective factors and key strengths are to help guide you with the treatment planning process (Selekman, 2002; Prochaska, 1999). Forty percent of what counts for successful therapy outcomes has to do with the therapist's expertise in capitalizing on these client extratherapeutic factors (Hubble et al., 1999). Parents that have had multiple treatment experiences need to be placed in the expert role of informing you both specifically what was helpful that former therapists tried with them and what they did that made matters much worse with their problem situations. Parents can be asked the following questions:

- "Can you think of any specific things that former therapists or treatment programs tried with you or your daughter that you found to be most effective?"
- "How specifically was that helpful?"
- "If you tried that strategy again with your daughter today, do you think it could be as helpful?"
- "You have seen a lot of therapists before me. What did they miss or overlook with your situation that is important for me to know?"
- "If we address that issue, how specifically will that be helpful to your daughter?"
- "What sorts of things did your past therapists do that you disliked the most?"
- "If you were to work with the most perfect therapist, what would he or she do that you would find to be most helpful?"
- "How can I be most helpful to you at this time?"
- "Let's say I were to offer you a menu of treatment options to choose from. Which of the following treatment options would you like to pursue first: participating in family therapy, a solution-oriented parenting group, or seeing you alone to address parenting issues?"

By asking these important questions, therapists can steer away from replicating the same unhelpful past attempted solutions and gain a clear understanding about how the parents would like to see the therapist conduct the treatment process, such as which issues to address first, who to include in sessions, which treatment modality they would like to begin with, and so forth. In former treatment experiences with their adolescents, challenging parents often had little say in the goal-setting or treatment planning process and felt disempowered. When they did not cooperate with the therapist or treatment team's recommendations, the parents were often blamed for the adolescent's lack of progress, accused of trying to "sabotage" their son or daughter's treatment, and labeled "noncompliant."

Even the most difficult parents possess certain key strengths that can be tapped and utilized to help them resolve their adolescents' difficulties. It is these parental strengths that were often overlooked by former therapists, because they did not fit with the dominant stories written about them as being "uncooperative," "noncompliant," and "defensive." Inviting parents to talk about their strengths, talents, areas of expertise, and past parenting successes sparks positive emotion and can instill hope and optimism about their ability to resolve their adolescents' difficulties. Parents can be asked the following questions about their signature strengths and past successes:

- "What are your key strengths?"
- "In what ways do you think you could tap your key strengths to better manage your son's difficult behaviors?"
- "How specifically do you think that will be helpful?"
- "How else do you think you can use your key strengths to help improve your relationship with your son?"
- "In what ways have your key strengths helped you in your work relationships that could be useful in the parenting department?"
- "Can you think of any strategies or consequences you used in the past with your son that worked and that we might want to experiment with in his current problematic behavior?"
- "When your older daughter experienced similar difficulties as a teenager, what did the two of you do to resolve her difficulties?"
- "How have you used your key strengths in the past to successfully resolve other difficulties with your son?"
- "Which of your key strengths did you find to be the most helpful in that particular situation, and why?"

These questions can create possibilities with even the most challenging parents because they are the ones generating the creative solution strategies, not the therapist. Therefore, they will be much more invested in trying to experiment with their own unique ideas and solution strategies.

Finally, another important extratherapeutic factor area is to accurately assess each parent's stage of readiness for change (Prochaska, 1999). If the parents are in *precontemplation*, the therapist should use relationship-building skills and alternate back and forth between restraining from immediate change (Fisch et al., 1982) and seeding useful ideas about the benefits of changing. Precontemplative parents typically do not think they have a problem or have anything to do with their adolescents' difficulties. They also may come to counseling in a demoralized state or not recognize the benefits of changing anything. Parents in the *contemplation* stage, on some level, recognize that there is a problem with their parenting style or strategies. However, they are feeling ambivalent about changing their attempted solution strategies, which they are fairly convinced will eventually work. Having the parent list on paper all of the advantages and disadvantages of continuing their attempted solution strategies can help them visually to get through their ambivalence and begin to entertain doing things differently. Some difficult parents are in the *preparation* stage and are very close to wanting to experiment with new parenting strategies. However, they will report that there are specific obstacles to embarking in the direction of change. These might include, for example, fears of retaliation by an explosive and violent son, fears that their daughter's eating-distressed behaviors will only get worse, or worries that they will not be able to work together as a team in implementing a new change strategy. On the other hand, some difficult parents may be so desperate at intake that they may come to the first session "in the starting blocks," already in the *action* stage of readiness to change. With these parents, once you have established a well-formed behavioral treatment goal, and know their theories of change and past attempted solutions, you can offer them a therapeutic experiment to try out immediately to get the change ball rolling. With difficult parents, in particular, it is important that you carefully match your in-session therapeutic actions and experiments with the unique stage of readiness for change that each parent is at. One of the major reasons why these difficult parents are so angry or pessimistic is that former therapists and treatment programs mismatched their interventions with the parents' unique stages of readiness for change, adopted a privileged expert role, and then blamed them for not cooperating with their treatment plans and goals. Even the most challenging of parents want relief from their oppressive difficulties and want to cooperate with us. However, it is important that we not fall into the trap of being resistant therapists!

CHALLENGING PARENTING STYLES AND TREATMENT ISSUES

Each of the various parenting styles and attitudes we describe that parents present with has its own implications for clinicians. Practical guidelines are presented for how to foster cooperative relationships with each type of parent. Case examples are provided.

Angry and Hostile Parents

Angry and hostile parents can be some of the most challenging clients we will work with and are quite skilled at testing the integrity of the therapist. We all know these parents. We may hear them screaming at their kids in the waiting room, they may get in our faces and tell us at the start of treatment that counseling has been a waste of time in the past and that whatever we have to offer them will probably not work, they may verbally bash and blame the adolescent client in front of the rest of the family; and they may react in rage if they feel criticized, misunderstood, or are encouraged to change their interactions with the adolescent. Often these parents report being mishandled by their former therapists, treatment program personnel, and larger systems professionals. In some cases, they may have experienced institutional racism. These parents frequently are yelling at and punishing their kids, particularly the adolescent client. They believe that by using power or coercion that they can effectively control and successfully manage their adolescents' problematic behaviors. Many of these parents are feeling extremely frustrated by their and former therapists' inability to resolve their adolescents' behavioral difficulties; they may be struggling financially because of their possible unemployment situations and all of their adolescents' past treatment costs; or they may be grappling with unresolved family issues from their families of origin, and lack strong support systems.

Some of these angry and hostile parents view the adolescent client as the cause for all of the family problems and stress in their lives. They believe that the adolescent has "negative intentions" and is going out of his or her way to make their lives miserable. In some cases, a *negative sentiment override pattern* can develop in their families, where negative feelings about their adolescents completely overrides the potential for experiencing positive family interactions with one another (Dishion & Kavanagh, 2003; Weiss, Halford, & Kim, 1996). The parents will go out of their way to convince the therapist that the adolescent is the "problem." Unless the therapist agrees with their problem explanation, this may contribute to difficulties with building a therapeutic alliance and lead to a possible premature dropout situation.

These parents can be quite demanding, inflexible, and have highly unrealistic expectations for their adolescents. They may rarely express empathy and appear to lack sensitivity for their adolescents' expressions of emotions, needs, and expectations. More often than not, compromise and negotiation are not permitted. These parents may adopt a position of "It's *my* way or the *highway*!" Research indicates that this type of parenting style often produces children and adolescents who are fearful, anxious, impulsive, and moody (Baumrind, 1991). Shedler and Block (1990) found that adolescents who frequently abuse drugs had parents who were very critical and emotionally unresponsive when they were very young children. Gottman, Katz, and Hooven (1997) and Synder and Patterson (1995) found that parents who frequently lose control of their temper produce children who tend to be aggressive, have angry interactions with their parents, may have poor peer relations, have school behavioral difficulties, and may engage in delinquent behavior. Henggeler and colleagues (2002) have indicated that parents who are rated high on control and low on warmth measures tend to have adolescents who regularly engage in delinquent behaviors and substance abuse. In some cases, the adolescents' verbal abuse and aggressive behavior toward the parents may activate in the latter unpleasant memories of past abuse from their own parents, which can trigger their fight responses (Greene, 1998). Similarly, some adolescents encounter difficulties by misreading social cues and have a cognitive bias toward assuming hostile intent, which can fuel excessive verbal abusiveness and aggressive behavior toward their parents (Dodge, 1991).

What is most important to remember with angry and hostile parents is that there are many good reasons why they are so upset and on the defensive. They may feel that past therapists and treatment program personnel robbed them of their freedom to define the goals of treatment, to express their expectations and engender respect for their unique cultural differences in their parenting practices, or to have any choice in the type of treatment modalities they wanted to pursue. They also may be struggling to cope with tyrannical adolescents that are constantly verbally abusing them and noncompliant with their rules and expectations. We need to honor their *commitments*, or why they are clinging to certain problem explanations and attempted solutions (Kegan & Lahey, 2001). Through the use of curiosity, we can explore with the parents the thinking and stories behind their commitments to help us better understand their unique perspectives and how best to establish a cooperative relationship with them. In addition, we can easily lose sight of their strengths and resourcefulness, such as being persistent and committed as parents and not giving up on seeking help for their adolescents. However, even the most seasoned of therapists can find themselves becoming too reactive and defensive with these parents when we are met by the fury of their anger and hostility. By providing empathy and validation, giving them plenty of room to ventilate their upsetting thoughts and feelings about their frustrating and stuck situations, and inviting them to share their long problem-saturated stories about their plights, they are more likely to become less defensive and be open to hearing what we have to say and collaborate with us. To help normalize the parents' long struggles, it can be quite useful to share with them how other parents you had worked with in the past who had similar difficulties were able to resolve their chronic problem situations with their adolescents.

Treatment Guidelines with Angry and Hostile Parents

1. Join with the parents by inviting them to share with you what their key strengths, talents, and areas of expertise are.

2. Have the parents share with you their problem stories, theories of change, attempted solutions (theirs and past therapists' treatment programs). Most importantly, find out what former therapists missed with their situation and what they had done that was not helpful and contributed to making their situation worse.

3. Inquire about their pretreatment changes and past successes. Explore with them whether it would be worthwhile to experiment with increasing the frequency of new self-generated problem-solving strategies or testing out with the present adolescent problem situation a past successful consequence or parenting strategy.

4. Determine what stage of readiness for change each parent is in. Match your questions and proffered experiments to the stage each of them is presently in.

5. With parents in the *precontemplation* stage, begin by restraining from immediate change by saying: "Your son's/daughter's difficulties have been pushing you around for a long time. So, we need to take it nice and slow with carefully planning out what we want to try." This can be followed by beginning to plant helpful ideas in the parents' minds about the benefits of changing their behavior—for example, presenting to the parents recent research on positive emotion and its benefits for children, demonstrating how it greatly contributes to enhancing their problem-solving and coping abilities and contributes to their becoming more resilient (Fredrickson, 2002; Seligman, 2002, 2003). It also can be useful to present the research on the deleterious effects of negative emotion on children as another way to raise their consciousness for changing their parenting style. The therapist needs to alternate back and forth between restraining and seeding helpful ideas about the benefits of changing until the parent moves into the *contemplation* stage. These parents also deserve compliments for being persistent and committed and for their continuing efforts to try to find the *best* treatment possible for their adolescents.

6. With contemplative parents, the use of the *decisional balancing scale* (Prochaska et al., 1994) can help them begin to look at the advantages and disadvantages of continuing to persist with the threats, yelling, hitting, and grounding for months on end. Since people learn best through visual means, this in-session experiment may hit home for them once they see that there are many more disadvantages than advantages to continuing these unproductive attempted solutions. At this point, the parents may be receptive to abandoning what has not worked and more willing to discuss new parent management strategies if they have ad-

vanced into the *preparation* stage. Another useful experiment for contemplators is to have them play supersleuth detectives like Sherlock Holmes and Miss Marple and have them observe on a daily basis for clues or signs of any encouraging or responsible behaviors they see occurring with their adolescent.

7. Parents in the *preparation* stage are getting closer to taking action, but they will report that there are specific obstacles that may get in the way of changing their situation. Our job is to collaborate with them in accurately trying to identify what the correct obstacle or limiting factor is that is keeping them stuck from taking action or trying a new parenting strategy with their adolescent. The therapist can ask parents the following questions: "What specifically do you think is holding you back from trying something new with your son/daughter?" "What is standing in your way?" "What else could be the problem?" Once we have defined with the parents what the correct obstacle or limiting factor is, we can begin to identify specific baby steps that can be taken to remove it. For example, one obstacle for parents may be their conflicts about their individual parenting styles and lack of teamwork. As an experiment and an attempt to unify them more as a team, you can have each parent separately on a daily basis observe what the other parent does with the adolescent and other children that they really liked, thought was effective or creative, and make a mental note or write their observations down. Ask them not to compare notes until the next appointment. If the limiting factor for the parents is their own fear about not using their coercive power to assert their authority with their son or daughter and the possibility of having a crisis on their hands, as an experiment they can "play detective" a few times over a week's time—minus the threats, yelling, and hitting—and notice how their adolescent responds differently to them and changes his or her behavior in other contexts. The parents may be pleasantly surprised to discover that by changing their dance steps in relationship to the adolescent his or her behavior improves.

8. The *do something different* experiment (de Shazer, 1988) also can be quite effective with parents who are moving from the *preparation* to *action* stage. The therapist can point out to the parents that their responses to the adolescent, when he or she acts up, are far too predictable, and can stress that what is needed is an injection of novelty into their problem situation with their adolescent. Whenever the adolescent pushes their buttons or they are tempted to rescue him or her, they are to experiment with different responses that can be off-the-wall, outrageous, or different from anything they have previously tried. This experiment is quite effective with parents who are constantly getting trapped in power struggles, are too emotionally reactive, and are easily exploited and manipulated by their adolescents.

9. If none of the above proposed strategies is working or a therapeutic alliance has not developed, we need to employ curiosity and explore with the parents what is keeping us from moving forward. The therapist can ask the following questions: "How do you think we each are contributing to keeping us stuck in our efforts to work together?" and "What did we each do or not do that got us to this place?" The therapist can ask an older child or adolescent sibling in the room observing our interactions together: "How would you describe in a neutral and nonblaming way what each person is contributing that is keeping us stuck?" The parents may be more willing to listen to and act on a sibling's feedback than what the adolescent client would have to say. Individually, you as the therapist should ask yourself, "What would the parents say I am doing that is contributing to our difficulties working together?" Once we have a better understanding of the interactive *contributing system*, we can each see what we need to avoid or change in our interactions in the future (Stone, Patton, & Heen, 2000).

10. When stuck, it is always helpful to *go back to basics* and reflect on our own actions. We can ask ourselves the following questions: "Is our treatment goal too big?" "Are we working on the *right* problem?" "Have I been inaccurate in my assessment of the parents' stages of readiness for change?" "Have I proposed therapeutic experiments that the parents feel uncomfortable with or are not ready for?" "Do we need to go for smaller changes?" "Are my expectations too grand for these parents?" "Do I feel like a bad therapist?" "Is the real customer for change not present in our sessions?" Once we have critically explored in our minds potential answers to these questions, we can check out with the parents what they think about our thoughts and try and figure out together where we possibly got derailed and adjust our therapeutic stances appropriately. As therapists, it is important to regularly critically evaluate our work and be willing to change our way of thinking about and intervening with our clients.

11. Expanding the system and recruiting other family members and key members of the family's social network can be useful when feeling stuck. The parents can be asked: "On a scale from 1 to 10—with 10 being most concerned about you—what numbers would you give absent family members, extended family members, your clergyman, other involved helping professionals, or your closest friends?" "Which of these individuals do you think it would be most beneficial to bring in to help us out with generating some fresh ideas and gaining some added support?" If working solo, another way you can expand the system is to get permission from the parents to have your colleagues serve as a reflecting team to see how we are getting stuck and to offer some new ideas (Andersen, 1991).

12. Other useful questions we can ask the parents to help us get unstuck and uncover potential secrets that may be blocking the change process are: "I am presently working with another family just like yours—

exactly the same situation—and I am feeling really stuck. Do you have any advice for me about how I could best help that family out?" "It appears that we have run into a brick wall at this point in our work together. Is there something we have not talked about up to this point that you think I need to know about?" "If we talked about it, who would be the most troubled and why?" "I am curious, was there something that you told yourselves before you came in to see me for the first time that you were not going to talk about in our meetings together?"

13. If a blame–counterblame pattern of interaction continues to occur in the family sessions, it is most helpful to disrupt this process by dividing up the session time and seeing the parents separately from the adolescent. The use of videotape playback also can be very beneficial to these families in that they can see how they set one another off, observe how destructive their interactions can become, and help increase their awareness of what works in their interactions with one another. Like therapists, parents and adolescents have their blind spots, and in the midst of our heated interactions with one another we can't fully hear and see ourselves and the effects of our behavior on others.

14. Another therapeutic option we have to counter the family's victimization by this negative blame–counterblame pattern is to externalize it (Selekman, 1999; White, 1985; White & Epston, 1990). The therapist can introduce the idea to the parents that sometimes patterns of interaction have a life all of their own and are intergenerational. We can begin the externalization process by asking the parents what they would call this pattern they fall prey to in their relationship with their adolescent. Second, we can explore with them how this "blaming," "arguing," or "putting down" (client's words) pattern got the best of them and their parents while growing up. The therapist can ask the following questions of the parents: "In what ways does 'blaming' force you to jump on your son's case?" "How else does 'blaming' wreak havoc in your relationship with him?" "Does it ever poison your relationship and truly shake things up there?" "Can the two of you think of any times lately where you both stood up to 'blaming' and did not allow it to brainwash you to dictate your reactions to your son?" A family ritual can be set up where the family is working together to conquer the "blaming" pattern. When externalizing the problem with clients, it is most important that it be based on their description or beliefs about it. In addition, this new frame or explanation about the problem has to be acceptable or come close to fitting the parents' belief system. Therefore, we need to carefully read and listen to the client's nonverbal and verbal feedback to know whether or not we are on target with the interventions we have tried.

15. Teach these parents how to be better negotiators. Have them identify their emotional hooks—that is, the issues that get them the most upset and irrational—and advise them on how to pick and choose their

battles, be better listeners, how to attack the problem and not their adolescents, and how to persuade without coercing (Brown, 2003). Research indicates that the best negotiators avoid getting highly emotional and losing control of their tempers (Rackham & Carlisle, 1978).

16. An important therapeutic rubric to remember with angry and hostile parents is to *never argue with, or intimate blame,* with them. Often these parents already feel like failures, have been blamed by former therapists and treatment program personnel, and have little faith in and a major distrust for therapists or the mental health care system in general. Therefore, we need to be very sensitive to and regularly validate their feelings throughout the treatment process. If they do not follow through with proposed therapeutic experiments, we need to normalize their experience and take responsibility for jumping the gun and pushing too hard for change before they were ready for it. This may also be an indication that we need renegotiate our treatment plan, establish much smaller treatment goals, deemphasize therapist authority and guidance, and offer therapeutic experiments designed to bolster client self-control, self-direction, and require minimal overt action on the part of the client (Beutler & Harwood, 2000; Beutler et al., 2002).

Case Example: Robert and Elizabeth

Robert and Elizabeth were referred to me by their 16-year-old son, Tim's dean at his high school for "keying [scratching a car with a key] his teacher's car," "disrespect for authority," "poor grades," and "fighting with peers." Tim had been suspended three times before for "fighting with peers." I also discovered from the dean that he had "a long treatment history" and that his parents were "very difficult to work with."

My first taste of Tim's difficult parents was in the waiting room of my office, where the father blew past me without a handshake, stating loudly that this was a "waste" of his time. Elizabeth gave me the third degree and asked me about my professional qualifications and credentials. She shared with me that she was surprised that I turned out to be a social worker, because all of their former private therapists were licensed psychologists. After this warm and delightful greeting by Tim's parents, I was saying to myself that this was going to be a really long session. It also helped me understand how Tim could have difficulties with authority figures. At this point in the family session, I attempted to join with each family member by inquiring with them about their key strengths, hobbies, and interests. The father made it clear to me that he was not in my office to talk about his situation. Thank goodness I had a little better luck with Elizabeth. She loved to play doubles tennis and had won some tournaments with her partner. I asked what she thought their recipe for success was. She pointed out that they talked to one another a lot on the court, did a nice job of backing each other up, and were good up at net. When we came to Tim, I discovered that he used to be "a nationally ranked junior tennis player" and also had "won a number of tennis tournaments." The father abruptly chimed in that Tim's "attitude" problem got him "kicked out of tournaments" as well. When asked if he had a serve-and-volley or a baseline game, Tim shared with me that he had a big serve and would follow it up to net. I asked Tim if he and his mother ever played together, and his mother pointed out that she would not stand a chance on the court with him.

At this point in the session, I asked the family what they saw as the problem and what they wished to change. The father asserted loudly again that Tim had an "attitude" problem. I asked him to define what he meant by an "attitude." Robert defined the "attitude" as "not talking to adults in a respectful way," "swearing," "arguing," and "not cooperating." I took a risk with the family and asked if anyone else in the family gets pushed around by the "attitude." Elizabeth shared that she thought that her husband shows an "attitude" at times. Robert got defensive and disagreed with Elizabeth's observation. I decided to take another risk and ask Elizabeth if she could think of a time recently where the "attitude" seemed to get between her and Robert and somehow got them to lock horns with each other. She brought up how "Robert was on a mass rampage removing everything out of Tim's bedroom and locking it up because of his suspension and then grounded him for 6 months." Elizabeth felt that he was being "totally outrageous with his ways of managing" Tim's difficulties. At this point, Robert began to verbally attack Elizabeth. I had Tim step out of the room and decided to capitalize on this hot parenting disagreement.

It turned out that Robert and Elizabeth rarely agreed with each other about how to best manage Tim. I cut off Robert from blaming his wife for being "too soft" and stressed how they could make a good doubles team if they combined his power game with her great use of spin and love for teamwork. Finally, I got a smile out of Robert. When I asked him about what I had said that made him smile, he pointed out that the last time they had played doubles together they had lost in the finals of their club championship due to his not communicating well with her on the court. Since I had successfully broken the ice with Robert and had begun to better connect with him, I asked the couple if they would be willing to revisit the extreme consequences that Tim had received for his suspension. I stressed that lengthy and extreme consequences can foster resentment and sneaky behaviors with adolescents. Robert agreed to revisit this issue with his wife. Apparently, Elizabeth had long thought that Robert had been "way too hard on Tim." Robert agreed with his wife. He also pointed out to me that he had recently been "demoted at work after 25 years" with his company, which he was quite angry about. By the end of the session, I was able to get Robert and Elizabeth to agree to work with me on coming up with new consequences, ways to avoid getting into power struggles, and creating a more inviting home environment for Robert.

Highly Pessimistic Parents

Some parents come to us feeling demoralized and lack the hope that our treatment experience with them will differ from all of the other therapists they have seen and the treatment programs they have had their son or daughter unsuccessfully treated in. Their repeated lack of success trying to resolve their adolescents' chronic behavioral difficulties can eventually lead them to adopting a *learned helplessness* stance—that is, attributing their failures to *global* and *permanent* aspects of themselves (Seligman, 1998, 2002). By the time we meet these parents for the first time, they may be just about ready to give up on their adolescents, place their adolescents in a residential treatment program or boarding school, or have their adolescents live with relatives. Not only do these parents have a tendency to blame themselves, but they also may blame their partners, extended family members, and former therapists for their depressing situation. These parents may have a tendency to only dwell on the negatives with their adolescents and not notice any of their strengths and responsible behaviors. They may have already thrown in the towel at home and are emotionally unavailable to and provide no monitoring or limits for their adolescents.

Seligman and his colleagues (1995) found in their research that children directly learn their pessimism from their parents, which can set the stage for their later falling prey to clinical depression and anxiety difficulties. The parents' criticisms implying pessimistic causes have a cumulative effect on how children view themselves (Peterson & Park, 1998). In a similar fashion as their parents, these children will start to believe that their setbacks or difficulties they experience are unchangeable and will eventually undermine other areas in their lives. Even when the situation was not their fault, they will perceive the situation as unchangeable and will not put forth any effort to try to change it (Seligman et al., 1995).

Treatment Guidelines for Highly Pessimistic Parents

1. Implement guidelines 1–7 of the earlier section on angry and hostile parents.
2. If the parents cannot identify any pretreatment changes or have great difficulty in responding to the *miracle question* (de Shazer, 1988) in your attempt to establish a well-formed behavioral treatment goal, first try using *coping questions* and, if necessary, try *pessimistic questions* (Selekman, 2002; Berg & Miller, 1992). The parents can be asked the following

questions: "It sounds like at times your situation must feel pretty grim for you. Tell me: what steps have you taken to prevent things from escalating further and getting much worse?"; "Are you aware of how you did that?"; "What else are you doing to prevent your situation from getting much worse?"; "Some parents in your situation would have thrown in the towel a long time ago. They may have sent their kid off to a military school, tried to make their kid a ward of the state, or even put their kid up for adoption! What has stopped you from pursuing any of those options?" "Who will attend your son's funeral?" "What do you think the eulogies will be?" "What will life be like for you and your husband when your son is no longer around?" By better cooperating with and exaggerating the parents' pessimism, we can open the door for possibilities.

3. Another useful question to ask highly pessimistic parents is a *subzero scaling question* (Selekman, 2002). The parents can be asked the following questions: "On a scale from –10 to –1—with –10 being that your situation is unsolvable and –1 your situation can improve a little bit—where would you have rated your situation 4 weeks ago?" "At a –10." "How about 2 weeks ago?" "At a –7?!" "What steps did you take to get to a –7?" "What else did you do that was helpful?" "How has that made a difference?" "Where would you rate your situation today?" "At a –5." "Are you aware of what you did or what you told yourself to get that to happen?" "Let's say we get together in 1 week's time, and you come in here and tell me you took some further steps up to a –4; what will you tell me you did?" This type of scaling question can raise the parents' hope and expectancy levels that their adolescents' problematic behaviors can be eventually resolved.

4. Once a therapeutic alliance has been developed, the therapist can begin teaching the parents how to become skilled disputers when their own irrational or self-defeating thoughts start to push them around in the parenting department. Parents can be taught how to search for *evidence* to dispute or debunk these irrational or self-defeating thoughts, *alternative explanations* for their behaviors and their adolescents' behaviors, and the *lack of usefulness*, or disutility, of clinging to certain thoughts they have that may be fueling excessive worrying or negative thoughts (Seligman, 2002, 2003). Parents also can be taught how to *decatastrophize* by learning how to use self-talk and asking themselves the following questions: "What is the worst thing that might happen?" "What is one thing I can do to stop the worst thing from happening?" "What is the best thing that might happen?" "What is one thing I can do to try and make the best thing happen?" "What is the most likely thing that will happen?" "What can I do to handle the most likely thing if it happens?" (Seligman et al., 1995, pp. 219–220). Once parents become more optimistic and skilled at disputing their own self-defeating thoughts, they can be put in charge of teaching

their adolescents disputation skills and how to decatastrophize. Learning the powerful tools of disputation and decatastrophizing will greatly benefit the adolescent in not falling prey to depression and effectively coping with life stressors.

5. If a parent continues to be pessimistic, family members can be invited to challenge this parent's unhelpful thoughts and outmoded beliefs. Family members can be asked: "What indications have you observed that would tell you that your wife is not ready to throw in the towel with your daughter?" "How else has your wife showed you that she is not ready give up on your daughter?" "Do you think your mother is ready to give up on your sister?" "How can you tell that she still cares about her?" "What keeps you hanging in there with your daughter, Paul?" Through the use of family members' challenging alternative views on the problem situation, you can help loosen up the pessimistic parents' rigid beliefs and alter their viewpoint on the problem situation.

6. The *do something different* experiment can be useful if the pessimistic parent continues to find him- or herself nagging, yelling, or worrying too much. This experiment can help strengthen that parent's reflective skills and help him or her be less reactive to the adolescent's challenging behaviors (Selekman, 2002; de Shazer, 1985, 1988).

7. Another effective therapeutic experiment for highly pessimistic parents is to have them daily, over a week's time, list all of the reasons why they think their problem situations with their adolescents are not much worse (Molnar & de Shazer, 1987). Often this experiment helps them become more self-aware of their own creative problem-solving and coping strategies for managing their adolescents' behavioral difficulties. In addition, the experiment can raise their hope and expectancy levels that their situations can improve.

8. If the parents continue to feel oppressed by their adolescent's chronic presenting problem or their *hopelessness and despair*, both of these difficulties can be externalized (Selekman, 2002; White & Epston, 1995). By doing so, the therapist can unify the family members' efforts as a team to liberate themselves from the problem.

9. Follow guidelines 9–16 that were recommended for angry and hostile parents until you find a treatment strategy that works.

Case Example: Barbara and Paul

Barbara and Paul were referred by a former client for help with their 18-year-old son, Steve, who was "heavily abusing alcohol," not consistently following their household rules, had had some "brushes with the law for traffic violations," and was being "verbally abusive" with Barbara and his 16-year-old brother, Kent. Steve grudgingly agreed to attend our second family session. Of the two parents, Barbara was much more pessimistic about Steve's ability to change. It was easy to see how Barbara's pessimism was fueling Steve's anger and disrespect for his mother. Barbara had a tendency to live in the past, when Steve's behavior was a lot worse, and in the present tended to notice only what he was doing wrong. Paul was quite upset with "Barbara's negativity" and "feeling at a loss about how to change her." He felt that she was "always on Steve's case about everything." Barbara, on the other hand, felt "unsupported by Paul" in dealing with Steve's difficult behaviors, particularly his abuse of alcohol. At this point in the family session, I employed curiosity with Barbara to explore with her the history of her *commitment* (Kegan & Lahey, 2001), or professing of concern about Steve's abuse of alcohol. Barbara disclosed that she was "fearful" that "Steve would end up like two of her brothers" who "had serious problems with alcohol and drugs in their teens and early-twenties." Apparently, this was the first time that Steve had heard that his uncles had serious problems with alcohol and drugs. He made it quite clear to his mother that he had "no intention to allow the drinking to get too out of hand," nor was he planning to start abusing other drugs at this time.

Although Barbara acknowledged that she was encouraged by hearing this from Steve, she brought up another concern she had with Steve. Barbara had a good sense of humor, and she could laugh about her pessimistic outlook on life. I secured her permission to involve other family members' perspectives on how they viewed Steve's behavior. Both Paul and Kent identified a number of "recent signs" that "Steve was taking more responsibility," "not going out with his friends and drinking as much," and "talking to everyone in the family more, including Barbara, in a "more respectful way lately." Steve shared with his mother that if she would only "acknowledge the good things" he did more often it would help them get along better. Barbara found the family feedback to be quite beneficial and agreed to work on her pessimistic mindset. I taught her a variety of disputation tools and how to decatastrophize to practice over the next week. In addition, I had her play supersleuth detective and with her imaginary magnifying glass notice daily every encouraging and responsible step that Steve would take. Both these treatment strategies paved the way for Barbara to be more optimistic and better at catching Steve at his best!

Laissez-Faire Parents

Laissez-faire parents are often far too permissive, rarely provide or consistently enforce rules and consequences with their adolescents, may abdicate their parenting responsibilities to relatives and other adults in their social network, may be self-absorbed and emotionally disconnected from their adolescents, and can be overindulgent with them. In some cases, laissez-faire parents may believe that "being friends" with their adolescents—that is, not providing limits and giving them lots of freedom—will help gain their cooperation and reduce the occurrence of problems. Some laissez-faire parents are averse to experimenting with new parenting strategies and appear to be committed to doing more of what works for them, even if it is further exacerbating their adolescents' difficulties. Finally, with some of these parents, we may find ourselves more worried and involved in trying to save their adolescents from dire and life-threatening situations than they are.

Laissez-faire parenting can create major life difficulties for their adolescents. Most importantly, the adolescent may not learn the skills for regulating his or her emotions, may have little frustration tolerance, and may become explosive when he or she does not get his or her way. Research indicates that laissez-faire parenting can produce adolescents who are more rebellious, aggressive and domineering with peers, and are heavy drug abusers and frequently engaged in delinquent behavior (Reivich & Shatte, 2002; Henggeler et al., 2002; Steinberg, Darling, Fletcher, Brown, & Dornbusch, 1995).

Treatment Guidelines for Laissez-Faire Parents

1. Implement guidelines 1–7 that were recommended for angry and hostile parents.

2. If you find that you are much more alarmed by the adolescent's extreme high-risk behaviors than the parents are or are working a lot harder than they are to try to save their kid from dire or life-threatening consequences, *creating intensity* with the parents can be most useful (Minuchin & Fishman, 1981). The therapist can share the following: "If your son continues to heavily abuse drugs and cut himself, one of these times he will slice a vein or artery, and it will be all over." "My fear for your son is not so much the drugs he is abusing but the people behind them." "I once worked with another kid who was heavily abusing and scoring drugs on the rough westside of Chicago and he had a sizable drug debt. The dealer had his house burned down!" It is easy to see how comments like these can raise the parents' anxiety and motivation levels to take action to prevent a tragedy from occurring with their son or daughter.

3. In a similar fashion, the use of *pessimistic questions* can be used to energize the laissez-faire parents to take action. The therapist can ask the parents about who will be attending their adolescent's funeral, what the eulogies will be, and what life will be like for them when their son or daughter is no longer around (Selekman, 2002; Berg & Miller, 1992).

4. Another useful strategy with laissez-faire parents is to use curiosity and ask a lot of open-ended questions to invite the parents to help you out with your confusion about their parental beliefs and style of parenting. Like the TV detective Columbo, we want to have them produce enough clues that they will begin to confront themselves about the necessity for

changing their parenting style and interactions with their adolescents (Selekman, 2002). For example, the therapist can ask the parents the following questions: "Help me out . . . I am confused (*scratching your head*). I hear you saying that you want Johnny to stop abusing cocaine. I think that's great. Help me understand how you think that can happen if it's okay for him to drink at home with his buddies? Maybe I'm nuts or something—that's what my wife tells me sometimes—but I wonder if he thinks if it's okay to drink, it's okay to do cocaine. What do you guys think? Maybe that sounds pretty far-fetched to you—I could be wrong."

5. If it appears that the parents are too emotionally disconnected from their adolescent, family connection-building rituals can be employed to help reconnect them in a meaningful way. For example, in the family session, have the adolescent take a ride in your *imaginary time machine* back to a time when she was a lot closer to her father. The next step is to have her apply all of her senses to the experience, including color and motion (Selekman, 1997; 2002). The therapist can ask the following questions: "Where are you together?" "Who else is there?" "How are you all dressed?" "What are you doing together?" "What are you talking about?" "What is most special about this experience?" When the adolescent rejoins us from her time travels, we can discuss how to reinstate these positive interactions and activities in the present-day relationship with her father.

6. With single-parent laissez-faire parents, it can be quite effective to recruit their partners, adult siblings, and even the adolescents' *inspirational others* (caring and committed adults outside their homes) to help empower them, give them more leverage with their adolescents, and create more structure in their homes.

7. If still stuck, follow guidelines 9–16 that were recommended for angry and hostile parents until you find a treatment strategy that works.

Case Example: Peter and Linda

Peter and Linda were referred to me by their 15-year-old son, Mark's school social worker for "burning and cutting himself," "severe anxiety," and "problems with depression." Mark had an extensive treatment history, including 4 inpatient psychiatric hospitalizations for his self-harming behaviors and severe depressive episodes. Mark's parents divorced when he was 9. Peter had been seeing him every 2–3 months. Initially, I had started family therapy with Mark and Linda. Although Peter had been invited to participate in our family sessions, he contended that his work schedule would make it impossible for him to attend. According to Mark, since his parents had divorced, his father had not been present very actively in his life, and Mark greatly disliked his new wife.

What was most surprising to me was Mark's parents' complete lack of anxiety or reaching out with emotional support after a self-harming crisis at school where he would repeatedly stab himself with a pencil or some other sharp object. The school social worker also found herself "more alarmed and involved in trying to comfort Mark than the parents." Linda was struggling with "a lot of personal issues" that she openly admitted got in the way of being more emotionally available to Mark. She had just broken up with her boyfriend that she had planned to marry when she found out that he was cheating on her. She had also just lost her job and was struggling financially to support Mark and his brother. Mark had previously disclosed that his mother was never really very supportive of him and was typically focused on taking care of herself. His other beef with her was that she was "always complaining" and constantly "nagging" him.

At this point in treatment and with Mark's support, I decided to see if I could engage his father in treatment and try to facilitate connection building between them. Mark was longing to reconnect with his father. Apparently, before the parents' divorce Mark and his father "used to be very close" and "went fishing a lot" together. Once I eventually got Peter to join Mark and me for a family session, I worked really hard to make a good connection with him and spark his interest in attending future sessions. As a way to begin the connection-building process, I had Mark take a ride back in time in my *imaginary time machine* to a place where he had had a really special time alone with his father. Mark went back to his most memorable fishing trip with his father, during which he had "caught five bluegills" at the age of 8. He described his father's sporting a big smile on his face and telling him how proud of him he was. Both Mark and Peter brightened up noticeably when we began to discuss this important event in their relationship. I asked Mark what aspects of this special event in his life he would like to reinstate in his relationship with his father. He definitely wanted to "start going fishing" with his father again. Mark began to tear up and disclose to his father that he would like to feel that he "cared more about" him. When asked what specifically his father could do now to start showing that more, Mark requested that his father could try to see him more often. Our family therapy session ended up being quite successful in that, as a consequence, Peter started calling and seeing Mark more often. The biggest surprise was Peter's requesting that "Mark call" him whenever he was having a hard time coping with stressors at school or at home. Over time, Mark's behavior improved significantly, due to his increasingly feeling more *a sense of place* in his father's life.

Parents with Mental Health or Substance Abuse Issues

With some adolescent case situations, it will not be so obvious early in treatment that one or both parents are struggling with an untreated mental health or substance abuse problem. In some cases, this may be a family secret, and in a heroic way the adolescent may be protecting his or her parent with mental health or substance-abuse difficulties by keeping concerned therapists and larger systems professionals focused on his or her own dramatic acting-out behaviors (Selekman, 2002). Sometimes we will pick up on innuendos or a family member will disclose that one or both of the parents' mental health or substance abuse difficulties are contributing to the high family stress level and the adolescent's behavioral problems. One of the major consequences for adolescents who have parents that are underfunctioning due to their mental health or substance-abuse difficulties is that they may become *parentified* beyond their developmental abilities (Selekman, 2002; Perez-Bouchard, Johnson, & Ahrens, 1993). Being locked in this family role can emotionally overburden the adolescent and exacerbate his or her own behavioral problems. Finally, adolescents who have parents that have serious problems with substance abuse are at high risk for developing this problem themselves (Perez-Bouchard et al., 1993).

Treatment Guidelines for Parents with Mental Health or Substance Abuse Issues:

1. Implement guidelines 1–7 that were recommended for angry and hostile parents.

2. If the parents eventually identify their mental health or substance-abuse difficulties as interfering with their parenting roles or their own abilities to cope with stress or other problems in their lives and are in the *preparation* or the *action* stages of readiness for change, the therapist can offer couples therapy or individual treatment with each parent if they would find that to be more helpful.

3. In some cases, the involvement of a psychiatrist could be beneficial if a parent is displaying vegetative, psychotic, or severe anxiety symptoms and requires medication. If one of the parents admits that he or she has lost control of his or her abuse of alcohol or drugs and is experiencing severe physical consequences and withdrawal symptoms, an outpatient or inpatient detox may be in order. With both of these case situations, the therapist would need to actively collaborate with the psychiatrists involved to unify treatment efforts.

4. If you suspect or have good evidence for the parents' mental health or substance problems acting as a barrier to changing the adolescent's problems, the therapist can use curiosity and adopt TV detective Columbo's style of interviewing by asking such questions as: "You know what really confuses me about this whole situation with Charlie? You [the parent] always seem so concerned and worried about your son—and I can

see how much you love him—but somehow he keeps getting into trouble after school and on the weekends. What do you suppose we are missing here? My wife, for example, has been telling me a lot lately that I have been slipping up with staying on top of house projects. Is there something we have not talked about up to this point that, if we discussed it, would help clear up my confusion about your situation?" Through the use of curiosity and interviewing parents as Columbo might, you can, in a nonthreatening way, encourage parents to open up about their individual difficulties or secrets, be more accountable for their actions in helping to maintain their adolescents' problems, and be more active in the change process.

5. In a similar fashion, you can invite a few of your colleagues to serve as a reflecting team (Andersen, 1991) and wonder aloud about the *not yet said* (Anderson & Goolishian, 1989)—that is, family secrets—which can possibly open the door for the symptomatic parent to begin talking about his or her individual difficulties or other emotionally distressing family concerns.

6. Another useful team strategy is the *therapeutic debate* (Selekman, 2002; Papp, 1983). This team strategy is particularly useful with families that are plagued with chronic problems, rigidly entrenched patterns of interactions and fixed beliefs, and possible secrets. The team members will join you and the family in the therapy room and will debate about the advantages and disadvantages of changing their present problem situation. One team member will represent the parents' position, while the other will represent the adolescent's position. This powerful team strategy also can open up space for family members to begin to address the specifics about what is keeping them stuck, which may turn out to be family members' concerns with a parent's emotional difficulties or problems with substance abuse.

7. If it appears that the adolescent shares the same presenting problem as one of the parents, it may be useful to externalize it (Selekman, 2002; White & Epston, 1990; White, 1995). The therapist can ask the following questions: "How long has 'depression' been pushing all of you around for?" "How does 'depression' create a Grand Canyon of distance in your relationship [mother–daughter relationship]?" "Tell me, Marjorie [the mother], did 'depression' also weigh down your relationship with your mother when you were growing up?" "What effect did that have on you?" "Can you think of things you used to do as a teenager to stand up to 'depression' and not allow it to weigh down your relationship with your mother?" "How about with friends?" "When you were victorious over 'depression' as a teenager, how did you begin to view yourself and your situation differently?" Through externalization of the problem and capitalizing on past and present *sparkling moments* or important victories over the

problem, you can empower the family to liberate themselves from the shackles of their intergenerational difficulties.

8. If still stuck, follow guidelines 9–12 and 16, that were recommended for angry and hostile parents until you find a treatment strategy that works.

Case Example: Mary

Mary was referred to me by her daughter, Deborah's, school social worker for "cutting herself," "suspected substance abuse," "poor grades," and signs of depression. The social worker, the dean, and two of Deborah's teachers were quite "alarmed by the cut marks on her arms" and wondered if she was possibly "suicidal." The parents were divorced, and the father refused to participate in family therapy, because he did not believe counseling worked. Although there were a number of stressors in Deborah's life, such as her father's putting heavy pressure on her to get A's in school, peer rejection issues, and the loss of her grandfather, she contended that the number-one stressor in her life was her "mother's drinking problem." Deborah had shared this with me in confidence. According to Deborah, when her mother would get intoxicated, she would "yell and nag" her more. She felt that the alcohol was creating a wide chasm in their relationship. After about four family sessions, I was successfully able to stabilize Deborah's self-harming behavior, and she was beginning to improve in most areas of her life. However, her mother's drinking problem was getting much worse. In our fifth family session, I allowed my curiosity to wander and explored with Mary about what stressors in Deborah's life we had not talked about yet. The timing of this question was right on target in that Mary began to disclose about how Deborah was "concerned about" her "drinking" and how she too was starting to see how it was creating personal problems for her as well. Deborah complimented her mother after she admitted that she had a problem with alcohol abuse.

At this point in the family session, I decided to meet alone with Mary and capitalize on this great window of opportunity to see if I could gently move her from the *preparation* stage to the *action* stage of readiness for change. Since alcoholism problems ran in her family and she had been heavily abusing whiskey and vodka on a regular basis, I was concerned about her having severe withdrawal symptoms and experiencing *delirium tremens*. Mary agreed to see my psychiatrist, who was a specialist on addiction problems and could possibly do an outpatient detox with her. She also agreed to contract with me on learning how to establish an alcohol-free lifestyle and learn relapse prevention tools. Once alcohol-free, Mary was better able to maintain a full-time job and be much more emotionally available to Deborah.

SUMMARY

Working with difficult parents can be a therapist's worst nightmare. However, it is important to remember that these parents did not fall into their provocative and rigid styles of interacting overnight. They are often feeling stuck and at a loss for what to do with their kids. In addition, if we respectfully take the time to invite them to share their oppressive stories and multitude of unsuccessful attempted solutions, and guide us on how best to cooperate with them, we will be able to co-create a therapeutic climate ripe for change.

Six

Effective Engagement Strategies with Difficult Adolescents

There comes that mysterious meeting in life when someone acknowledges who we are and what we can be, igniting the circuits of our highest potential.

—Rusty Berkus

Engaging the difficult adolescent can be an arduous task for even the most skilled therapists. Frequently, these youths have been labeled "resistant," "uncooperative," "anti-authority," "noncompliant," and "unmotivated" by the referring person and other helpers. With many of these case situations, past therapists have attempted "more of the same" solutions (Watzlawick et al., 1974) with these adolescents, for instance, needlessly antagonizing them by "putting the parents in charge" of their adolescents without attending to their needs in relationship to the parents. Often, past therapists have done the majority of their intervening through the parents and have not joined well enough with the adolescent, or have failed to ascertain from the adolescent specifically what he or she would like to get out of therapy. It is my contention that it is possible to generate changes on the parental and adolescent levels simultaneously. In this chapter, I present 10 engagement strategies that capitalize on the strengths and resources of the adolescent and help foster a cooperative therapeutic relationship. These are:

1. Humor and surprise.
2. Utilization.
3. Working the other side of the fence.
4. Bringing in a friend.
5. Using the adolescent as an expert consultant.
6. Validation and empathy.

7. Self-disclosure.
8. The Columbo approach.
9. The two-step tango.
10. Honoring and respecting silence.

Case examples are provided to illustrate the utility of these engagement strategies with difficult adolescents.

HUMOR AND SURPRISE

The therapist's use of humor has been empirically proven to be an effective tool for engaging difficult adolescents (Alexander, Barton, Schiavo, & Parsons, 1976; Newfield, Kuehl, Joanning, & Quinn, 1991; Parsons & Alexander, 1973; Selekman, 1989a, 1989b, 2002). Adolescents have reported liking therapists that have a good sense of humor, are playful, and create a lively therapeutic climate. With every new adolescent case, I listen carefully for the humorous twists in the family's story that I can utilize in the joining and therapeutic experiment design and selection process. I also like to capitalize on the humorous bodily posturing of the adolescent to further enhance the engagement process. For example, I have conducted some family sessions slouched ridiculously low in my chair to mirror the adolescent's nonverbal behavior, which typically prompts smiles and laughter from the family and the youth. I purposefully disclose humorous experiences from my own adolescence to normalize the adolescent client's present struggles with a particular developmental task. Finally, I may share a humorous joke that offers the adolescent and parents a new way of looking at their situation and can lighten up the atmosphere in the therapy room. The following case example demonstrates how the therapist's use of an appropriate joke that, in some ways, mirrors the family's story can generate new possibilities in the family's way of viewing their situation.

The parents had brought Jim in for therapy because of his "antisocial attitude" and abuse of alcohol and marijuana. According to the parents, Jim would "blast his terrible music for hours" after school. They felt his heavy metal music was "fueling his antisocial attitude" and substance abuse. For 1 year, the parents had been having major power struggles with Jim over his heavy metal music and substance abuse. The excerpt below is from the first family session. Because the atmosphere was tense, I decided to take a risk and share a humorous heavy metal music joke I had heard.

THERAPIST: I was recently at a comedy club downtown and heard a heavy metal music joke that I would like to share with all of you that I believe you will get a kick out of. I'm sure all of you have heard about all of the controversy on TV regarding the subliminal messages that heavy metal records are supposed to give to teenagers, such as: "Jump off the bridge," "Shoot your dog," and so on. Well, imagine this scene . . . The teenagers are rushing home from school and playing their heavy metal records backwards, and the subliminal message is "Cut the grass!" "Cut the grass!" And all of the teenagers are mowing their lawns! The parents are freaking out and fainting . . .

FATHER: *(laughing)* That's funny!

MOTHER: *(laughing)* I would probably faint!

JIM: *(with a smile on his face)* That would really trip them out if I mowed the grass . . . I hate cutting the grass. *(turning toward his mother)* You would really faint if I cut the grass?

M: You haven't cut the grass since you were 10 years old . . .

F: I would probably faint because you rarely do anything around the house.

T: *(turning to Jim)* It sounds like your parents don't think you can do it, but I agree with you that it would really "trip them out" if you cut the grass. Which one of your parents will be the first to faint?

J: Probably Dad would.

F: Thanks, son, but you're probably right. I am more sensitive to big surprises than Margaret [mother] is.

T: When your dad faints after you have cut the grass, will you dump a bucket of water over his head to revive him?

J: That would be funny . . . . *(laughing)* No . . . I think I would wait to see how tripped out he will look when he sees the great job I did on the lawn.

After discussing in great detail the parents' reactions to Jim mowing the lawn, the atmosphere in the therapy room had lightened up and the family interactions had greatly changed. The parents and Jim mutually agreed that his mowing the lawn would be a good initial treatment goal. In 1 week's time, not only did Jim mow the lawn, but he kept the volume level of his stereo down, and the parents reported no signs of substance abuse. As a reward for his great week, the parents took Jim to one of his favorite Italian restaurants and bought him some headphones so he could "blast his music as loud as he wanted to into his own ears."

In therapy sessions with adolescents, I try as much as possible to keep our meetings upbeat and make room for improvisational surprises. One of my former cases provides a good example of how my therapy sessions take the form of an improvisational theater production.

William, a white 15-year-old "depressed" high school freshman, was referred to me for "fleeting thoughts of suicide," "poor social skills," and "failing grades." William and his mother came to the session very concerned about his problems. After asking the miracle question (de Shazer, 1988), I successfully generated a number of useful exceptions and co-created a context for change with the family. One important exception was that William attended a martial arts class. To further empower William and challenge the dominant story (White & Epston, 1990) that he was "depressed," I had him give the team (behind the one-way mirror) and me a live demonstration of his best judo and karate moves. Following William's great performance, the team came into the room from behind the one-way mirror, and together we gave him a standing ovation. After the team left the room, I commented to the mother how she "must feel safe with William around." I also asked William if I could feel his biceps. When complimenting William at the end of the session, I shared with him that the team and I would like to take martial arts lessons with him. This compliment produced a big smile on William's face. Over four sessions of therapy, William successfully improved his grades, made two friends at school, and no longer displayed any signs of being depressed.

UTILIZATION

The engagement strategy of *utilization* was developed by Milton H. Erickson (Gilligan, 2002; O'Hanlon, 1987; Havens, 1985; de Shazer, 1985; Erickson, 1965; Erickson & Rossi, 1983; Erickson, Rossi, & Rossi, 1976; Gordon & Meyers-Anderson, 1981). While establishing rapport with his clients, Erickson would listen carefully for specific strengths and resources, key client words, beliefs, themes, and metaphors he could utilize in their therapeutic conversations and channel into presenting problem areas. Erickson believed that therapists should enable their clients to do what they do best by capitalizing on their strengths and resources (O'Hanlon, 1987; Gordon & Meyers-Anderson, 1981). The following case example illustrates the therapeutic usefulness of the utilization strategy with a challenging adolescent case.

Ramón, a 16-year-old Latino male, was brought for therapy by his mother, Juanita, for his aggressive and violent behaviors at school and at home. For 3 years, Ramón had been getting into fights at school, arguing with teachers, punching holes in his bedroom wall, and threatening to strike his mother. Ramón had been in individual therapy twice before, but none of his behaviors had changed. Juanita had been "divorced from Ramón's father for 5 years." She attributed Ramón's aggressive and violent behaviors to his father's past physically abusive behavior. Apparently, the father used to beat Juanita in front of Ramón and disciplined Ramón harshly with a belt. Ramón had not had any contact with his father since the parental divorce.

Early in the first interview, I discovered that Ramón was a very talented artist. In fact, I had the opportunity of seeing some of his best drawings in his sketchbook that he brought to the session. Ramón loved to draw Marvel Comics superheroes like the "Hulk," "Fantastic Four," "Thor," and so forth. However, over the past year, Ramón had been using most of his artistic talents for drawing evil-looking "supervillains" that would "kill the good guys" and "take over the universe." While admiring Ramón's drawings, I noticed that he took pride and joy in his work and liked the fact that I was taking an interest in his artistic abilities. Ramón also shared with me that some of his most creative moments in coming up with new "supervillains" occurred "after a fight" with his girlfriend or his mother, or after "a bad day at school." After hearing this important exception material, I began to think about how I could use Ramón's artistic abilities and constructive coping strategy in the problem area. Before meeting alone with Ramón, I spent session time with Juanita to explore exceptions and past helpful attempted solutions. Juanita could neither identify any exceptions nor envision future miracles with Ramón's behavior. Prior to our first family session, Juanita had called the police on Ramón for threatening her.

Ramón had begun to blame his mother for his aggressive behavior by claiming that she "yells at" him "too much." Juanita agreed that there had been times when the more she would overreact to Ramón, the more he would escalate his aggressive behavior. While meeting with Juanita, I explored with her whether she would like an experiment to try that could assist me in helping her son. Juanita decided to experiment with the observation task (Molnar & de Shazer, 1987) that I wanted to give her, which would focus her attention on exception patterns in Ramón's behavior.

During my individual session time with Ramón, I decided to capitalize on his artistic abilities, particularly at drawing evil-looking supervillains. I asked Ramón if he would be willing to do an experiment that would be fun and that would "blow your mother's mind." I also pointed out that another benefit of doing the experiment would be having his mother "yell at" him less. Ramón agreed to try my experiment. I gave him the following instructions: "Whenever you are mad about anything or at anybody [bad day at school, girlfriend, Mom], I want you to zoom up to your bedroom and draw some of the most evil-looking 'supervillains' that your creative mind can come up with. I want you to keep drawing until you are no longer mad. I will be looking forward to seeing all of your new 'supervillain' characters in your sketchbook next week."

I concluded the family session with compliments for Juanita and Ramón. One week later, Juanita came in reporting a big reduction in Ramón's temper outbursts and threatening behaviors. She had not received even "one call from the school." Juanita was most surprised by Ramón's "not fighting back" with her. Ramón reported that his mother was "yelling less" and they "hardly got into it" over the week. The biggest surprise for me was hearing that Ramón had decided to extend his experimental behavior to the school context as well. Ramón proudly showed me his new "supervillain" entries in his sketchbook. Future sessions consisted of prescribing more of what was working, consolidating gains, and collaborating with concerned school personnel.

WORKING THE OTHER SIDE OF THE FENCE

In my clinical practice with difficult adolescents and their families, I have found it to be quite advantageous to provide the adolescent with individual session time. Research indicates that both the adolescent and his or her parents expect therapists to do this (Selekman, 2002; Newfield et al., 1991; Selekman, 1989a, 1989b). The individual session time can be used to further join with the adolescent, negotiate the parents' goals, establish a separate goal, find out what he or she would like you to change with the parents' behaviors, and elicit from the adolescent the privileges he or she would like to get from the parents. The majority of difficult adolescent clients I have worked with have been quite surprised when I asked them, "How can I be helpful to you?" In their previous therapy experiences, their parents' wishes for how they "should act" or what they "had to change" took precedence. They were never asked questions such as "What would you like me to change with your parents?" or "Is there a privilege you would like me to go to bat with your parents for you?" These types of open-ended questions can provide the therapist with invaluable information that can be utilized in negotiating a quid pro quo contract with the adolescent's parents. By working the other (adolescent's) side of the fence, the therapist can greatly strengthen his or her therapeutic alliance with the adolescent and be an effective intergenerational negotiator for the family. In the following case, I will present an excerpt from my first family session with Julie.

Julie had been on probation for the past 3 years for shoplifting, possession of marijuana, and truancy. She had been involved in multiple therapy experiences since age 11. Now, at age 16, the parents were seriously contemplating shipping her off to boarding school. During the first half of our session, I was able to secure the parents' treatment goal for Julie, which was for her to get up on time in the morning to catch the school bus at least twice over the next school week. The excerpt below is from my individual session time with Julie.

THERAPIST: You know, I have heard a lot from your parents about what they want to see you change, but what I would really like to know from you is how can I be helpful to you?

JULIE: Well, they are always bitching at me about every little thing. I need some new clothes, and they tell me, "Tough!" Even when I do things right—like go to school or come home on time—they never notice.

T: That's got to be frustrating. So, if there was one thing you would like me to change with your parents, what would that be?

J: Well, if you can get them to stop bitching at me so much . . .

T: During 1 week's time, how many days out of seven do they usually "bitch" at you?

J: Seven days!

T: Now, since they have been bitching at you for such a long time and so frequently, how many days out of seven would be realistic for them in terms of making a small amount of progress? How many days out of seven could they cut back on the bitching that would be a good start for them?

J: If they could go at least one day without bitching at me I would be happy.

T: When they are not bitching at you, what will they be doing instead?

J: Maybe saying something nice to me for once, like "Good job!" or "I can tell you are trying." See, I never hear these kinds of things anymore.

T: So, in the past, they used to praise you?

J: Yeah . . . before I got on probation.

T: What were you doing differently back then that made them want to praise you?

J: Well . . . I was doing better in school, I didn't party . . . you know, smoke weed . . . those kinds of things.

T: Back then, how did your parents praise you, and what other kinds of things were they doing differently that you liked?

J: Well, they told me that they were proud of my good report cards, Mom took me out to buy clothes, my dad used to joke around with me more.

T: We are running out of time, but I want to thank you for letting me know about what you want for yourself and how together we can work on changing your parents' "bitching." Their goal for you, which sounded pretty easy, was for you to set your alarm clock and get up on time to catch the school bus at least twice over the next week. My hunch is, if you really wanted to blow your parents' minds you would do this at least a few times over the next week.

J: No problem! If I really wanted to, I could get up on time for the bus and stay in school at least three times over the next week.

After complimenting the family, I gave an observation task that consisted of each family member keeping track of what each member did that they wanted to continue to have happen. The family came back 1 week later more hopeful, positive, and reporting a number of exceptions. Julie had had 5 days of getting up on time to catch the school bus. She noticed that her parents were "bitching" at her "less" and actually "praised" her at the end of the school week. Besides amplifying all of the family changes, I successfully negotiated with the mother and Julie a time for them to go shopping together.

When utilizing this engagement strategy, it is important that the therapist join well with the parents and demonstrate his or her commitment to helping them achieve their goals with their adolescents. By carefully working *both* sides of the fence, the therapist will be in a better position to negotiate realistic goals, expectations, and privileges.

BRINGING IN A FRIEND

Some adolescents are more likely to open up in counseling if one of their best friends can accompany them to the session. Today, since peers and their "crew" or "homies" have become in some cases much more significant to them than their own families, for engagement and therapeutic leverage purposes it can be quite advantageous to try to secure written consent to involve the adolescent's closest friend(s) in his or her individual or family therapy sessions. I have devised a *significant other consent form* to get written permission from the adolescent's parents to involve his or her friends in treatment. The rules of confidentiality are explained, and there are several lines for signatures provided on the consent form. We secure signatures from the client, his or her parents, the friends, and the friends' parents on the consent form. Besides being concerned and committed to our clients, these friends can offer some novel ideas and creative problem-solving strategies that they and their parents used successfully to resolve their difficulties. They also may have come up with useful ideas for coping with peer rejection and bullying.

Stuart, a white 17-year-old with a long history of self-harming behavior and depression, had been referred to me by his school social worker. Stuart was frequently bullied at school, which would result in his grabbing anything sharp and stabbing himself repeatedly on his arms. He had been psychiatrically hospitalized several times and was on a variety of medications. In our first few sessions, it was quite difficult to get Stuart to open up about his issues or assert himself with his parents, whom he felt invalidated him a lot. I brought up the idea of Stuart's bringing in one of his closest friends for support and some fresh ideas. Both Stuart and his parents thought this was a great idea. He decided that he would bring in Tania, who used to "cut herself" and have "big-time problems with depression." I had them sign off on the significant other consent form and make sure that Tania and her mother signed off on it as well. In our next family session, I tapped Tania's wisdom and expertise at being able to conquer similar issues that Stuart was grappling with. She talked about how her parents started to "listen more" to her, how she "took more risks" with "standing up" for herself when peers would reject her, and she did "yoga as a way to relax" herself when "stressed out." Tania also started taking guitar lessons after school. The session proved to be quite productive, and Stuart was much more talkative in the session.

Tania's involvement in this and future family sessions had successfully brought out Stuart's voice more, offered him some valuable coping strategies, and empowered him to resolve his difficulties.

USING THE ADOLESCENT AS AN EXPERT CONSULTANT

Difficult adolescents who have had multiple therapy experiences have a wealth of knowledge about what therapists should and should not do with them and their parents. I may ask the adolescent, individually or with the family, the following questions: "You have seen many therapists before me, what do you suppose they missed or overlooked with you?" "What should a new therapist do with you that will make a difference?" "If I were to work with a teenager just like you, what advice would you give me to help him or her out?" These open-ended questions invite the adolescent to tell the story of past therapy experiences, convey the idea that therapy with me is collaborative, and foster a cooperative working relationship.

Barbara, a white 16-year-old bulimic, had been in three inpatient psychiatric eating disorder programs and had had five outpatient treatment experiences with psychologists and psychiatrists. The parents brought Barbara to see me after her discharge from an inpatient psychiatric 3-month eating disorder program. According to the parents, Barbara had "relapsed" shortly after getting out of the hospital. She was "bingeing and purging again." While meeting with the whole family, I asked the miracle question (de Shazer, 1988), which created hope for the parents and helped them more clearly articulate what they needed to do differently around Barbara. Barbara, on the other hand, had very little to say regarding what her "miracles" would look like. After meeting briefly with the parents to explore their attempted solutions and treatment goals, I spent some individual session time with Barbara to better connect with her and explore what she would like to get out of therapy.

THERAPIST: I thought it could be helpful if you and I had a little bit of individual space and time together without your parents around. They really talk up a storm!

BARBARA: You're not kidding! That's part of the problem . . . They always do this in counseling . . .

T: Talk up a storm?

B: Yeah . . . all of the counselors let them talk too much—you know, like my mom goes off on a long speech on all of the new books she has read on bulimia and anorexia and how she saw so and so on the Oprah show the other day . . . This is why I usually don't say too much in counseling . . .

T: So, past counselors have allowed your parents to talk too much in your family sessions. What other things have your past counselors or doctors done with you that you didn't think were helpful or turned you off?

B: Well . . . some of the doctors I saw in the hospital were always trying to get inside my head. I hate that! Tell me how you feel? You know, stupid shit like that. I had this one psychologist put words in my mouth and said that I "binge and purge to get even" with my parents because they go away on vacation a lot. That's a crock of shit! Basically, a lot of my friends do this throwing up thing to lose weight so we can get into those tight skirts.

T: Barbara, can you think of any other things I should do differently with you and your parents that former counselors failed to do?

B: Yeah, with my parents . . . don't let them talk so much about what they have read or saw on TV—they begin to sound like all those other counselors. I know my parents love me, but try and get my mom to stop worrying so much about me. Everyday I hear: "Are you okay, honey?"; "Should I not buy potato chips and cookies at the store today?"; "Can I help you with your homework?" This drives me crazy!

T: Which one of those things would you like to see changed first with your parents, the long monologues or getting your parents to worry about you less?

B: The last one. I get real nervous when they worry about me a lot. That's when I really pig out and purge, when I'm real nervous.

T: Any other things that your parents do that make you feel like pigging out and purging?

B: When they try and pick my friends for me. Like, they tell me to stay away from two of my closest friends because they have the same problems.

As the reader can clearly see, placing Barbara in the expert position opened the door for her to tell her story about why past treatment experiences did not help her. I learned what I needed to do differently with Barbara and her parents. The added bonus was discovering the specific parental behaviors that inadvertently maintained the bulimia problem. Through the use of pattern intervention (O'Hanlon, 1987) and having Barbara keep track of what she did to overcome the urge to "pig out" (de Shazer, 1985), we were able to resolve the bulimia problem.

VALIDATION AND EMPATHY

Most of the adolescents who present with severe behavioral difficulties and have closely affiliated themselves with a *second family* (Selekman, 2002; Taffel & Blau, 2001) in the community, such as a street gang, often feel invalidated and emotionally disconnected from their parents or other key caretakers in their lives. As they put it best, they feel "dissed"—not listened to—and feel insignificant to these key adults in their lives. This can fuel rage and aggressive and serious self-destructive behaviors. Unfortunately, the second family they had sought refuge in often consists of other invalidated or emotionally disconnected youth who may be a lot worse off. It is critical as therapists that we not inadvertently repeat these kinds of parent–adolescent experiences with these youth. Being a good listener, consistently validating their thoughts and feelings, and staying connected to the adolescent unconditionally can help promote the healing process and empower them.

Miguel, a 16-year-old member of the Latin Kings street gang, was brought in by his mother after being expelled from school for seriously hurting a rival gang member who also attended his high school. He also had a long history of explosive and violent behavior and heavy marijuana and alcohol abuse with his "homies." Throughout most of his childhood, Miguel's father, Carlos, was both emotionally and physically abusive toward him. The father also would constantly compare him to his 14-year-old brother, Raul, who was a "straight-A student" and "star athlete." Miguel reportedly had a long history of bullying his "angelic" brother. During the miracle question inquiry portion of the session, Miguel reported with an angry tone in his voice and with watery eyes that his "father will never change!" At this point in the session, I decided to meet alone with Miguel and give him plenty of space to share his long emotionally painful story of victimization by the father. He reported several emotionally painful experiences dating back to the age of 5. As I used validation and empathy with Miguel, he began to cry and grieve his shattered dream of wanting to have a different kind of relationship with his father. He also began to make some important connections about how his involvement with the Kings and bullying his brother were all related to the way his father had mistreated him. Following our highly productive session, Miguel made a commitment to work on his anger management, try to land a job, and improve his relationship with his brother. Neither Miguel nor his mother wanted me to try to engage the father for family therapy. I respected and honored their request. I also provided them with the name and address of a shelter near their home in case violence erupted in the home.

Two weeks after our initial session, not only did Miguel secure two part-time jobs, but he began taking a GED preparation class so that he could get his high school diploma. Miguel also stopped running around with his Latin King "homies" as well. However, the biggest growth step and most emotionally moving highlight of our work together was in our sixth session, when Miguel asked for his brother's forgiveness for all the years he had bullied him. After his brother accepted Miguel's apology, they gave each other a big brotherly hug.

SELF-DISCLOSURE

The purposive use of self-disclosure has been shown to be a useful therapeutic tool with difficult adolescents (Selekman, 1989a, 1989b, 2002; Newfield et al., 1991). It is crucial that the therapist's self-disclosed material fit with the adolescent client's presenting dilemma. Adolescents have reported that they like counselors that "had been there," in terms of experiencing similar struggles as a youth. However, not all therapists have experienced stormy adolescent periods in their lives, nor are they familiar with street lingo. These therapists can use themselves in other ways, such as using humor, telling stories, and sharing their gut reactions or absurd ideas in the interviewing process with the adolescent. The case example of Steve demonstrates how purposive use of self-disclosure can normalize the adolescent's present struggles and also offer the young person some new ideas for problem solving.

Steve, a white 17-year-old substance abuser, had a long history of treatment for delinquent acting-out behavior. He and his mother were currently at an impasse over his spending too much of his free time with his girlfriend. The other hot issue for the family was Steve's refusal to cut his long hair in order to get a job. The excerpt below is taken from the first family interview with Steve during my individual session time with him.

THERAPIST: So, your mom has been on your case a lot lately about your girlfriend, cutting your hair, and getting a job?

STEVE: Yeah, I'm sick of her damn harping! She's always ragging at me about everything. I've got a few possible jobs lined up. I ain't going to cut my hair for nobody! I went to this one picture framing store.

T: You know, when I was your age, I was a bad dude too. I had a long maxi army coat, high-top black leather boots, a big 'fro out to here *(physically showing him how round and high my afro used to be)*. My parents wanted me to get a job too. I also said "I ain't going to cut my hair" to get a job. But, you know what? I got turned down left and right by employers because I looked like a wild man from Borneo!

S: *(laughing)* You're wild, dude!

T: Once I trimmed that 'fro down, I finally nailed a job. Then, I had money to take my girlfriend out instead of bumming off my parents all of the time.

S: Maybe you're right, because I'm kind of sick of bumming money from my mom, and lately she hasn't given me anything. Karen [Steve's girlfriend] has had to pay for us lately, which is kind of a drag for me.

T: The bottom line is that no employer is going to hire a young person that looks like a wild man—you know, like a stoner [drug abuser]. The other thing about getting a job is that you'll have money to buy yourself things that you like—you know, CD's and clothes.

S: That sounds cool. Okay, dude. The next time you see me hopefully I'll have a job, but I will cut my hair.

Because I connected well with Steve earlier in the family session, I decided to make use of self-disclosure to normalize his struggles regarding not wanting to cut his hair and shared with him my own solution to this dilemma as a youth. My self-disclosed material was acceptable to Steve's belief system because it mirrored his own situation. Two weeks later, Steve came to the second session sporting a stylish-looking haircut and happily reporting that he had landed a job working in a video store.

THE COLUMBO APPROACH

Some difficult adolescents make us feel highly incompetent as therapists. Often, these tough adolescents are court-ordered to family counseling or have had a long history of involvement with mental health professionals. The TV police detective Columbo has taught me some valuable skills for engaging some of the toughest adolescent clients. Columbo has no trouble allowing his clumsy and incompetent style to show with potential suspects. He likes to readily free-associate about his wife, and others have been regularly letting him know how he is slipping with certain responsibilities and what a bungler he can be. He also convincingly empathizes with the suspect's loss of the murder victim and how emotionally distressing the situation must be for him or her. While joining with a potential suspect, Columbo uses compliments to butter up him or her. Throughout the entire investigation process, Columbo asks questions from a position of "not knowing" (Anderson & Goolishian, 1988b, 1991b) and presents himself as being confused about who committed the murder and how it occurred. This keeps potential murder suspects off-balance and eventually leads them to help Columbo solve the crime through leading him to important clues or incriminating themselves in some way.

David, an African American 16-year-old, was court-ordered for 1 year of family therapy for stealing car radios, home burglary, and suspected gang involvement. In the first session, David was accompanied by his mother and his 12-year-old brother, George. Ever since David had been arrested for stealing car radios and home burglary, he denied engaging in any of these behaviors. The mother reported that she thought that David was probably "running with a gang." This was her biggest concern at intake. David had already been in therapy five times for his acting-out behavior. Two of these times, he had refused to go for further sessions after the initial interviews. During the majority of our first session, David had very little to say about why he had to go for counseling or what he saw as the problem. The excerpt below is taken from my individual session time alone with David.

THERAPIST: It must be a real drag for you to have to go for counseling again. *(fidgeting with my pad of paper)* Whoops! *(dropping my pad of paper)*

DAVID: What's wrong with you, man?! Are you nervous or something?

T: Well . . . a little. I'm surprised that my supervisor gave me your case. I mean your situation is way over my head. I don't get it. The judge ordered you to go for counseling. For what reason? I mean you say that nothing happened and the police got the wrong guy. I'm really confused. *(looking puzzled)*

D: Well . . . well, I didn't break into that man's crib, that was some other brothers that did that. I grabbed me a few car radios in the 'hood, but I don't do the other things.

T: *(playing dumb)* "Crib?" "'Hood?" What do you mean? Maybe I'm old-fashioned or something.

D: You don't know nothing, man! Crib means house. A 'hood is where you live, you know.

T: Oh . . . now I see. You mean neighborhood. Help me out . . . oh, by the way, thanks for the help with the new words you taught me. Anyways, help me out . . . did the judge or the probation officer tell you what they wanted you to accomplish in counseling?

D: Well . . . I think he said I got to stay away from the Vicelords [street gang] and not get busted anymore.

T: Did they mention anything about what you're supposed to do at your "crib?"

D: You're a trip man! *(laughing)* You're something else, man. Follow the rules. Go to school, you know.

The Columbo approach proved to be quite effective for helping me get in the door with David. My bungling therapist style made it difficult for David to feel threatened by me. I also made it clear to him that I was neither a social control agent nor an extension of the court system.

Future therapy sessions focused on helping David steer away from the street gang lifestyle, assisting the mother with some new parenting skills, and collaborating with the probation officer. Because boxing was one of David's strengths, I hooked him up with an adult friend of mine who coached talented Golden Gloves boxers.

THE TWO-STEP TANGO

Most court-ordered visiting/precontemplative adolescents are not even window-shoppers for counseling, because they "do not have a problem." However, the adults in their lives have a problem with their behavior. Therefore, rather than coming across like all the other concerned adults in his or her life, lecturing and trying to get him or her to change, it is important to do a *two-step tango*. On the one hand, we need to restrain the adolescent from changing, and, on the other hand, begin to seed or plant helpful ideas in his or her mind about the benefits of changing (Selekman, 2002; Prochaska, 1999; Fisch et al., 1982).

Sean, a white 17-year-old, had been court-ordered to see me for 72 hours of DUI (driving under the influence) counseling after being arrested driving home from a party heavily intoxicated on hard liquor. According to the parents, Sean had continued to drink despite getting the DUI and losing his driver's license. With his beard and weathered appearance, Sean looked a lot older than his age. Intergenerational alcoholism problems ran in the family on the father's side of the family. As soon as Sean walked in the door, he made it quite clear that he "hated social workers" and that this was "a waste of time." Sean had an extensive treatment history for his oppositional, aggressive, and alcohol-abusing behaviors. He had been in an adolescent chemical dependency program in the past. Clearly, based on his strong family background of alcoholism, his recurrent blackouts, shakes, physiological costs due to the alcohol abuse, and inability to stay abstinent, I felt a detox was in order. The case transcript below demonstrates the effectiveness of the two-step tango with clients like Sean.

THERAPIST: Sean, I know this is a real drag for you, and you made it quite clear to me that you particularly "hate social workers." I hear you loud and clear. I just want you to know that I am not going to tell you what to do and that there is no hurry to change here. After all, you really "like to party" with your friends and you "like to drink." Did you know that among long-time alcohol-abusing men, over time, their male sex hormone testosterone declines and their female sex hormone estrogen rises, meaning that you can potentially develop small breasts and lose your facial hair!? Can you imagine picking your girlfriend up for a date and having small breasts and blotches of skin where your beard used to be!?

SEAN: (*with a frightened look on his face*) You mean, that could happen to me?!

T: Yeah. I have worked with some alcoholic adult men where that has happened to them. Yeah, it can really scare you when that happens. (*I am shaking my head and looking down.*) Hang tight. There is no hurry to change. After all, we have 71 more hours to work together! Let's take it nice and slow. By the way, did you know that alcohol is like Liquid Drano—you know what that is?

S: Yup.

T: Well, anyway, your cells in your body actually change to get used to having alcohol in your system. If you are physically hooked on alcohol and suddenly take it out of your body for a period of time, your body can go into shock and you can get the DTs!

S: What's that!?

T: That's *delirium tremens*. Your breathing and heart rate slow down, and you experience tactile hallucinations—that's when you feel like bugs are crawling all over your body! You can actually die!

S: (*looking scared again*) Hey dude . . . could that really happen to me!?

By the end of our session, Sean agreed to go in for a detox and began to look at the necessity of maintaining an alcohol-free lifestyle. He appeared to be quite shaken up about the serious consequences of his continuing to abuse alcohol. I framed the detox experience as being an opportunity for him to pursue a different direction in his life.

HONORING AND RESPECTING SILENCE

As Bohart and Tallman (1999) have pointed out in their important therapy process research, silent clients are not being passive recipients of our efforts to help them, nor are they being resistant. On the contrary, the wheels in their minds are turning, they are sizing us up and carefully determining whether or not they can trust us or we can be of *real* help to them. Often, therapists assume that the silent adolescent is being "resistant," "uncooperative," or "anti-authority." For adolescents who have had many negative past experiences with therapists and treatment programs, why should they trust us?! The biggest complaint that I have heard from these adolescents coming for treatment with thick fork-lifted file folders is that their confidentiality had been repeatedly violated by their former therapists or treatment program personnel. It takes a lot of effort and patience to sit quietly and listen to a therapist talk for an hour. A lot of adults could not handle going a whole hour without saying a word. The adolescent's silent behavior needs to be honored and respected.

Willie, a 15-year-old African American, was referred to me by his high school dean for "fighting with fellow students," being "verbally abusive toward his teachers," and "involvement with the Vicelords street gang." His going for counseling was serving as "an alternative to being suspended for violent behavior." According to his mother, Latisha, "counseling has not worked in the past," and she ends up "doing most of the talking." In the first half of our initial family session, history began to repeat itself with me, in that Latisha was "doing most of the talking." I decided to meet alone at this point with Willie to see if I could get in the door with him. I asked the following questions: "How can I be helpful to you? Is there anything you would like me to work on changing with your mother? Are there any privileges for which you would like me to go to bat for you with your mother?" Willie did not respond and continued to sit with his arms tightly folded across his chest. I empathized with his desire to remain silent and how this makes sense based on the fact that he had had a lot of past negative counseling experiences. I also offered to help get the dean off of his back. This was met with more silence. By the end of the hour, I complimented Willie on his ability to endure a whole hour of listening to me talk. This produced a smile on his face. I am thinking, "A breakthrough!" I further complimented him on his respectful listening abilities and asked him if he planned to use the same listening strategy the next time we got together.

In our next family meeting, Willie smiled when I greeted him in the lobby, shook my hand, and said, "Hello." He also surprised me during our individual session time by revisiting my idea about "getting the dean off of his back." By respecting and honoring his need to be silent and staying connected to him through continuing to talk, despite his silence, I helped pave the way to building trust in our therapeutic relationship.

SUMMARY

In this chapter, I have presented 10 useful engagement strategies for difficult adolescent clients. With the majority of my difficult adolescent cases, I have found it helpful to use a combination of these engagement strategies in the first family interviews. The various engagement strategies selected for any one particular case are based on the unique cooperative response pattern of the adolescent, the family's goals, and on what I need to do differently as a therapist in relationship to the adolescent that can help generate a therapeutic change. No matter what setting you work in, readers will find these engagement strategies to be quite effective in rapidly fostering cooperative working relationships with adolescents.

Seven

The No-Problem Problem Mandated Family

Eighty percent of success is showing up.
—WOODY ALLEN

Most clinicians dread being referred mandated juvenile offenders and their families. This is mainly due to unhelpful stereotypes about these clients that have been perpetuated by the mental health literature, which has roots in the deficit perspective. Frustrated helping professionals working in the trenches with this treatment population often vent their disgruntlement by giving kids such labels as "antisocial," "resistant," "in denial," "noncompliant," "defensive," and "difficult to treat." When therapists accept and adopt these labels, they often fall into the trap of trying to convince the clients they have problems, not honoring their stories and goals, not taking a strong interest in their key strengths and special talents, and mismatching their therapeutic interventions with the clients' stages of readiness to change, which can all lead to the treatment system getting stuck, clients requesting new therapists, or premature dropouts.

No-problem problem families are often mandated clients who may or may not come to us under duress and do not think they have a problem that warranted the need to go for family counseling. However, a juvenile court judge or a child protective worker, both of whom have the power to enforce response and action, are putting pressure on the family to comply with their treatment recommendations. There are two types of no-problem problem mandated families. The first type consists of first-time juvenile offenders that may be doing pretty well in other areas of their lives, and this may be the first time they have been in family counseling or in any kind of counseling (Selekman, 1997; Eastwood, Sweeney, & Piercy, 1987). At all costs, we need to be careful not to invent or create problems for these families. Therefore, as therapists we need to strongly empathize with their dilemma of being forced to go for counseling for the length of the adolescents' probation terms when—were it not for their breaking the law and being court-ordered to go for treatment—they would not be in counseling to begin with. These cases become difficult when therapists treat them as though they were like any other family in their caseload, and at the start of treatment assign and expect them to comply with therapeutic interventions, which they may not follow through with. The no-problem problem family members are often in the *precontemplation* stage of readiness to change (Prochaska, 1999) when they begin treatment. So, assigning them between-session therapeutic experiments, for example, is only a recipe for frustration.

The second type of no-problem problem family has had extensive treatment experience and involvement with helping professionals from larger systems, including the juvenile justice system, before. However, what may have contributed to family members' feelings of demoralization, hopelessness, and despair and the youth's continued legal involvement was the mismatching of past treatment modalities and interventions with their stages of readiness to change and theories of change (Prochaska, 1999; Hubble et al., 1999). Also, former therapists' goals may have been driving the treatment process or there may have been a lack of sensitivity to important client cultural issues. In addition, severe financial difficulties, parental substance abuse and mental health issues, lack of a support system, and living in a decaying and rough community can also contribute to families' being stuck in a *precontemplation* stage of readiness to change as well (Prochaska, 1999).

With no-problem problem mandated families, therapists need to first create a therapeutic climate in which family members feel genuinely listened to, respected, and understood. Therapists need to take a deep interest in each family member's concerns, positions on why they think they were referred, their theories of change, cultural values and expectations, their key strengths, unique talents, and what they are most passionate about in their lives. Since these families are often eager to extricate themselves from this counseling ordeal as quickly as possible, the therapeutic emphasis needs to be placed on what specific family members' key strengths and talents can be tapped to empower them to take the necessary steps in the future to satisfy the probation officer, judge, or any other involved larger systems professionals that their adolescent will stay out of further trouble and not need to go to counseling anymore. Finally, as therapists we must compliment them and acknowledge the fact that they are already taking these steps simply by just showing up for their first appointment.

In this chapter, I discuss how to conduct strengths-based wellness conversations with no-problem problem mandated families that promote therapeutic cooperation and change, present a variety of questions that elicit family members' expertise and assist them with establishing well-formed behavioral treatment goals, and describe how to establish successful collaborative relationships with probation officers, judges, and other involved helping professionals from larger systems. Two case examples are presented to illustrate how to co-create possibilities with both types of families in these situations.

COAUTHORING SOLUTION-DETERMINED WELLNESS STORIES TO PROMOTE COOPERATION AND CHANGE

By adopting a wellness mindset with these families, we demonstrate to them a genuine interest in learning more about family members' key signature strengths, talents, and passions in their lives. Simply by inquiring about these meaningful and important areas in family members' lives, we are eliciting their expertise and inviting them to compliment themselves on their resourcefulness. To further expand on this wellness conversation, we can invite family members to share how they have successfully tapped their key signature strengths and talents to overcome adversity or other challenging life events in their past. The therapist also can explore with family members the constructive pretreatment steps that they have already taken to help the adolescent stay out of further trouble, such as the adolescent's deciding to stay away from certain peers and places, the parents more tightly monitoring their daughter or son, and any other preventative measures they have taken. In addition, through this wellness inquiry we will learn which key family member signature strengths and talents we can harness and utilize to empower the family to rapidly work their way out of counseling. They will be more likely to cooperate with the proposed change strategies we offer them when they are couched in their language and draw upon their strengths and talents. Wellness conversations like these can create a therapeutic reality of cooperation in which we become partners for change.

At the first appointment, family members may have difficulty in identifying any pretreatment changes or how they envision using their signature strengths and talents to help them succeed in counseling and work their way out of the juvenile justice system. With the help of future-oriented questions, we can have family members project themselves into the future to preview how they can successfully complete counseling and terminate the probation process and then have them walk their way back to the here and now, spelling out the systematic steps they took to accomplish these objectives. Not only is this type of questioning useful for goal setting, but also it generates from family members useful information about any overlooked pretreatment changes and potential solution strategies that can be implemented immediately. This future-oriented inquiry can be taken a step further by asking family members to focus 9–12 months down the road and have them share with you what specifically each of them is doing to stay on track and further improve his or her situation, both individually and as a family. To help bring this future visualization more to life for them, it important to have them describe in great detail the *who, what, where,* and *how* of their successes.

Some parents will not be surprised or may be even glad that their son or daughter finally got arrested and charged with a crime, especially if they were feeling that their adolescents were totally disregarding their rules and limits. Other involved helping professionals from larger systems may also be pleased with this outcome with the hope that the adolescent will finally be held accountable for his or her troublesome actions. Up to the point of arrest and being charged, the adolescent may have been getting away with criminal activity, having some difficulties in school, and was forewarned by the parents to stop hanging around with a negative group of peers. In these case situations, I may reframe the adolescent's getting into trouble as being *a valuable lesson in choice making* or as *a reminder that honesty is a virtue*. By doing this, counseling becomes a context for wisdom and learning how to make better choices, be honest, keep the lines of communication open across generational lines, and the parents can learn from their son or daughter what they need to do differently that can help prevent future legal involvement and behavioral difficulties. If the parents had similar difficulties with an older sibling, it could be quite useful to find out what problem-solving strategies they used that worked that may be worthwhile trying with their son or daughter who is currently in trouble. In addition, the therapist should further explore with that sibling how he or she was able to turn around the situation and get back on track.

Finally, it may be beneficial to find out from the presently troubled adolescent what key resource people in his or her social network can be recruited to help out with staying out of further trouble both in and out of our family sessions. This could be an *adult inspirational other* (Selekman, 2002; Anthony, 1987) who deeply cares about and provides support to the adolescent and longtime friends who are not a part of the negative peer group. In some cases, the therapist can have the inspirational other (a caring and concerned teacher, for example) and the adolescent's friends serve as a *consultation support team* in a social context in which he or she is having difficulties, such as at school.

For families that continue to cling to the position that the adolescent's offenses were flukes or that counseling is a waste of time—despite your best efforts to connect with them or move them from the *precontemplation* stage of readiness to change (Prochaska, 1999)—it is worth the risk to put them in the expert position and ask their advice about how best to work with other families like them. For instance, the therapist can ask the following questions:

- "I really would like your suggestions. I am currently working with a family just like you guys—exactly the same situation—and I am feeling really stuck. Do you have any advice for me about how I can best help that family out?"
- "If I had all of you sitting in as expert consultants with that family, what would you recommend I say or do that you think that they would find to be most helpful?"
- "If you were me, what would you suggest or try to do with the parents?"
- "Charlie [the client], if you were me, what should I share with my client that could help him stay out of further trouble?"

The bonus of having the clients take a meta-position to another stuck family just like them is that it brings forth their expert knowledge and resourcefulness in generating their own unique solutions for their own situations. Furthermore, the therapist will learn how to cooperate better with these more challenging families.

If this strategy does not work, once again we can employ the tactics of TV detective Columbo as a way to help family members find important clues for how they got into this predicament and how they can draw upon their expertise and creativity to resolve their dilemma. The following case example illustrates how to use Columbo tactics in the interviewing process.

Melissa, a 16-year-old, had been court-ordered for 9 months of family counseling after being caught shoplifting $1,000 worth of women's clothes from an exclusive department store. This was the first time that Melissa, an A and B student in high school, had ever been arrested or had had any legal problems. The parents (Bob and Carol) told the probation officer that they rarely had any difficulties with Melissa at home. They believed that the state's attorney and judge were being too extreme in court-ordering both 9 months of probation and family counseling. Melissa felt the same way as her parents and really thought family counseling was a waste of time. The transcript begins midway into our first family session.

THERAPIST: It really sounds like your having to come and see me is a big headache for all of you. I felt like this last weekend when my wife made me clean the garage. I can't say I blame her—I have been putting off this awful job for the past year! (*Bob and Carol are laughing.*) Melissa, I am very confused about how this whole situation happened. (*scratching my head and looking confused*) Your parents and probation officer both told me that you are a very good student and have never been arrested before. How is it that you somehow ended up being caught with $1,000 worth of merchandise in your possession?

MELISSA: I don't know.

T: I mean . . . you could have had one or two items, but you had five very expensive clothing items!

M: I really did not pay attention to how much I had taken.

BOB: I think the problem is that Melissa just plain made a bad call. I mean, maybe this is a teenage thing. I really think Judge Robinson and the state's attorney were being a little too extreme with the consequences here.

CAROL: Melissa is a really good kid, and we don't have any family problems. Can you tell Mr. Lanier [the probation officer] that family counseling is really unnecessary?

T: I can put in a good word for you with Mr. Lanier, but I don't think he is going to buy it. He comes from the old school and believes that a little counseling can't hurt.

M: Fuck! You mean we're going to have to do 9 months of these meetings?!

C: Watch your mouth!

T: Well, I am glad to help you out in any way I can. I can tell Mr. Lanier that you all really think that family counseling is a waste of time. However, I don't think he is going to like the sound of this. The last family I worked with who wanted me to relay this message to him resulted in Mr. Lanier's riding my client like a bronco buster. He would make many more surprise visits up to his school, at his home, and would have the local police occasionally tail him when he would leave the home.

M: You mean that could happen to me?! (*Looks scared.*)

T: Yeah, Mr. Lanier is quite good at turning up the heat with his court kids, especially when he thinks they are hiding something from him. I always tell my court kids that it is better that I find out about their secrets before he does. Tell me, Melissa, was there something you told yourself before you came in here today that you were not going to talk about with me along these lines?

M: Well . . . this was not the first time that I have shoplifted for myself and my friends. Yeah, they let me know what they want, and I will get it for them.

T: How many times before have you done it?

M: I would say that I have done it about 10 times before.

B: I am really shocked to hear this from you! Where are you hiding all of the clothes?

M: In the storage closet in the attic. Sometimes I will just mix the new clothes in with my old ones.

C: How come I have never seen these new clothes in your closet or in the dirty wash?

M: Well, I remove the tags and sometimes keep my new clothes at friends' houses. Haven't you noticed that I have started to wash my own clothes?

C: So, that's why you started washing your own things! Which one of your friends is involved with this mess?

M: Tara, Kim, and Stacy.

C: My God! I would have never suspected any of them would participate in this kind of thing.

B: I am really shocked by this. We have given you so much freedom.

T: I must say, Melissa, you are very clever that you have been able to pull this off for so long. Well, before I call Mr. Lanier today, do you think we now have something to work, on or should I still tell him that you think family counseling will be a waste of time?

As readers can clearly see, by using Columbo tactics I was successfully able to get Melissa to talk about her long history of shoplifting and elicit concern about this problem from the parents. By the end of our first family session, everyone agreed that they wanted me to avoid at all costs telling Mr. Lanier that family counseling was a waste of time. Another positive outcome from this session was the parents moving from a laissez-faire parenting style to providing more structure and limits for Melissa. In fact, not only was Melissa grounded for a month, but the parents called all of her friends' parents to let them know about the shoplifting and the stolen clothing items and brainstorm how to best handle the situation.

The next case example illustrates how to foster a cooperative relationship with the second type of no-problem problem mandated family. In addition, the case demonstrates the advantages of placing therapy-veteran families in the expert role to guide therapists in not replicating attempted solutions by former treatment providers and finding out what to do differently with them.

Leon, a 14-year-old African American, was referred to me by his probation officer, Mr. Smith, for "suspected gang involvement," "substance abuse," "vandalism," and "not following his parents' rules." Leon had been placed on 9 months of probation for violating his court supervision. Leon had been under court supervision and performed community service for vandalizing cars in his neighborhood. However, he recently got arrested with other members of "his crew" for "possession of a small quantity of marijuana." According to Mr. Smith, Leon and his family had been in counseling "several times before," but "nothing had changed" with Leon's behaviors or his parents'. He described the parents as being "burned out" with parenting, all of "Leon's difficulties," and "tired of having to see counselors."

Leon's parents, Ken and Ruby, had cancelled our first scheduled appointment because their son had conveniently disappeared when it was time to head out to my office. One week later, Leon came with his parents and his 10-year-old younger brother, Ted. I could tell by the looks on family members' faces that they were not too thrilled about having to see me—after all, I was the fifth therapist they had been to in the past 3 years!

RUBY: You counselors can't help my son unless he wants to help himself.

THERAPIST: I agree with you, Ruby. I would greatly appreciate if you can better help me understand what you've been through with your past counselors so I don't make the same mistakes. What did they overlook or miss with Leon or your situation that would be important for me to know?"

R: They bought into Leon's jive talk. He's a player.

T: What do you mean by that?

R: Leon talks a good game. He says one thing and does something else outside all of your offices—you know what I mean?

T: Do you mean that he is not "a man of his word?"

R: Yeah he never does what he says he's going to do in these meetings you all have for him.

T: What did past counselors do with you and Leon that made you upset or made your situation worse?

R: They let him slide way too much!

T: Would it help if I were much more active as a counselor and more closely monitored Leon's being "a man of his word" outside of this office?

R: Maybe.

KEN: Listen, I'll be honest with you, I don't believe this counseling thing works at all. If Leon ends up in jail, that's his problem.

T: I hear you loud and clear. I would probably feel the same way if I had already been to four counselors and nothing had worked. Getting back to what I had just asked Ruby, do you think it may help a little, as long as Leon is court-ordered to see me, if I more tightly monitored his follow-through with things we asked him to do outside of here—you know, held him more accountable for his actions—that it could help a little bit?

K: I don't know . . . maybe.

T: Do you also think it could help if I worked more closely with Mr. Smith than your other counselors had done?

R: Definitely. I think some of the old counselors didn't do that enough.

T: What do you think, Ken?

K: Probably.

T: Leon, I appreciate your being such a respectful listener when your parents and I were talking. I would think, like your parents, this must be a real drag for you to have to see another counselor again. How can I be helpful to you so we can make this your last time with a counselor?

Leon: I don't know.

T: I just want you to know that I have a great relationship with Mr. Smith, so I can help you out there. He is open to hearing my suggestions and helps my people out when they are delivering—you know, staying out of trouble.

L: Will I have to go to the juvie if I get busted again?

T: That sounds like Mr. Smith's style. He doesn't mess around.

By giving the parents plenty of room to share their concerns about past therapists, counseling, and validating their feelings, they were able to clearly spell out their expectations of me as a counselor. I learned what to avoid doing with Leon and them that would be considered "more of the same." The parents also pointed out that my being more active as a therapist in closely monitoring Leon and regularly collaborating with Mr. Smith could help. In addition, I did explore with Leon and his parents how they felt about working with a white therapist. Neither Leon nor his parents voiced any concerns about this. It appeared by the end of the family session that the parents and Leon were more hopeful about our being able to do some productive work together.

EMPOWERMENT QUESTIONS THAT ELICIT CLIENT EXPERTISE AND REALISTIC TREATMENT GOALS

In this section, I present a variety of client empowerment questions that can invite families to think about creative ways they can draw from their key strengths, talents, past successes, and what they are most passionate about to help them stay out of further trouble and achieve future successes. It is important to remember, when establishing treatment goals with no-problem problem mandated families, that they should take the lead in determining the goals for treatment, which may be completely unrelated to the adolescents' offenses and reasons why they were being referred for counseling to begin with. In addition, these questions also can be employed as a way to have family members begin to think about the steps the probation officer, the judge, and other involved helping professionals would like to see them take that would indicate to them that they really changed and no longer needed to be involved in their lives. Furthermore, with families that present with longstanding difficulties and multiple areas of concern, therapists need to have them prioritize where they would like to begin and negotiate with them a very small and realistic behavioral goal in their selected target area. Finally, it is helpful to remind these families that their identified initial treatment goal is the *start of something new*, not the immediate end to their prioritized areas of concern. I present below examples of three types of client empowerment questions: *referral process*, *goal-setting*, and *future-oriented questions*.

Referral Process Questions

Referral process questions invite family members to speculate why and how it came about that they were referred for counseling. As part of this inquiry, it is helpful to explore with the families their past history of being referred to other therapists and their present and past involvement with other larger helping systems:

- "Do any of you have any idea why the judge court-ordered family counseling for you?"
- "What do you think he was hoping you would accomplish in counseling that would make him think it was a good decision for you to do this?"
- "When you see Judge Brown in 6 months, Jimmy, which one of the changes you accomplished in counseling will really surprise him the most?"
- "What specifically do you think your probation officer wants to see you work on in counseling that would indicate to him that you really changed and did not need to be in counseling anymore?"
- "What else do you think he wants you to work on changing?"
- "Let's say your probation officer were sitting right here 3 weeks from today; which change that you made happen will he be the most pleased to hear about?"
- "How will that change make him really believe that you are taking your probation situation seriously?"

- "Bill and Barbara [Jimmy's parents], what changes that Jimmy had made will you be the most eager to share with his probation officer in 3 weeks' time?"
- "How about as parents? What will you share with the probation officer that you had been doing differently with Jimmy that he will think really helped him to stay out of further trouble?"
- "Jimmy, what will your dean and school social worker be telling your probation officer that you are doing that will make him a true believer that you have really changed for good?"
- "Have you ever been referred for counseling before?"
- "How do you think that came about?"
- "What steps did you take as a family to make that counseling experience successful or meaningful for you?"
- "Have you ever had any involvement with the court system in the past?"
- "Were there any aspects of your past experience with the court system that you really did not like?"
- "What aspects?"
- "What would you like me, as your counselor and advocate, to do to help this court system experience be less stressful and better for you?"

Goal-Setting Questions

As mentioned earlier, first-time offending and no problem-problem families that have been in counseling before often are not working with well-formed behavioral treatment goals, which leads to the exacerbation of their difficulties or the treatment system getting stuck. In some cases, their treatment goals previously were too lofty or vague, or the therapists' goals were driving the treatment. *Clients need to take the lead in defining their treatment goals.* Our job is to help them negotiate realistic and solvable treatment goals. The following questions can help us to secure our clients' ideal treatment outcome pictures and collaboratively establish well-formed treatment goals with them:

- "Suppose tonight while all of you are sound asleep a miracle happens and Linda is no longer on probation. You wake up the next day, and each one of you notices that things are different. What will have changed in your ideal miracle pictures?"
- "Are you aware of how you got that to happen?"
- "What else are you doing differently, Linda, that is helping you stay out of further trouble?"

- "In what ways have your parents changed that is helping you get along better with them and stay out of trouble?"
- "Mom and Dad, what adjustments will you be making with your parenting that will be helping Linda stay on track?"
- "I'm curious: are any of the pieces of the miracle happening a little bit now?"
- "Are you aware of how you pulled that off?!"
- "How has that made a difference?"
- "What other pieces of the miracle are happening?"
- "How will you know that you really succeeded in counseling?"
- "Now that I know you wish to continue to do further work on your arguing problem, I would like to first get a rating from each of you where the arguing situation was at 4 weeks ago. On a scale from 1 to 10—with 10 being that you are rarely arguing and 1 you are arguing all of the time—where would you have rated your situation 4 weeks ago?"
- "A 1 and a 2, respectively?"
- "How about 2 weeks ago?"
- "A 4 and a 5, respectively?!"
- "What specifically did each of you do to get up to a 4 and 5?"
- "How was that helpful?"
- How about today: what would each of you rate the arguing situation?"
- "Wow! At a 6 and 7, respectively!"
- "Are each of you aware of how you did that?!"
- "What else are you doing that is helping you not argue?"
- "Let's say we got together in 1 week's time and you came in here and told me that you had taken further steps to get up to a lucky 7 and an 8. What will you tell me you did to get that to happen?"
- "Which of your key strengths and talents will you tell me you used to help you achieve your goal?"
- "How have you used your key strengths and talents to resolve other difficulties you were faced with in the past?"

Future-Oriented Questions

The most powerful aspect about the future is that it has not happened yet, thus making it fertile soil ripe with possibilities. Most mandated families enjoy talking about how life will be like for them when they no longer have to deal with judges, probation officers, sitting in court, and having to go for counseling. The more details we can elicit from families about the constructive steps they will be taking in the future to get out of the juvenile justice system and counseling, the more likely we will be able to co-create with them positive self-fulfilling prophecies. The following future-oriented questions help set positive client self-fulfilling prophecies in motion:

- "Let's say we run into one another at the local grocery store 1 year from today, and you proceed to tell me the steps that you took to successfully complete counseling and terminate your probation. What will you be telling me you did to accomplish these big achievements?"
- "How was that first step you took most helpful to you?"
- "What difference did that change make for further improving your situation?"
- "If Mr. Smith [the probation officer] also just happened to show up at the grocery store and joined us in this conversation, and began to reflect on your case situation, what specific changes will come to mind first that he really thought made the difference in turning your situation around?"
- "Let's say he was right on target with what really worked for you; which one of those changes will you tell him has helped the most and why?"
- "Let's say that you gained some good wisdom from your experiences in counseling and on probation. What would you share with him that you learned and have put into practice in your lives?"
- "Let's say we have returned back to the grocery store 1 year from now, and we were continuing to have our great conversation with the probation officer. What will you [Mary's parents] be sharing with the two of us that you are currently doing that is helping Mary stay on track and making your relationship better with her?"
- "How about you, Mary. What specifically will you be telling us that you are doing that is helping you stay on track and get along better with your parents?"
- "If your old peers that you used to run around with were to walk into the grocery store right now and I asked them how you have changed, what would be two or three things that they would tell me that changed about you that would make them not want to hang out with you anymore?"
- "Now that you have made so many important gains with taking responsibility and getting along better with your parents, how are you viewing yourself differently now as compared to the former you who used to be on probation?"
- "What new ideas have you gotten about yourselves as parents now that you have helped pave the way for Mary to turn things around?"

COLLABORATING WITH PROBATION OFFICERS AND JUDGES

When collaborating with probation officers and judges, we need to respectfully listen to their stories of involvement, honor their concerns and expectations of us, and convey a strong desire to work together to help our mutual clients not reoffend and function better in other areas of their lives. As therapists, we need to use our curiosity to elicit from the probation officers involved their *commitments* (Kegan & Lahey, 2001) or positions on why they think the clients got into trouble to begin with and what specifically they need to change to successfully end probation. Although we may disagree with the probation officers' problem explanations and lofty goals for our clients, we need to suspend judgment and honor their opinions. We can, however, in the short run attempt to negotiate with the probation officers smaller indicators or signs of progress that we can help our clients try and achieve that could get us on the pathways toward achieving those lofty goals. The following questions are useful when goal setting with probation officers:

- "What do you think I need to address first with Willie and his parents that can help put him on the road to change?"
- "How do you think that change will make a difference for Willie?"
- "What will you need to see Willie do that would convince you he would not have to go to counseling anymore?"
- "What will be some small signs of progress that will tell you that Willie is really trying to turn his situation around?"
- "Let's say we all got together with Willie and his family in 2 weeks' time. What small change would you be the most pleased to hear about?"
- "How will Willie's parents show you that they are doing a better job of managing him?"
- "Is there anything else that you think I need to address with the parents that can further help Willie improve?"
- "In the past when you have worked with other young men like Willie, what advice have you given the therapists involved that seemed to help them do a good job with your clients?"
- "What do you think I should avoid trying to do with Willie and his parents that will definitely not work?"
- "When you worked with other therapists in the past, what did you appreciate the most about the way they collaborated with you?"
- "How do you think that made a difference in your work together and with the future outcomes of your clients?"

Questions like these can help us negotiate small, realistic treatment goals with the probation officer and establish successful collaborative relationships with them. Like our clients, we want to harness the probation officers' strengths, talents, and wealth of professional experience and wisdom to help us do effective clinical work. When probation officers feel that their professional expertise and opinions are respected and valued by the therapists involved, a cooperative working relationship will quickly develop.

Another important way therapists can establish solid collaborative relationships with probation officers and judges is to try to schedule monthly lunch dates or meetings. In these meetings, we can discuss how well we are working together and what improvements need to be made with our communications and service delivery. It is most advantageous to have an open-door policy, enabling the probation officer to participate as often as he or she desires in family counseling sessions. In fact, as frequently as I can, I like to have probation officers and any other involved helping professionals attend my initial family counseling sessions so that from the start the family is clear on what the helpers are expecting them to accomplish in treatment.

With judges, the more familiar they become with our treatment approaches and values as therapists, the more receptive they will tend to be to our case input. Although this can be accomplished with each judge individually, it is more practical to arrange an hour-long presentation on your treatment approach for a group of judges at your local juvenile court. It also is advantageous to welcome judges' concerns about our therapeutic approaches and elicit from them any adjustments they think we should make to be more effective with juvenile offenders and their families. In addition, some judges may be receptive to the idea of having you sit in juvenile court and have your first family contacts with your soon-to-be-referred new clients right after their first encounters with them. This kind of arrangement can make the engagement process go much more smoothly with even the toughest of mandated families.

SUMMARY

In this chapter, I have presented several practical guidelines and therapeutic strategies for successfully engaging challenging no-problem problem mandated families. Since many of these families have had past negative treatment experiences or antagonistic relationships with involved helpers from larger systems, it is critical that we provide them with ample floor time to share their problem stories and elicit their theories of change and treatment expectations to help foster cooperative relationships with them. For those families that are new to counseling or the adolescents are first-time offenders, therapists need to be careful not to fall into the role of social control agents, but instead, capitalize on their strengths and co-create with them compelling future realities of success. Finally, it is important that therapists take the time to cultivate solid working relationships with child protective workers, probation officers, and judges in their communities who can offer the necessary support and leverage needed with tougher no-problem problem mandated families.

Eight

Co-Creating a Climate Ripe for Transformative Dialogues with Helping Allies from Larger Systems

Appreciation is a wonderful thing: It makes what is excellent in others belong to us as well.

—VOLTAIRE

Long before second-order cybernetics (von Foerster, 1981; von Glasersfeld, 1984; Keeney & Ross, 1983; Maruyama, 1974) thinking became the new epistemological framework for family theorists, Auerswald (1968, 1972) had stressed the importance of therapists' adopting an ecological perspective, that is, focusing on the interactions among clients, their families, helpers from larger systems, and the community. Auerswald's (1968, 1972) pioneering theoretical ideas provided the groundwork for later prominent family theorists to expand on his ecological perspective. The Milan associates (Boscolo, Cecchin, Hoffman, & Penn, 1987) developed the idea of the "significant system," that is, they believe it is necessary for the therapist to intervene with all those individuals involved in trying to solve the client's problem, as well as to consider the impact of the therapist's own thinking and interventions on the other members of the "significant system." Coppersmith (1985) refers to the significant system as being a "meaningful system." Goolishian and his colleagues have described the significant system as being a "problem-organizing, problem-dissolving system" (Anderson & Goolishian, 1988b). Bogdan (1984) contends that problems are an "ecology of ideas."

The Milan associates were heavily influenced by theoretical ideas from the field of cognitive biology (Maturana & Varela, 1988) and from radical constructivist theorists (von Foerster, 1981; von Glasersfeld, 1984), particularly the latter group's notion of "observing systems" rather than "observed systems" (Boscolo et al., 1987). For the Milan associates, the therapist needs to include him- or herself as part of the observation of the client system being treated. When other helpers are involved with a therapist's case, these helping professionals are considered part of the problem system and community of observers that have coalesced around an identified problem. The client system is no longer being viewed as a separate observed entity requiring major repair work by a privileged therapist who knows what is "best" for the client.

Independent of the Milan associates, family therapy teams worldwide have developed their own unique systemic approaches for working with the family–multiple helper problem system. At the Houston–Galveston Family Institute, Goolishian and his colleagues (Anderson, 1997; Anderson & Goolishian, 1988b, 1991a, 1991b; Anderson, Goolishian, Pulliam, & Winderman, 1986; Goolishian & Anderson, 1981) have developed a highly respected therapeutic approach for working with chronic and difficult family cases in which multiple helpers are involved. In Europe, the Milan associates and the innovative work of Goolishian and Anderson have been highly influential on treatment teams in Ireland, Norway, and Germany. The Dublin group has applied these theorists' ideas to the challenging therapeutic context of working with incest victims, their families, and the network of helpers involved with these cases (McCarthy & Byrne, 1988; Kearney, Byrne, & McCarthy, 1989). Andersen and his colleagues in Tromso, Norway, have developed an innovative reflecting team consultation approach for treating difficult and stuck cases in which multiple helping professionals were involved (Andersen, 1987, 1991). Deissler (1989, 1992), in Marburg, Germany, has done some pioneering work with psychiatric clients, their families, inpatient treatment teams, and the larger mental health delivery system. More recently, Seikkula and his colleagues in Finland have developed what they call an *open dialogue* consultation approach with psychotic older adolescents and adults, their families, and involved helpers, which is backed by strong empirical evidence that their model can prevent psychiatric admissions and sustain clients in their homes (Seikkula & Olson, 2003; Seikkula, Alakare, & Aaltonen, 2000).

In this chapter, I present an ecological approach for working with the family–multiple helper problem system, offer practical suggestions on how to cultivate cooperative and collaborative relationships with helpers from larger systems, discuss the role of the therapist, present some useful collaborative questions to employ in family–multiple helper meetings, and provide six case examples.

The difficult adolescent client often has had frequent encounters with representatives from the juvenile justice system and local police departments, with school personnel, mental health and drug rehabilitation programs in the community, and some involvement with child protective workers. In any one community, a therapist will typically find that the communications are poor among these larger systems, the coordination of services is disjointed, and disagreement is a common phenomenon that occurs between the larger systems' representatives and the family. The family and the concerned helpers can become polarized around problem explanations, theories of change, and what the *best* form of treatment should be. This can lead to what I call *family–helping systems knots* occurring (Selekman, 2002). Because of such difficulties, I have found it useful to go out into the community and proactively develop close working relationships with helpers from larger systems and attempt to create bridges between my clinic and the representatives from the various helping systems. I have also found it useful in my clinical work to collaborate regularly with clergy, community leaders, and adolescent clients' peers and inspirational others.

Over the years, I have worked with a number of adolescents that have been involved with the police and the juvenile justice system. Besides making the time to go out and visit local police departments to familiarize myself with the youth officers and meet police social workers, I have found it useful to schedule occasional lunch dates with these key individuals. I try to schedule monthly lunch dates and office meetings with probation officers as well. I like to use these lunch meetings to build rapport and to find out ways we can cooperate better on cases. I am very interested in learning from helpers what I need to do differently as a therapist and cocollaborator and what I should continue to do with them in our mutual cases together. With some court-involved adolescent cases, my good rapport with judges helped make a difference in treatment outcomes. It is essential for therapists to find out from judges their views regarding treatment for youth and their expectations of therapists.

When interfacing with school personnel, I have found it useful to conduct meetings over lunch to address communication problems and generate new ways to cooperate better. Not only is it important to develop good working relationships with the administrative staff and school social workers, but it is helpful to secure the guidance department and teaching staff's input with cases and treatment expectations as well. Regularly making oneself available to manage school crises and offering to run groups or co-lead them with school social workers are two other effective ways we can cultivate solid working relationships with schools.

With representatives from psychiatric and drug rehabilitation programs, I like to become familiar with their treatment philosophies and program components, as well as secure information from the treatment teams about what their follow-up aftercare expectations are with cases being referred to me. Many of the agencies and hospital-based programs that have referred cases to me have welcomed family transition sessions prior to the youth's discharge from the program. If aftercare groups and other services are being provided to my clients, I extend invitations to involved program therapists to participate in our family therapy sessions or family–multiple helper meetings.

Once I have conducted a macrosystemic assessment with the adolescent and the family to determine the individuals that constitute the problem system, I have the family sign consent forms so I can freely converse and collaborate with these key individuals during our family–multiple helper meetings and when providing advocacy for clients in the community. Organizing family–multiple helper meetings is tedious work, particularly trying to coordinate everyone's schedules for joint meetings. Whenever possible, I try to engage as many as possible of the key members of the problem system that the family wanted to be present in our meetings together. Sometimes, however, this proves to be a futile task with some helpers because of their oppressive caseloads or schedules. In these situations, I will have my clients prepare a one-page summary of the highlights of the family–multiple helper meeting and mail copies to the absent helpers. I also set aside some time in my schedule to try to arrange separate meetings at the absent helpers' various offices. With involved and busy psychiatrists or other doctors, I have had success using the conference calling system in the office where the family–multiple helper meeting is being conducted so they can actively participate in our meetings without being physically present. Unless this outreach work is done by the therapist, the absent helpers may become stuck viewing the client's problem situation in one particular way and engaging in the same unproductive attempted solutions, which can contribute to the maintenance of the problem. We need to maximize the opportunities for the concerned helpers involved with our adolescent clients to notice changes and hear their original problem situations be communicated about differently (Anderson et al., 1986) by significant others in the adolescents' social ecologies.

THE ROLE OF THE THERAPIST

The first and foremost responsibility of the therapist in the context of the family–multiple helper meeting is to co-create a safe conversational space that makes room for both multiple problem views and concerns and the co-construction of new ideas. This process can only evolve through the therapist's use of *multipartiality* (Anderson, 1997; Anderson & Goolishian, 1988b)—that is, the therapist sides simultaneously with the family members' and helpers' varied views of the problem situation. He or she accomplishes this through being nonjudgmental, conversing in the client's and helpers' language, and offering his or her therapeutic opinions as tentative ideas rather than as the ultimate truth. The therapist is a respectful listener, a co-collaborator, and is prepared at any point in the therapeutic conversation to change his or her opinions or ideas.

Hargrove (1999) suggests that one effective way to co-create possibilities for action with a group is to employ "crazy wisdom," or a more intuitive approach, asking the question "What would be some 'crazy things' we could do with this situation?" Questions like this can tap collaborative meeting participants' creative and intuitive minds to focus upward and laterally toward free space, departing from existing views and creating new possibilities.

Another useful therapeutic tool to use in collaborative meetings is *suspension* (Selekman, 2002; Isaacs, 1999; Bohm, 1985). Inevitably, in the context of family–multiple helper collaborative meetings, we will encounter helpers who are extremely pessimistic or clinging to highly pathological explanations about the parents' or the adolescent's behaviors, which provokes in us a strong negative emotional reaction. Our reactions to these helpers may compel us to want to defend or protect our clients from them. To share our emotional reactions or concerns with these helpers might not only put them on the defensive and silence their voices but also could lead them to not wanting to attend future collaborative meetings. With suspension, the therapist pretends as though he or she has an empty cartoon-like cloud overhead that is filled up with the angry and frustrated feelings he or she may have toward these helpers. By doing so, the therapist has the opportunity to pause, carefully examine thoughts and feelings, reflect on where these ideas come from, and invite others in the meeting to share their thoughts about what these helpers have just said.

Two other tools closely related to suspension that we can employ to critically examine our thinking in the collaborative process are *the ladder of inference* and *the left-hand column exercise*. With the help of the ladder of inference (Hargrove, 1999), we can trace from the bottom rungs of the ladder the data we select, the meanings we add, the assumptions we make, and conclusions we draw from this information. This, in turn, leads to our adopting certain beliefs that govern our actions (see Figure 8.1).

The left-hand column exercise (Hargrove, 1999; Argyris, 1986) can help us become more aware of how our thinking and defensive routine maneuvers help us to avoid conflict and prevent transformative learning from occurring in our collaborative relationships. There are four steps to the left-hand column exercise:

1. Describe in one short paragraph a major difficulty you are experiencing with a particular involved helping professional from a larger system.

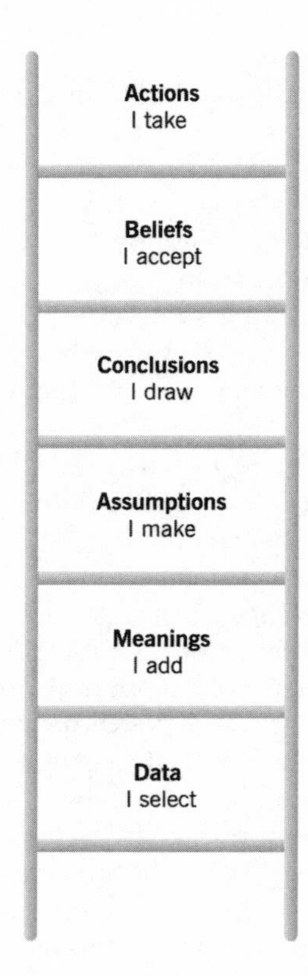

FIGURE 8.1. The ladder of inference.

2. In addressing this difficulty, describe in this same paragraph a strategy you would employ with this helper either individually or in the next family–multiple helper collaborative meeting.
3. On a separate sheet of paper, divide the page into two columns. In the right-hand column, write how you would begin the conversation: what you would actually say to the helper. Then write down what you believe the helper would say. Next, write your response to his or her response. Continue this process for two pages.
4. In the left-hand column, write down any thoughts or feelings that would be triggered in response to what the helper is saying but that you would not communicate to him or her for whatever reason.

In Figure 8.2 I present an example of how I employed the left-hand column tool (particularly in steps 3 and 4) to help me get unstuck in my collaborative relationship with a highly anxious and pessimistic school social worker and other involved school personnel. The client was a 15-year-old self-harming adolescent named Carrie, who despite going 6 weeks straight without cutting herself, was still a major concern of the school social

My Thoughts and Feelings	Actual Conversation
	Therapist: When I spoke to you earlier in the week, you seemed very concerned about Carrie starting to cut herself again. Is there something you think I am missing with her situation that I need to address with her in my next family session?
It seems as though every time I speak with William, he is anxious and pessimistic about Carrie's ability to change. I wonder if he realizes that his anxiety and pessimism could possibly set in motion a negative self-fulfilling prophecy in his interactions with Carrie. However, I should be supportive and address his concerns.	**William:** I think Carrie is going to start cutting herself again. Lately, she appears more anxious and brittle. This is why we decided to have her check-in with me and shadow her from class to class daily.
	Therapist: Is the "shadowing" idea designed to prevent her from cutting herself or to provide added support for her?
This "shadowing" idea is really overkill. It may be increasing Carrie's stress level and set the stage for another cutting episode. They probably have to do this because of school liability issues. I better not rock the boat by challenging them on how these prevention strategies can potentially backfire.	**William:** Having Carrie check in with me every morning was simply not enough. We thought combining the check-ins with the shadowing would be the best way to prevent her from cutting herself again
	Therapist: I have been teaching Carrie a lot of coping tools to help prevent her from caving into the impulse to cut herself again. As far as I know, we have gone 6 weeks without a cutting episode!
I feel as though William and other concerned school staff do not think I am doing a "good enough" job with Carrie. I am feeling really stuck. Maybe I need to stop making so many assumptions about William and the school staff and ask more questions, such as: • How can I be more helpful to them? • How can we work together more effectively? • Would it be helpful for me to collaborate with Carrie's teachers?	**William:** That sounds good, but we are not seeing her use those "coping tools" here. Occasionally, she has shared with me and others her thoughts about wanting to hurt herself. She also is failing a few of her classes.

FIGURE 8.2. The left-hand column exercise.

workers, some of her teachers, and her dean. Besides being quite anxious and very pessimistic about Carrie's ability to maintain self-control, they decided to implement two risk management strategies with her. One was for her to check in with the school social worker daily to assess how she was functioning and whether or not she had any issues to talk about. The second strategy was for all the concerned school personnel to take turns "shadowing" her from class to class. With the help of the left-hand column tool, I was able to critically examine my thinking and how it was blocking me from truly listening to and respecting the social worker's and other school staff's concerns.

We also need to honor and be sensitive to involved helpers' *commitments* or meaningful stories behind their concerns (Kegan & Lahey, 2001). There are good reasons why involved helpers cling to certain problem explanations or attempted solutions in their interactions with our clients. Unless we respectfully give these helpers plenty of space to share their stories of concern, they will continue to cling to certain problem explanations and actions that may be inadvertently exacerbating the adolescent and her family's difficulties. Once these meaningful stories are shared and reflected on by other meeting participants, the concerned helpers' fixed beliefs may loosen, they will feel embraced and respected, and new possibilities for action can be generated.

Finally, the therapist asks questions from a position of "not knowing" (Anderson, 1997; Anderson & Goolishian, 1988a, 1991b). Buddhist students were taught by their ancient masters the value of "Don't know mind," which describes a mind forever fresh, open, and fertile with possibilities (Mitchell, 1988). Lao-tzu taught his students the following piece of wisdom: "Wise men don't need to prove their point; men who need to prove their point aren't wise. The Master doesn't seek fulfillment. Not seeking, not expecting, she is present and can welcome all things" (in Mitchell, 1988, p. 15). If we expect that family members and involved helpers will be receptive to our ideas and propositions for action, we have to be equally willing to look critically at the limitations of our own views and be open to adopting co-collaborators' perspectives and suggested pathways for action. When hosting family–multiple helper collaborative meetings, therapists can ask themselves the following questions to maintain an open mind for all possibilities:

- "Do I share with the participants of the meeting how I arrived at my understanding of this problem situation?"
- "Have I encouraged others to reflect on my ideas?"
- "Do I listen to really hear?"
- "Do I seek to truly understand other participants' views?"
- "Do I explore, listen, and offer my views in an open way?"

I present a variety of collaborative questions below that therapists can use as tools for helping facilitate transformative dialogues in their family–multiple helper meetings.

COLLABORATIVE QUESTIONS

The way we ask questions in our family–multiple helper collaborative meetings can either pave the way for *transformative dialogues* or promote a constrictive atmosphere where family members and involved helpers are fearful of taking risks with one another and sharing the *not yet said* or significant *undiscussables*, such as family secrets and upset feelings or personal views family members and helpers may have toward one another (Selekman, 2002; Kegan & Lahey, 2001; Gergen & McNamee, 2000; Bohm, 1985; Anderson, 1997; Anderson & Goolishian, 1988b). The use of the miracle question (de Shazer, 1988) and externalization of the problem (White & Epston, 1990) also can be useful in family–multiple helper meetings to help establish ideal treatment outcome goals and for co-creating possibilities with complex and difficult adolescent cases. On a cautionary note, when using these two powerful categories of questions, they need to be presented in a tentative way so that they are not perceived by more skeptical or pessimistic family members and helpers as though you are parading a *more privileged or correct way* of viewing the problem situation. If this should happen, the more skeptical or pessimistic participants may think you are not taking the problem situation seriously enough, you are not open to hearing their concerns and problem views, and that perception may possibly disrupt the conversational flow. Questions that promote transformative dialogues tend to be open-ended, capture meeting participants' interest and curiosity, and help generate new meanings and possibilities for action. Although this is not an exhaustive list of collaborative questions, the questions below have been particularly useful in my meetings with concerned helping allies from larger systems.

- "What is it that you want to learn more about and hope to achieve in these meetings?"
- "What strengths will we come to know about your family in our work together?"
- "What are your best hopes that will grow out of our work together?"
- "Sometimes ideas just pop into my head. I was thinking: what if somehow a miracle happened, and all of the concerns and problems we have been talking about were resolved. How would things be different with this situation?"

- "While I was closely listening to what you were saying about how difficult your situation seems, a strange idea entered my mind. I wondered if all of us are being pushed around by this attention-deficit disorder thing that seems to have taken on a life of its own, especially the various ways we all have been frenetically scrambling to come up with the *best* solutions to try and control it at school, at home, and in the community. Have any of you had that thought or felt like that at times?"
- "What's missing with this situation that, if provided, will make a difference?"
- "What led you to that way of seeing things?"
- "You may be right, but I'd like to understand more. What leads you to believe . . . ?"
- "When you said that, what did you mean?"
- "Is there something that needs to be talked about that we have not touched on yet?"
- "What are the issues we have not addressed with one another?"
- "What do you think has kept that issue from not being talked about?"
- "Are there any specific chapters of your family's story that you think we should know about that can help us gain a better understanding of your situation or concerns?"
- "What are we doing or not doing that may be contributing to this situation's getting worse?"
- "What have you appreciated the most about your involvement with . . . ?"
- "How can we apply all of our strengths and resources to make the biggest difference with this situation?"

When participants in the family–multiple helper meetings respond to these questions, new meanings can be sparked, untold chapters of the family's story can be revealed, and new possibilities for action can be generated, any of which can serve as the catalyst for change.

Harlene Anderson, co-developer of the collaborative language systems therapy approach with Harry Goolishian (Anderson, 1997), had the following to say about the importance of adopting the respectful therapeutic position of "not knowing":

> Not-knowing freed us from having to be experts on how clients ought to live their lives, the right question to ask, and the best narrative. We did not have to be content-knowing experts. This freedom to not know, in turn, led to an expanded capacity for imagination and creativity. (p. 64)

Change occurs in the family–multiple helper therapeutic context when the following happens: new narrative meanings about the client's problem situation are generated, and the participants are communicating about the original problem situation differently. Over time, the originally co-constructed idea that there was a "problem" is dissolved in the collaborative process. With the dissolution of the problem comes the dismantling of the problem system (Anderson, 1997; Anderson & Goolishian, 1988b, 1991a).

CASE EXAMPLES

Suicidal—or Déjà Vu?

Laura, a white 16-year-old high school junior, was referred to me by her school social worker for what was described as a "severe depression." The school social worker shared with me in our initial telephone conversation that Laura had been "looking very depressed" for the "past month." Her academic performance had "dramatically declined" due to her "failure to complete homework assignments." Laura's English teacher was also quite "worried about" the former's "depressed state." The English teacher had reported to the school social worker that she had observed Laura "sitting in the far corner of the room with her head down" on several occasions. The assistant dean of the high school had also been made aware of Laura's "depressed condition" by the school social worker and agreed that she was a "high-risk" student requiring "immediate therapeutic intervention." Over the past month, Laura had had two counseling sessions per week with the school social worker.

In my first interview with Laura and her mother, I explored with them their understanding about how they had gotten referred to me for family therapy. The mother shared with me that the school social worker was "overreacting" and "too intrusive" with Laura. She further added that Laura was "having a hard time adjusting" to her recent "relationship break up with John." They had been "going steady" for 2 years. Laura agreed with her mother's interpretation of her situation and voiced her upset feelings about being "shadowed" by the school social worker. Laura openly admitted that she was "very bummed out" about John's breaking up with her, but that she would not take her life because of it. According to Laura, the school social worker had asked her in every one of their counseling sessions together if she had "suicidal thoughts." The mother reported that she had called the assistant dean numerous times to complain about the school social worker's "overinvolvement" with her daughter and had "requested that she not see her any more for counseling."

In this initial session, besides exploring what Laura and her mother were doing to better cope with her "relationship breakup," I conducted a macrosystemic assessment with the family to determine with them who the key members of the problem system were. We mutually agreed that the problem system consisted of myself, the school social worker, the English teacher, the assistant dean, Laura, and her mother. We also decided that it would be most advantageous to combine individual family therapy sessions with joint family–school meetings. To close out our first family session, I had Laura and her mother sign written release of information forms that would allow me to discuss their case situation with the school members of the problem system.

Present at the first family–school meeting at the high school were the school social worker, the English teacher, the assistant dean, Laura, her mother, and myself. Because the school social worker had referred Laura's case to me, I began the meeting by inviting her to share her story of involvement with Laura and the events that had led to her referral. I also asked her: if she could rewrite her original story about Laura, what would a good outcome be? For the school social worker, a good outcome for Laura's story would be "a young lady not depressed and back on track with her academics." I asked similar questions of each of the meeting participants and asked them if they wished to reflect on one another's comments. Laura's mother shared her concerns that the school had "greatly overreacted" to her daughter's situation and that Laura was "not suicidal!" The mother's ideal outcome story for Laura was that Laura would be "completely over the loss of John" and that the school would be "off Laura's back." Laura shared with the group that she was already "taking steps" to get over breaking up with John and was "catching up" with her school assignments. Her ideal outcome story was that she would begin to date again and she would no longer be "shadowed" by the school social worker.

At this point in the meeting, I explored with the school social worker the story behind her commitment (Kegan & Lahey, 2001) to trying to help Laura be less depressed. She began to cry and self-disclose her painful untold personal story about how her "16-year-old daughter had committed suicide." This was the first time the assistant dean, the English teacher, Laura, her mother, and I had ever heard this. Through the use of curiosity and exploring the story behind the school social worker's commitment, we learned what was compelling her to try to save Laura and not lose another adolescent to suicide. Once the school social worker began to disclose her painful story, I noticed a dramatic shift in both Laura and her mother's defensive position toward the school personnel, particularly the school social worker. Spontaneously, Laura and her mother offered their deepest sympathies to the school social worker. The assistant dean and the English teacher were also highly supportive. By the end of the meeting, we all mutually agreed that I would continue family therapy sessions to further help Laura get over the loss of her boyfriend, John, the school social worker would discontinue her counseling sessions with Laura, and that we would have another family–school meeting 1 month later to assess further case progress.

During the month-long interval, I conducted two more family therapy sessions to further amplify Laura's effective coping strategies in putting the loss of John behind her. By the second family therapy session, Laura had not only "caught up" with her "school work," but she had also met a "cute guy" on the football team. In our second family–school meeting, everyone—from the school social worker to the mother—reported observing considerable changes in Laura's behavior. We decided as a group that we would discontinue the family–school meetings because of Laura's progress and that I would offer the family one more check-up session 3 months later.

Breaking Free from the Gang Lifestyle

Anna and her son, Pedro, a 14-year-old Latino, had been referred for family therapy by his probation officer for car radio theft, assault and battery charges, chronic curfew violation, and gang involvement. Anna was born in Mexico, and since she had moved to the United States she had experienced both emotional and financial hardship. Her ex-husband, Ramón, was an alcoholic, was physically abusive, and had had many affairs while they were married. As much as she wanted to go to college to pursue a professional career, Anna had to surrender this dream because of her child-care responsibilities and stressful waitressing job. Anna had four children from her relationship with Ramón; Pedro being the oldest sibling, José the middle child, and Jorge the youngest son; Isabella, 5 years of age, was the only daughter in the family. Anna's only support system in the community was her priest and two Latino girlfriends.

Pedro boycotted my first family therapy session. Anna reported in the initial family session that she was most concerned about Pedro's gang involvement and his coming in after midnight on the weekends and some weekday nights. I explored with Anna her attempted solutions in trying to resolve Pedro's problematic behaviors and elicited from her the key members of the problem system. Anna reeled off a long list of family friends and helping professionals. The family–multiple helper problem system consisted of the following individuals: myself, a local police officer, the probation officer, the school social worker, two of Anna's girlfriends, the priest, a child protective worker, the school principal, and the leader of the community crisis team. I invited Anna to tell me if she thought it would be helpful to bring some of these important people together to assist us in resolving Pedro's difficulties. Anna thought that joint meetings with all of these key individuals would be a great way of working together. I had her sign release of information forms and pointed out that we would need Pedro's signature and cooperation with this method of working, as well. Anna made it clear to me that she would make sure that Pedro came to our next family session.

One week later, Pedro came to our session but maintained a defensive posture throughout most of the interview. When I met with Pedro alone, he became less defensive and liked the idea that the family–multiple helper meetings would ultimately "help get some of these adults off of his back" once they noticed the progress he would "be making while we are working together." We also talked about how the local police department had him "pegged as a gang banger" and how "they will be closely monitoring every move" he makes "on the streets." After our brief conversation, Pedro readily signed several release of information forms. Finally, I asked Pedro if there were any other key individuals he would like to include in our family–multiple helper meetings. Pedro was in agreement with his mother's list of the individuals who should be included in meetings.

After 2 weeks of playing telephone tag with the key members of the problem system, I finally was able to schedule our first family–multiple helper meeting. The following individuals came to the meeting: the school social worker, the probation officer, the child protective worker, a concerned local police officer, the priest, the team leader of the community crisis team, Anna, and Pedro. Just prior to this meeting, Pedro's father died of a heart attack, and Pedro was suspended from school after getting caught with a bottle of Jack Daniel's whiskey in the boys' restroom. The whiskey incident occurred soon after Pedro found out about his father's death.

I began the meeting by briefly connecting with each provider. Because the probation officer had referred Pedro to me, I started the meeting by having him tell the story of how he decided to refer the case to my clinic. Besides sharing with the group all of the reasons why Pedro had been placed on probation, he also pointed out that he thought "Anna could greatly benefit from learning some parenting skills." His outcome goal for Pedro was for the latter to stay out of further legal difficulties by steering clear of the Latin Kings street gang. At this point in the meeting, the school social worker brought up Pedro's whiskey-related school suspension and said she was "concerned about how poorly" he was "coping with the loss of his father."

Suddenly, Anna took the floor and shared her story about her past relationship with Ramón (Pedro's father) and why they had divorced. All members of the family–multiple helper meeting, including Pedro, had their eyes fixed on Anna and were listening intently to her story. Anna shared with the group that Ramón was "very loving with Pedro" when he was a toddler but that Ramón began to "distance himself from the family" when he started "abusing alcohol and marijuana." Pedro and the rest of the group got a chuckle out of hearing about the time that Ramón gave Pedro a sip of his beer and Pedro immediately rushed into the bathroom to spit it out. Pedro asked his mother, "Did I really do that?" Following this amusing chapter in Anna's story about Ramón, Pedro heard for the first time all of the reasons why his mother had divorced his father. This included Ramón's physical and emotional abuse of Anna, as well as the multiple extramarital affairs he had had before Pedro reached his adolescence. After hearing this painful material, Pedro began to shed a few tears and put his arm around his mother for support. This was the first time I had observed Pedro showing affection toward his mother.

Prior to ending this highly productive meeting, the probation officer shared with Pedro that he would not bring him before the judge for the possession-of-alcohol incident. Pedro gave a big sigh of relief and smiled. I brought to the group's attention that Pedro had resolved his curfew violation problem and had not gotten in any further legal difficulties. We all gave Pedro a big round of applause for the behavioral progress he had been making. Another change in Pedro's behavior was that he had stopped beating up on his 13-year-old brother, José. The last time Pedro had beaten up his brother, the child protective services were called in to intervene. The family priest shared with Pedro that he would explore with his colleagues if there was some work that he could do around the church. We all agreed to meet as a group in 4 weeks.

Subsequent family–multiple helper meetings served to further empower Anna and Pedro. The priest found some odd jobs for Pedro to do around the church to help keep him off the streets. Anna had saved up some of her money, and I helped her secure some scholarship funds from a local community college to take a few classes. Pedro continued to make progress in all areas of his life and successfully terminated his probation. He also discontinued his involvement with the street gang. A total of six family–multiple helper meetings, one every 4 weeks, were held over a 6-month period.

"With a Little Help from My Friends"

Adolescent clients' peers can be an invaluable resource for brief therapists to utilize when co-constructing solutions with families and when stuck in family therapy (Selekman, 1991a, 1995, 2002, 2004). With some of my stuck cases, I will utilize an adolescent client's peers as an expert consultation team to help offer us some fresh ideas. The following case illustrates the power and creative ingenuity of peer-generated solutions with stuck adolescent cases.

Liz, a white 16-year-old adolescent, was referred to me by her probation officer for possession of marijuana, substance abuse, chronic violation of parental rules, and school truancy. Liz had participated in Narcotics Anonymous (NA) meetings in the past and found them to be "boring and unhelpful" for relapse prevention. She also had been in a 28-day inpatient chemical dependency program. Two weeks after being discharged from this program, Liz returned to marijuana use.

After two sessions of brief therapy, the parents and I had collaboratively disrupted the problem-maintaining pattern of superresponsible parental behavior around Liz, which in the past had led to superirresponsible behavior on the part of Liz. For example, the more the parents rescued Liz from experiencing the consequences of her truancy from school by interceding with powerful school officials, the more she skipped detentions and school. Despite the parental changes, Liz was having great difficulty in maintaining marijuana abstinence. She would go for 3 days and then use marijuana 1 or 2 days of the week. In brainstorming with Liz what resources she had outside the family that we could utilize for relapse prevention, she mentioned "three close friends" who were reformed "drug addicts." Together, we decided that it might be useful to bring in her friends to the next session, pending her parents' approval, to see what creative ideas they might have for "staying straight."

Liz's parents also thought this was a great idea. Because Liz's parents knew the parents of two of the peers, her parents agreed to call them to get approval for their daughters' participation in the next therapy session. Liz decided on her own to meet with the third friend's parents to discuss the situation and have them get in contact with her own parents.

Because the probation officer and school social worker were very involved with Liz's case, the family and I thought it would be a good idea to include these key members of the problem system in our future sessions as well. In the first interview, I had secured signatures on release of information forms from the family in order to collaborate with these concerned helpers.

In the third session, both the probation officer and school social worker reported noticing some important changes in Liz's behavior. According to the probation officer, Liz was "putting forth more effort" and "showing more responsible behavior." The school social worker shared with us that Liz "clearly had a better attitude" and was "attending school regularly." Despite all of Liz's changes, the parents, the probation officer, and school social worker were all very concerned about her inability to "stay straight." Earlier in the session, I had introduced Liz's three friends—Sara, Linda, and Holly—to the parents and helpers. Both the probation officer and school social worker agreed that NA was not for everyone, and they were open to the idea of using Liz's peers for relapse prevention purposes. At this point in the interview, I had the peers share their ideas about how they could help Liz "stay straight." Sara began the discussion by sharing with us her story about how "keeping busy" during her leisure time was the key to how she "protected" her sobriety. Linda reported to the group that she found "aerobics" to be a great "natural high" activity. Linda got a laugh out of the group by sharing how she was "now addicted to aerobics!" Holly shared with the group that she now stays away from the "stoners at school" and also avoids "going to parties." I thanked the peers for their "helpful words of wisdom" and complimented them on what "caring friends" they were. After giving the peers compliments for their helpful consultation, we decided to give Liz and her friends 3 weeks to plan and outline a relapse prevention strategy that would be carefully tailored to Liz's lifestyle.

During the 3-week interval, Liz was doing aerobics classes twice a week, not allowing herself even one free minute during her leisure time to think about using marijuana, and she was avoiding the temptation to interact with any of her "partying" friends. At the next scheduled family–multiple helper meeting, the school social worker, probation officer, parents, and peers all reported marked changes in Liz's behavior. Liz was following her parents' rules, maintaining her drug abstinence, going to school regularly and keeping up with her homework, and was looking for a part-time job after school. Liz gave her friends a big hug in the session and acknowledged how instrumental they were in helping her change.

Because the probation officer and I had a close working relationship, he allowed me to determine the frequency of visits and the duration of therapy. As a group we all agreed that three future checkup sessions over the remainder of Liz's 9-month probation period would be useful to further consolidate family gains. By the last checkup session, Liz had secured a part-time job, improved her grades, and, best of all, she had remained drug-free with the help of her friends!

Living on the Edge

Nichole, a white 16-year-old acting-out adolescent, had been referred to me by her probation officer for shoplifting, substance abuse, school truancy, sexual promiscuity with older males, and chronically violating her mother's rules. Betty, Nichole's mother, had been divorced from her father for 5 years. Nichole had had very little contact with her father after the parental divorce. According to Betty, her ex-husband was a "cocaine addict." Nichole's 14-year-old brother, Bill, was a "jock" at school and had no behavioral difficulties.

I began my first family interview by exploring with Betty and Nichole their understanding of how and why they were referred to me. I also invited each family member to share her individual stories about the family drama. Betty was quick to point out that Nichole had a "bad attitude," "never follows" her "rules," was "not going to school," and was a "thief." According to Betty, Nichole had a long history of "stealing money" from her, and she was recently "arrested" at a department store for "trying to steal clothes." Nichole agreed with her mother that it was this most recent shoplifting incident that led to her being placed on probation for 1 year. Nichole further added that she hated the special therapeutic day school that she was "forced to attend," because they were "always on [her] case about everything."

Throughout the family interview, Nichole and Betty got into some heated arguments. Betty was angry at Nichole for "not coming home the other night" and for "not going to school." Nichole was angry at her mother for "always yelling" at her and not giving her a "weekly allowance." Betty also disclosed that she felt family counseling was a "waste of time" because it has "never helped in the past."

I asked the family to share with me what they liked and disliked about their three past counseling experiences. The family offered me some helpful advice about what I needed to do differently with them as a therapist.

At this point in the interview, I decided to spend some individual session time with Betty and Nichole. While meeting alone with Betty, I was able to provide support, hear more about the family story and her concerns, and elicit from her an initial treatment goal. Betty wanted Nichole to stop "ditching" school. During my individual session time with Nichole, I explored how I could be helpful to her with Betty and the school situation. Nichole disclosed that she would not steal from her mother if she got a "weekly allowance." She also reported not liking the probation officer's always "checking up" on her at the school and his making "surprise visits at the house." I offered to help get the probation officer off Nichole's back because of my good relationship with him. Nichole appeared to warm up to this helpful service I could provide for her. I also shared with her that I would be glad to go to bat for her with Betty to try to negotiate the privilege of earning a weekly allowance. I shared with Nichole that I could only pursue these activities if she were willing to attend school more regularly. Nichole took a risk and shared with me what some of the major stressors at school were for her. She reported several negative encounters she had had with the school principal, the social worker, her teacher Mrs. Smith, and some rival gang members who also attended the school. I provided support and asked Nichole if she thought it might be helpful for me to advocate for her at the school. Nichole thought it was "worth a try" to collaborate with the school staff.

To close out the first family interview, I provided compliments for both Betty and Nichole and conducted a macrosystemic assessment with them. The family felt it would be in their best interest for me to collaborate with the school principal, the social worker, Mrs. Smith, and the probation officer. I had Betty and Nichole sign consent forms so I could collaborate with these key members of the problem system.

Present at the first school meeting were the probation officer, the principal, the social worker, and Mrs. Smith. I began the meeting by inviting the school staff to share their stories about Nichole and her family. For the majority of the meeting time, each school representative had nothing but negative and pathology-laden stories to tell about Betty and Nichole. The principal called Nichole "unmotivated," a "sociopath," and in need of "psychiatric hospitalization." In fact, he had been making arrangements with the school's psychiatric consultant to try to have Nichole admitted at a local psychiatric hospital. According to the school social worker, Nichole's mother was "neglectful," "irresponsible," and had "failed to show up at several" of their "scheduled appointments." Mrs. Smith felt that Nichole had an "I don't care" attitude about school and herself. While I was listening to the school staff members' stories of hopelessness about this family, I began to wonder whether it would be possible to establish a collaborative relationship with them. The school staff seemed ready to throw in the towel with Nichole and her family. I used suspension (Isaacs, 1999; Bohm, 1985) as a way to avoid getting defensive with the pessimistic helpers and to carefully examine how my thoughts and feelings could get in the way of my deeply listening to their concerns and respecting their frustrations. Despite my discomfort with the school staff's stories about Nichole and her mother, I could empathize with their dilemma of having to work with students with long histories of behavioral difficulties and their families. Prior to the conclusion of our meeting together, I asked if the school staff had any helpful suggestions about how we could cooperate in the therapeutic change effort with Nichole and her mother. The school principal recommended that I have the mother "check her insurance to see if it would cover inpatient treatment for Nichole." The school social worker commented that she would be "willing to do family therapy sessions together," but that "they really don't want to change." At this point, the probation officer entered the conversation and stressed the importance of "team work" and giving Nichole "support at school." The school staff reluctantly agreed to have another meeting in 3 weeks.

While driving back to the office with the probation officer, he shared with me that in the past he had had great difficulty in establishing a collaborative working relationship with this school staff in some of his other cases. After hearing some of the probation officer's past case experiences, I no longer felt alone in my concerns about being able to enlist the school's support in the change effort. We both agreed that Nichole was "living on the edge" through her acting-out behavior and that she was clearly one of the school's toughest students to manage.

During the 3-week interval, Nichole had gone to school almost every day and was consistently following her mother's rules. In our third family session, Nichole's behavioral progress was officially rewarded by her mother with the presentation of her first $10 weekly allowance. Nichole was thrilled and voiced a strong desire to keep up her good work. Nichole was also shocked to hear that her probation officer had advocated strongly for her in the school meeting. Hearing this important information appeared to give Nichole a different view of her probation officer and greatly contributed to their having a better working relationship. Although the family experienced a few big arguments during this break period, they confidently reported getting quickly back on track again.

In my second school meeting, there was group consensus among the school staff members and the probation officer that Nichole was making good progress. However, the school principal was quick to point out that this was a "honeymoon period," which he had seen before with Nichole. Both the social worker and Mrs. Smith agreed with the principal that Nichole's changes had to be approached with "guarded optimism." I asked the school staff members if they were doing anything differently when interacting with Nichole that seemed to be helpful. Nobody reported having done anything differently when communicating with Nichole. Surprisingly, Mrs. Smith asked me if I had any suggestions of new strategies that she could try out with Nichole in the classroom. I recommended to her that she keep track of all of the various things she does with Nichole that seem to be helpful, and notice what Nichole does in the classroom that she would like to see Nichole continue. Mrs. Smith liked my suggestions and promised to have a progress report for me for the next scheduled meeting, in 3 weeks. It was also decided by the group that Nichole's mother be included in the next meeting.

One week prior to our next school meeting, Nichole's behavior took a turn for the worse. Nichole had stolen $50 from her mother, she "ditched" three days of school, and had been caught with a dime bag of marijuana in the school bathroom. She also failed to come home for two nights. According to Betty, she was out "whoring around" with some older teenagers. There were also rumors around the school that she had asked two of her gang-involved friends to slice the principal's car tires. The probation officer had phoned me to say that he had no alternative but to have Nichole placed in the juvenile detention center for 1 month.

In my fourth and fifth family sessions with Nichole and her mother, I did not see or hear any indications that she was heading for a major behavioral relapse. While Nichole was in the juvenile detention center, I visited her two times. On both occasions, Nichole appeared to be depressed and remorseful. I also discovered in our second visit together that Nichole's mother had agreed to allow her to drop out of school, provided that she would work.

After Nichole was released from the detention center, she was court-ordered to continue family therapy. Nichole was expected to look for a job actively, do chores around the house, and follow her mother's rules. For additional support, I put Nichole in contact with two former female adolescent clients who had also been on probation and had drastically changed their situations and become responsible young people. Not only did these two peers help Nichole secure a job at a fast-food restaurant, but they all became close friends.

In some of our future family sessions, I included the probation officer and the peers to reflect on Nichole's gains and for relapse prevention purposes. Our teamwork helped Nichole successfully terminate her probation and stay on track behaviorally.

Teacher Power

Todd, a white 14-year-old, was referred for family therapy because of his failing grades, poor "frustration tolerance level," "temper outbursts," "frequent confrontations with teachers," and "inability to respond to the teachers' limit setting." According to the school social worker, Todd had a long history of behavioral problems while in junior high. After receiving Todd's mother's verbal consent on the telephone to talk to the school social worker, I called the latter to gather more detailed information about the presenting problems and the school staff's attempted solutions. I recommended to the school social worker that it would be useful to set up a meeting with Todd's six teachers so that we could collaborate on the case. I also shared with him that I would need to get the parents' and Todd's written consent in order to collaborate with the school.

In my first family therapy session, I met with Todd, his younger brother, Steve, and his parents. According to the parents, Todd did not have major behavioral problems at home but would occasionally get "too physically rough" with Steve and also tested parental limits. We discussed the parents' and Todd's perspectives on the school difficulties. The parents were quick to share with me that Todd had an IQ of 130 and used to get A's and B's in all of his subjects before entering junior high. Over the past school year, however, Todd reportedly was receiving F's in his math, English, and social studies classes. The teachers in each of these classes had frequent phone contacts with Todd's mother regarding his temper outbursts, inability to respond to their limits, confrontations, and failing grades. Todd reported that his teachers were "mean" and quite "rigid" with him. He cited one example of his English teacher's rigid behavior in reaction to his turning in an assignment 1 day late and receiving an F on his paper. Both Todd and his parents gave me written consent to collaborate with the school social worker and the teachers.

At my first school consultation were Todd's six teachers, the school social worker, and the school principal. After I established rapport with each individual at the meeting, I asked the school social worker to share how he viewed Todd's situation and his decision to refer the case to me. I learned from the social worker that Todd "weekly" visited the "principal's office" for disciplinary reasons and that he frequently "blew off" his scheduled counseling appointments. Todd's English teacher was quite outspoken about what a "troublemaker" Todd was. She claimed he was a very "emotionally troubled young man." The math teacher reported that Todd was a "difficult student" and the "class clown." His social studies teacher saw similar behaviors in his class. At this point in the meeting, I explored with Todd's gym, art, and science teachers what their views of Todd's behavior were and how he was functioning in their classes.

Surprisingly, these three teachers viewed Todd as a "dynamic, bright, and hard-working young man." They reported how "cooperative" and "responsible" Todd was in their classrooms. I also discovered that Todd was receiving A's and B's in their classes. In the context of this discussion, the English teacher inquired of the more positive teachers what their "secret" was for "making Todd behave so well." The art teacher shared with the other teachers that it was important to be "laid back with Todd" and "avoid putting pressure on him." The science teacher agreed with this strategy and further stressed the need to "accentuate Todd's strengths." The gym teacher shared with the group that Todd has "great leadership abilities," and he found that by capitalizing on this strength he "earned Todd's cooperation."

While sitting in the meeting observing this productive cross-fertilization of ideas between the teachers, I was amazed by their creativity and problem-solving abilities. There was a strong sense of community among the six teachers, despite the fact that they had never sat together to brainstorm about how to best manage Todd in the classroom and to share their differing opinions about my client.

By the end of the first school meeting, the first group—the English, math, and social studies teachers—were eager to try out some of the new strategies they had learned from their colleagues. The art, science, and gym teachers (the second group) asked me if I had any suggestions for things they could do, as well. I reminded the second group that "if it works, don't fix it" and encouraged them to "do more of the same" with Todd. As an experiment, I offered the first group the following task to do between this consultation session and our next scheduled meeting: "Keep track of all of the things that Todd does that you want to continue to see in your classrooms. Also, keep track of what you do that works with Todd during those times." I asked the teachers to "write those things down and be prepared to discuss them in our next meeting." We also all agreed that Todd and his parents should attend our future meetings. The second school meeting was scheduled for 3 weeks later.

Two days after the school consultation, I met with Todd and his parents. Todd's mother reported that she had noticed that her son was "doing his homework." I shared with the parents and Todd what had been discussed in the school meeting. While meeting alone with Todd in the family session, I gave Todd the following task to do over the next 3 weeks: "Each day at school, I would like you to notice two things that your English, math, and social studies teachers do that you like, write those things down, and report those good things to your mother daily." Earlier in the session, I had shared with the parents my plans to give this task to Todd with the rationale that it could "help improve" their son's "relationships with his teachers." Todd's mother planned to buy a notebook to record her son's daily discoveries.

At the next school meeting, all six of Todd's teachers had nothing but praise for his great progress. The biggest surprise for the parents, myself, and the school social worker was hearing the English teacher's report about how well Todd was "performing" in her classroom. He was being "more respectful" toward her and "turning in his assignments on time." Todd shared with the English teacher that he had noticed that she was "nicer" to him. Both the math and social studies teachers also reported Todd's "considerable progress" academically and behaviorally. I spent the majority of this meeting amplifying the changes reported by the teachers and Todd. The parents thanked the teachers for being so "committed" to trying to help Todd out. Todd shared with the teachers and school social worker that he would continue to work on improving his grades and behavior. By the end of the meeting, it was decided that I would see the family two more times over the school year to monitor progress. No further difficulties were reported by the school or parents at each of our checkup sessions. Todd ended up finishing the school year with a B+ grade-point average.

Conquering a Stealing Habit

Mira, a 13-year-old East Indian Hindu girl, had been referred to me by her school social worker for her "chronic stealing and lying" behaviors and "academic decline with her grades," and for "what appeared to be clinical depression." According to Alice, the school social worker, Mira recently "got caught stealing valuables off the teacher's desk," and when asked to look through her hall locker "the school principal found stolen jewelry, calculators, and clothing items from other students." After this locker incident, Mira's hall locker was taken away from her, and an old doorless locker was brought into Miss Johnson's classroom so that she could monitor what went in and out of her new locker. This was the principal's attempted solution for the stealing problem. Although Mira found this situation to be very embarrassing, she had no choice or say in the matter. The principal also had considered having Mira evaluated by the district psychiatrist; however, he was willing to see if family therapy would work first. Surprisingly, neither the school nor the parents of students who had been robbed by Mira were going to press charges.

Mira had a popular twin sister at the school, Indira, who was an "A student," involved in athletics, and also a participant in the school drama club. Apparently, Mira used to be "a good student" prior to entering junior high school. The school social worker described the parents as being very strict and hard-working, particularly Mira's mother, Sunita. She was a nurse in a hospital unit with terminally ill patients. The father worked in a factory and spoke minimal English.

Prior to our first family-multiple helper meeting, I got permission from both Sunita and Mira to invite Alice, her student intern, Randi (who was providing some of the counseling with Mira), and her homeroom teacher, Miss Johnson, to our initial family meeting. Miss Johnson, out of all of Mira's teachers, was the most concerned about her and in many ways was like her inspirational other. Mira was delighted that I could get Miss Johnson to attend. Unfortunately, the school principal could not come because of an important administrative meeting he had to attend. The father also could not attend because of his work schedule.

When discussing Sunita's understanding of why Mira's stealing behavior was occurring and her best hopes that would come out of our work together, she blamed Mira for being "irresponsible" and "acting like a criminal." She had "no clue why" Mira would resort to such behavior. However, she was described as being "more emotionally sensitive" than her twin sister, Indira. Sunita also felt that Mira was being "an embarrassment to the family." Mira had a very sad look on her face and hung her head downward as her mother criticized her. At this point in the meeting, Alice, Miss Johnson, and Randi came to Mira's rescue by pointing out all of her strengths and the fact that she had not stolen anything for 2 weeks! I provided a little cheerleading and explored with the school staff as well as Mira how they were able to generate these pretreatment changes. However, despite the school staff's efforts to challenge Sunita's extreme pessimism and my successfully eliciting from them and Mira important details about what was promoting the changes, the mother continued to view Mira as the "main source of the stress in her life" and as requiring "a lot of help." Knowing that there had been some important self-generated pretreatment changes on Mira's part and that Alice, Randi, and Miss Johnson had contributed to these changes, I began to have a strong emotional reaction to Sunita's negativity and extreme pessimism. When this started to happen, I used *suspension* (Isaacs, 1999; Bohm, 1985) as a way to keep my thoughts and feelings in check and reflect on them in an imaginary cartoon cloud above my head. I began to think the following: how Sunita may be feeling about her inability to understand or change Mira's behavior, how within this particular culture Mira's actions and difficulties in school may be shaming the family, and the repercussions of Mira's difficulties on the marital relationship (that is, might the father blame or physically take it out on the mother for their daughter's problems?). Through the use of suspension, I was able to begin to view Sunita's parental dilemma in a new way and be more compassionate toward her. I used conversational questions (Anderson & Goolishian, 1988) to explore with her the impact of Mira's behavior problems on her and her husband and to see if she had any specific expectations of me or the school staff. By doing so, Sunita felt free to voice her concerns and expectations and appeared to feel more validated by all of us. I became increasingly more aware of how earlier in our meeting the mother might have felt unsupported by me and the school staff because of our optimism and enthusiasm about Mira's pretreatment changes.

I tried to bring out Mira's voice more in our meeting. However, she had a hard time opening up; she looked very depressed and spoke so softly that you could barely hear her words. At this point in the meeting, I took a risk and externalized the stealing behavior into the "stealing habit." I thought that, by offering the mother and the involved helpers an alternative way of looking at the problem situation, it might open up the door for possibilities. Sunita appeared to be intrigued by my new construction of the problem. I shared with the group how "stealing habits" take on a life all of their own, are very clever characters in the various sneaky ways they coach kids to take other people's possessions and lie about it, and really like to prey on "emotionally sensitive" kids like Mira. All of the school participants thought this new explanation made a lot of sense and were willing to work closely with Mira to conquer this stealing habit that was getting the best of her. Both Sunita and Mira smiled for the first time in our meeting. I proposed that we experiment with an *honesty test* (Epston, 1998) over the next week. This would entail teachers and family members leaving items out that would be visible to Mira and thereby test her ability to stand up to the stealing habit and not allow it to push her around. The whole group appeared to be quite enthusiastic about trying out the experiment at home and at school. We decided to meet again in 2 weeks.

I began the meeting by finding out what further progress Mira had made at standing up to the stealing habit and not allowing it to coach her to get into trouble. Alice, Randi, and Miss Johnson all reported that there was not even one stealing episode nor any instance of Mira's being caught in a lie over the break period. One sparkling moment reported by Miss Johnson was Mira's turning in a dollar in change that she had found on her classroom floor. I responded with "Wow!" "What did you tell yourself to not allow the stealing habit to convince you that you should have put that money into your pocket!?" Mira had a big smile plastered on her face and replied, "I wanted to do the right thing." Although Sunita was pleased with the progress at school, she still wanted to see "more effort" on Mira's part, specifically with "doing her chores." When asked about any indications of the stealing habit pushing Mira and other family members around, Sunita indicated that this had not been a problem. Across the board, the school team felt that Mira was "doing much better in her classes" and seemed "happier." The glow on her face indicated that Mira was feeling more "self-confident" and "happier." I asked Mira, "What percentage of the time are you now in charge of the stealing habit versus the stealing habit being in charge of you?" She reported being "90% in charge." The school team felt that she was at "90%" as well. I asked Mira where she would have rated the situation back when she first got into trouble, and she said that the stealing habit had been 80% in charge of her. I then asked the whole group what we would need to see happen to rate the situation 95–100%. Everyone, including Sunita, felt that if Mira continued to do more of what was working she would achieve this goal. Just to keep everyone on their toes, I warned the group about how the stealing habit may attempt to sabotage Mira's efforts to stay on track over our next break period. We decided to meet in 6 weeks.

At our final family–multiple helper collaborative meeting, both Mira and Sunita were sporting big smiles on their faces and in great spirits, and the school team was eager to report all of Mira's tremendous progress. First and foremost, Alice announced that Mira got her hall locker back! Not only did she get a "brand-new locker," but they "threw a locker warming party for Mira!" Alice, Miss Johnson, and the principal were all on hand to celebrate Mira's progress. Mira happily shared with all of us that the celebration party had really made her day! In addition, Mira's grades had gone up in all of her classes. On the home front, Sunita was delighted to report that Mira was "taking her homework more seriously," "doing her chores without reminders," and there were "no signs of theft." Having previously known about Mira's great progress at school, I ceremoniously handed her an achievement award certificate for conquering the stealing habit. By the end of our joyous session, we all agreed to discontinue our meetings.

SUMMARY

In each of the case examples described in this chapter, I attempted to co-create a safe and respectful conversational space with the families and involved helpers in which everyone's voice was heard and the generation of new narratives and creative solutions was made possible. Like a tribal healing community, the family–multiple helper meeting context can instill hope, combat feelings of isolation and impotence, and promote highly productive teamwork. As can be seen with all six case examples, through mobilizing and collaborating with the key resource people in the adolescents' social ecologies, therapeutic changes were not only co-produced rapidly but also were quite dramatic.

Nine

The Second and Subsequent Sessions

Guidelines for Consolidating Gains and Matching Therapeutic Experiments with Family Members' Learning Styles and Cooperative Response Patterns

> To keep our faces toward change, and behave like free spirits in the presence of fate, is strength undefeatable.
>
> —Helen Keller

In the second and subsequent sessions, our main job as therapists is to actively amplify and consolidate family changes and address concerns in such a way that these differences become more "newsworthy" to the family and continue to ripple on long after therapy is completed. When families return for their second sessions, there are four common positions they will present with that are based on the impact of the new ideas and therapeutic experiments they were offered in the first and subsequent sessions: on outcome, their situation is *better, mixed opinion, same,* or *worse.* In this chapter, I discuss therapeutic guidelines for experiment design and selection with each of these client positions, creative uses of consultation teams, and end of therapy rituals to celebrate therapeutic changes. Case examples are provided throughout the chapter.

BETTER FAMILIES

When families return for their second and subsequent sessions, I like to begin the sessions on a positive note by asking them: "So, what's better since I saw you last?" or "What further progress have you made?" If they report significant changes in their goal area or in other areas, I spend the majority of the session amplifying the exceptions and consolidating the family gains.

Through the use of cheerleading, solution-building questions, and highlighting differences with unique account and redescription questions (White, 1988b), I help make these important changes "newsworthy" to the family. When cheerleading, I give family members high-fives and handshakes, and respond to each exception with questions like:

- "Are you aware of how you did that?!"
- "What did you tell yourself to pull that off?!"
- "How did you come up with that clever idea?!"
- "Is that different for you to do that?!"

It is helpful to have family members make distinctions between their old patterns of behavior and their new patterns of interaction. I use consolidating and presuppositional questions (O'Hanlon & Weiner-Davis, 1989) to reinforce the new-exception patterns of behavior. Some useful consolidating questions to ask for reinforcing and amplifying family changes are:

- "At this point, what would you have to do to go backwards?"
- "What would you have to do to prevent a major backslide?"
- "What will you have to continue to do to get that [exception behavior] to happen more often?"
- "If we were to gaze into my imaginary crystal ball 3 months down the road, what further changes will we see happening in this family?"
- "Let's say over the next week the tension and stress levels are at an all-time high. What steps can the three of you take to prevent a major slip from happening?"
- "What steps can the three of you take to stay on track?"
- "What are you going to do over the next week to get up to a 7?"

As another way to highlight differences, I may also check with the parents and the adolescent as to how they presently rate themselves on the scale of their initial goal area. Failure to *cover the back door* with families in the *better* category—such as consolidating client gains, teaching them goal-maintenance and solution-enhancement tools and strategies, and intervening early when there are warning signs of clients slipping back into former problematic patterns of behavior—can set the stage for prolonged relapse situations and families feeling like they have returned back to square one in the change process (Selekman, 2002). As Prochaska and his colleagues (1994) have pointed out, clients often worry about slipping back into former negative patterns and habits once they enter the *maintenance* stage of readiness to change. By coauthoring with our clients highly structured goal-maintenance plans, consolidating their gains, and arming them with several solution-enhancement tools, we can maximize the likelihood of their being able to stay on track when the going gets rough.

Therapeutic Experiment Design and Selection

Some families will not request further therapy visits due to their significant changes or problem resolution. In this instance, I take an intersession break to "meet with myself" to construct compliments for family members or I have my team of colleagues observing from behind the one-way mirror come into the therapy room to reflect their compliments and ideas to the family. If the latter format is used, I have the family provide their reflections on the team's reflections and terminate therapy, if this is the family's wish. I always tell families that I have an "open-door" policy if they ever need to come in for a future "tune-up" session. I follow the same open-door format if I am working solo.

Other families may wish to continue in therapy in order to do further work in their initial goal area or work on a new goal. Besides having the team reflect their compliments and ideas to the family at the intersession break, I assess with the family whether they would like to continue using the same therapeutic experiment they were given in the first session or if they would like to be offered some new experiment options. The team and I share with the family our bias for *doing more of what works* by telling them, "We believe if it works, don't fix it" (de Shazer, 1985). If the parents request different therapeutic experiment options, the team and I may recommend to them an observation task (Gingerich & de Shazer, 1991; Molnar & de Shazer, 1987) so that they will "continue to notice what further changes they will make." We may also offer the adolescent the *secret surprise* experiment (O'Hanlon & Weiner-Davis, 1989) during our individual session time. During that portion of the session, I ask the adolescent to pick two surprises to do over the week or during the break period between sessions that will shock the parents in a positive way. I find it useful to have the adolescent try to identify some potential surprise ideas he or she may have in mind to help get him or her into the spirit of trying out this fun experiment. The adolescent cannot tell the parents what the surprises were. The parents are instructed to pull out their imaginary magnifying glasses like Sherlock Holmes and Miss Marple detectives and look for what those surprises were that "shocked them in a positive way."

Covering the Back Door with Families

Once clients begin to experience changes with their problem situations, they may take for granted early warning signs that the goal-maintenance process is beginning to unravel or unrelated difficulties are occurring in other areas of their lives. Solution-oriented therapists may also disregard these early warning signs or fail to address new client concerns because they are concentrating most of their efforts on amplifying and consolidating the clients' gains and steering clear of engaging in *problem talk* with them (Gingerich et al., 1988; Stalker, Levene, & Coady, 1999; Nylund & Corsiglia, 1994). To help prevent prolonged relapsing situations and major crises from occurring with our clients, it behooves us to regularly check in with them each session if there have been any warning signs of slipping backwards in the goal area or any new worries that they are concerned about. The earlier we can intervene when warning signs start to appear, the more likely we can empower our clients to make the necessary adjustments to stay on track and further improve their situations. It is important that we closely monitor and evaluate with the clients how the proposed adjustments or therapeutic experiments we offered them are working, need fine-tuning, or have not made a difference. In most cases, by attending to client concerns, having them make minor adjustments, encouraging them to increase their solution-maintaining patterns and use of past successful problem-solving strategies, or tightening up with the structure, we can rapidly help to prevent budding crises from occurring.

Longer Time Intervals

My colleagues and I have found it useful to give families longer time intervals between sessions as a vote of confidence. We increase the length of the time intervals between sessions until the family feels more confident to make a go of it on their own. For example, I may ask a family, "When would you like to come back—in 3 or 4 weeks?" The family is put in charge of deciding when our next meeting should be scheduled and the frequency of future visits. Palazzoli and her colleagues (1980) found that giving families longer time intervals between sessions gave the families more time to think about the new ideas introduced by the therapist and the consultation team. At the same time, longer time intervals between sessions can provide ample time for family members to notice differences and changes occurring within their family situations and in other social contexts. With court-referred families that have been committed to seeing me for a year by the probation officer or the judge, I do *brief long-term therapy.* Once I have negotiated with the probation officer or the judge the frequency of counseling sessions, I may see a family six to eight times over an entire year. I have also found the brief long-term therapy strategy useful with some chronic substance-abusing, eating-distressed, and self-harming clients, because it provides them with the confidence that they possess the strengths and resourcefulness to cope and problem-solve on their own. In addition, it offers us the opportunity to tighten up the structure during the adolescent's leisure time and strategize for how best to constructively manage inevitable future slips. I call these future scheduled visits "tune-up" sessions. Finally, a well-timed tune-up session can prevent a budding slipup situation from blossoming into a full-blown relapse.

MIXED-OPINION FAMILIES

When families return for their second session reporting concerns about the goal area or other difficulties that occurred in 1 week's time, I respectfully ask the family if before we address their concerns I could first hear about the times when the difficulties were *not* occurring. When exception material is produced, I amplify these changes through cheerleading and solution-building questions. If this strategy works, I use presuppositional questions to propel the family into a future reality without problems. I use either my trustworthy imaginary crystal ball or videotape metaphor (O'Hanlon & Weiner-Davis, 1989) to achieve this end. It also is helpful to explore with the parents and the adolescent where they presently rank themselves on the scale of goal attainment. If family members push to address their concerns, we need to respectfully honor their request by taking the time with the family to gather all of the important details about their concerns, such as what we need to attend to that was not covered in the previous session and needs to be immediately addressed. Once we have secured this important information, we can set a new goal and plan out together a new work project to address their concern area. I may also inquire with them: "What steps are you presently taking to prevent your situation from getting much worse?" Often, parents respond to this coping question (Berg & Miller, 1992) with important exception material. With every exception that is reported to me, I respond with cheerleading and solution-building questions. The original treatment goal established by the family may also need to be examined and renegotiated into a smaller, more solvable goal. In some cases, the parents may no longer want to address their original goal area and want to establish a new goal related to a more pressing concern.

Therapeutic Experiment Design and Selection

Besides giving compliments and sharing some of our ideas with the family, the team and I offer the family a menu of new therapeutic experiments that better fit with their unique cooperative response patterns and a renegotiated goal for them to choose from. The "do something different task" (de Shazer, 1985, 1988) is particularly useful with parents that are stuck doing *more of the same* (Watzlawick et al., 1974). If the exceptions appear to be happening spontaneously without any explanations for their occurrence, the team and I may offer the prediction task (Gingerich & de Shazer, 1991; de Shazer, 1988) as one option or some other experiment that can be performed on a random basis. With parents who are concerned that the adolescent may have future relapses or difficulties, the team and I share that "change is three steps forward and two steps back, but we will not be back to square one" (de Shazer, 1985). If adolescents are receptive to learning some solution-enhancement tools to help him or her to stay on track, I will teach them the following coping strategies as some possible options: visualizing movies of success, disputation tools to counter self-defeating "stinkin thinkin" thoughts, and mindfulness meditation.

Roger, a white 16-year-old, was brought to therapy by his parents for chronic rule violation, police involvement, and school truancy. The parents decided in the first interview that they wished for the "school attendance problem" to change. According to the parents, Roger would cut a few days of school with his "friends" and then attend 1 or 2 days per week. Neither the parents nor Roger could explain these spontaneous exceptions. Throughout the interview, I observed that the parents were highly conflictual and frequently put down each other's parenting styles in relationship to Roger. I used exception-oriented questions and had Roger leave the room, which seemed to help short-circuit this vicious pattern of interaction. After complimenting each family member on their strengths and coping strategies, I offered the family the prediction task (de Shazer, 1988) as a "useful experiment" for the week. Each night, the threesome were to separately predict whether Roger would be "staying in school" the next day and then, the day following the day predicted, to account for why this happened.

The family returned to the second session reporting that Roger had "gone to school four out of five days." I pulled out my imaginary pom-poms and acted like a cheerleader, and also amplified the exceptions. However, the parents began to criticize each other on how they had handled a "big blowup" about Roger. Roger had wanted to go to a party with some of his "troublemaking friends," and his mother had told him, "No!" The father, on the other hand, felt it would have been "okay for Roger to go" to the party. I asked Roger to sit in the lobby while I met alone with the parents. I complimented each parent on doing a fine job of getting Roger to "stay in school." I decided to give the parents an observation task for the next week in which each parent would separately observe what the other does about Roger that they liked and jot those things down so we could discuss their discoveries in the next session. The parents agreed with me that they "spent too little" time acknowledging "the good things" they each did with their son. After complimenting each family member, I recommended that they continue to do the prediction task with the rationale of "keep doing more of what works."

One week later, the family came in reporting a wealth of exceptions. Roger was going to "school daily," there were "no blowups," and the parents had not criticized or argued with each other for the entire week. When I met alone with the parents, each parent reported at least four things that he or she liked about the other partner's parenting abilities. As a vote of confidence to the family, I gave them a 4-week vacation from therapy. While on vacation, I asked them to "continue doing more of what works." We mutually decided to terminate therapy after the vacation break, due to problem resolution.

SAME FAMILIES

When families report no further improvement in the second and subsequent sessions, I first explore in a respectful manner whether there was at least one good day over the course of the week and attempt to amplify its exceptions. It is important to secure detailed information about all of the exceptions that occurred on the one good day because they may serve as potential building blocks for solution construction. If my solution-building inquiry produces negative client feedback and they wish to address their concerns first, I will honor their request. Similar to our therapeutic work with mixed-opinion families, we may need to establish a new focus for treatment so that their concerns do not escalate into crisis situations. I will also explore with the family members how they prevented things from getting worse. If the family members are still negative and pessimistic about their situation, I take this as important client feedback indicating that I need to do something therapeutically different. To begin with, it is helpful to keep things simple by investigating some basic areas with the family, such as whether we have a well-formed treatment goal. Whenever I feel we are stuck, I assess with the family whether our original treatment goal is too monolithic and needs to be broken down further, or whether we selected the wrong goal area to begin working on first. I may try utilizing the pessimistic question sequence (Berg & Miller, 1992) to help generate some exceptions. I also explore with the family whether anyone else needs to be participating in our therapy sessions who is not presently involved. In assessing customership with the family, I may ask the adolescent to rank on a scale from 1 to 10—10 being most concerned about him or her—how all family members and involved significant others not present in our sessions would be rated on the scale at the time. The answer to this question often provides me with important clues as to who I need to include in future sessions.

When trying to determine customership, I also will conduct a macrosystemic assessment (Selekman & Todd, 1991) with the family members to invite them to tell me what involved helpers from larger systems I need to collaborate with. If there are multiple helpers from larger systems involved with the family, I secure signed consent forms from the family and recommend that we have family–multiple helper meetings in the future.

Therapeutic Experiment Design and Selection

With some families, when I shift gears and ask, "How come things are not worse?," some important exceptions will be produced that can be utilized as building blocks toward co-constructing a solution with the family. The pessimistic sequence (Berg & Miller, 1992) can be utilized if no exceptions are produced. If the family continues to be pessimistic, I may shift gears and ask them to give me a videotaped description of the problem-maintaining sequence of interaction in the family. Pattern intervention (O'Hanlon, 1987; O'Hanlon & Weiner-Davis, 1989) is an effective therapeutic strategy for disrupting the problem-maintaining sequences of interaction in the family. O'Hanlon (1987) has developed a useful guide for how to disrupt problem-maintaining patterns in the client system. Some of his recommendations are:

1. Change the frequency/rate of the symptom/symptom-pattern.
2. Change the duration of the symptom/symptom-pattern.
3. Change the time (of day/week/month/year) of the symptom/symptom-pattern.
4. Change the location of the symptom/symptom-pattern.
5. Add or subtract (at least) one element to or from the sequence.
6. Change the sequence (order) of events around the symptom. (p. 36)

If the family warms up to the idea of experimenting with new change strategies that the team and I wish to offer them, we may propose the following options: pattern intervention strategies (O'Hanlon & Weiner-Davis, 1989; O'Hanlon, 1987), such as the do something different experiment (de Shazer, 1988); have the parents try to figure out and write down all of the reasons why their problem situation is not much worse (Molnar & de Shazer, 1987); or, if working solo, begin using a reflecting team format (Andersen, 1991; Friedman, 1995) in future sessions.

Fifteen-year-old Curt had been referred to me for family therapy by his school social worker for "failing grades," "disruptive behavior" in his classes, and "suspected substance abuse." According to the school social worker, Curt had been in counseling a few times before for his behavioral difficulties at home and at school. She felt that the parents were "not consistent with their limit setting."

In my first family session, Curt's mother, Helen, did most of the talking. Tim, the father, indicated to me that he was upset about having to miss work time for our appointment and did not think it was going to help. Curt sat quietly throughout most of our sessions with his head down, stretched-out legs, and his arms tightly folded across his chest. Helen voiced her concerns about Curt's behavioral difficulties and how she felt unsupported by her husband in trying to resolve their son's problems. When I asked the miracle question (de Shazer, 1988), I was met with silence from Tim and Curt. Helen, however, went on a long monologue about all of the changes she would see in her ideal miracle scenario. It was clear that the two men were in the *precontemplation stage of readiness to change*, while Helen was clearly in the *action stage* (Prochaska et al., 1994). The use of the coping and pessimistic sequence questions (Berg & Miller, 1992) with Tim and Curt was also met with "I don't know" and periods of silence from the men. I decided to meet alone with the couple alone to explore with them what the barriers were that prevented them from working together as a unified parental team. Tim opened up by criticizing Helen's parenting style with their son, that is, her "nagging and flying off the handle at him all of the time." Helen countered by questioning Tim's "boys will be boys" attitude and too laissez-faire a style of parenting with Curt. As we continued to talk about their lack of parental unity, Tim became more verbal and appeared to be moving into the *contemplation stage of readiness to change* (Prochaska et al., 1994). I decided to offer them an observation experiment in which both parents were to separately observe what the other parent did with Curt that they "liked," "thought was right on target," or "really worked." They were not to compare notes until our next family session. When I met alone with Curt, he remained silent for most of the time, and I got a few "I don't know" responses from him as well.

One week later, the family came back in reporting that their situation had "not changed one bit." The parents could not identify anything good or different about each other's parenting styles. Curt remained in the same posture and had nothing to say in the company of his family or when I saw him later in the session individually. I met alone with the couple again. I used problem-tracking questions (Palazzoli et al., 1980) to secure a detailed description of how they typically responded to Curt when he would get into trouble at school. The problem-maintaining pattern was as follows: Helen would confront him first, Curt would then mouth off to her, she would start lecturing and yelling at him about being disrespectful, Curt would storm out of the house, Helen would complain to Tim about Curt's disrespectful behavior and school trouble, Tim would get angry and blame Helen for Curt's difficulties, they would start to argue, and Tim would return home and not be given a consequence. I attempted to create some intensity (Minuchin & Fishman, 1981) with Tim about how his son was rapidly spiraling downward and Tim desperately needed to step up more and use his toughness to help him turn things around. It appeared that Tim got the message and was moving into the *preparation stage of readiness to change* (Prochaska et al., 1994). One thing I had discovered about Tim in our conversation was that when he had "gotten tough with Curt" in the past, Curt knew that his "father meant business!" We decided to try a few times over the next week to have Tim take the lead in setting limits and enforcing consequences with Curt and giving Helen a break. Helen was quite pleased that Tim was willing to "step up" and give her a "break from being the heavy."

The parents came in the following week smiling and much more hopeful about their situation with Curt. It only took two after-school surprise visits from Tim and a few other times when he delivered consequences to Curt to drive home the message that his father was "no longer going to tolerate phone calls from the school" and his disrespectful behavior toward Helen. The parents became a solid unified team. They also "took away Curt's driving privileges for a month" after they found "marijuana in his bedroom." Tim pointed out that, if caught again, Curt would lose use of the car for "6 months." By having Tim "step up" more, support Helen, and consistently set limits when necessary with his son, the therapy sessions resulted in Curt's behavior changing dramatically.

Some families, however, return to the second and subsequent sessions feeling highly pessimistic and demoralized by the presenting problem and other family difficulties. Many of these families have experienced multiple treatment failures and have been oppressed by the problem for a long time. Besides exploring what previous therapists might have overlooked or missed with them (storytelling), I externalize the problem (White & Epston, 1990). The team and I develop an experiment for the family designed to help empower them to conquer their oppressive problem.

Mr. and Mrs. Andrews sought therapy for their 17-year-old son, Steve, who had a long history of abusing drugs. Steve had been in two drug rehabilitation programs in the past and relapsed shortly after being discharged from the last program. Mr. Andrews viewed Steve as being "a druggie" because he refused to "stay straight." Mrs. Andrews felt that Steve had been "trying harder lately" to change. Steve shared in the first interview that kids at school were calling him a "stoner," which "pissed" him off. Steve's older brother, who was away at college, also had had a problem with drugs when he was in high school. My attempt to elicit exception material from the parents was met with negativity and pessimism. I quickly moved to asking the family the miracle question (de Shazer, 1988). The parents' miracles were Steve's maintaining drug abstinence, Steve and his father "getting along better," "less arguing" in the family, and Steve staying away from his "partying friends." I decided to meet alone with Steve to further develop my therapeutic alliance with him. I offered him two homework assignments due to his high level of motivation to do something about his drug problem. The first assignment was for Steve to notice all of the various things he would do to avoid the temptation to get "buzzed" (Steve's language) over the next week (de Shazer, 1985) and to write those things down for the next session. The second task was for Steve to pick 2 days over the next week to pretend to engage in miracle behaviors (de Shazer, 1991) so we could "blow your parents' minds!" After giving the family compliments, I asked the parents to pull out their imaginary magnifying glasses and try to guess days on which Steve was pretending to engage in miracle behaviors.

One week later, the family reported that minimal changes had occurred with their situation, and they were quite negative. An argument erupted in the session between Steve and his father over the former's voicing his desire not to change. I disrupted this destructive blaming cycle through externalizing the problem (White & Epston, 1990). I asked the family the following externalizing questions: "How long has the 'druggie' lifestyle been pushing your sons around?"; "What kinds of things did you do to help Bill [the older brother] escape from the 'druggie' lifestyle?"; "Steve, how long are you going to allow the 'druggie' lifestyle to invite the kids at school to call you a 'stoner'?" The atmosphere in the room greatly changed and my externalizing questions seemed to open up space for family members to view the problem situation differently. The parents began to talk about how this was a family problem. They had remembered that when Bill was grappling with the "druggie" lifestyle, they made a conscious effort to stop blaming him, which "seemed to work" in helping him change. Steve responded to my question about how he invited the "druggie" lifestyle to make the peers at school call him a "stoner" and "fry brain" with a lot of emotion. Steve commented: "I'm sick of those assholes!"; "I'm sick of being called a 'stoner'!"

Because I had no team, I took a break to "meet with myself" to design an appropriate experiment to offer the family. Each day family members were to keep track of the various things they did to stand up to the "druggie" lifestyle and not allow it to push them around, both at home and at school. I implemented this routine at school with the social worker and concerned teachers, as well. The family was also instructed to meet after dinner for half an hour to discuss their daily victories over the "druggie" lifestyle—what specifically they were doing to stand up to it, as well as how they were being pushed around by it. I explained to the family that "druggie" lifestyles do not die easily—so, the evening meetings were essential for strategizing and support. I asked family members whether they wanted to come back in 2 or 3 weeks. The family decided to come back in 2 weeks.

Two weeks later, the parents and Steve came in smiling and in good spirits. Steve had remained "straight for 2 weeks!" I fell out of my chair when Steve reported his tremendous accomplishment. There had been "no arguments" during the break period. The father, who was a Cubs baseball fan, said, "Steve is batting a thousand!" Steve's mother reported that she had seen him "doing his homework," which was a "big change." Steve reported that he found it useful to meet with his parents nightly for support and that he had steered clear of his "partying friends." After highlighting differences and amplifying the multitude of family changes, I recommended that they continue doing the task and that we meet again in 4 weeks as a vote of confidence in the family. I ended up seeing Steve's family two more times. For the last session, which was 2 months after the third session, I bought a cake to celebrate the Andrews's victory over the "druggie" lifestyle.

Managing Temporary Family Derailments

While on longer time intervals or mini-vacations from therapy, families may experience some slipping back from their improvement in the goal area, or fall back into their old problem-maintaining patterns of interaction in response to a slip. Once notified by the parents, I call the family in for an immediate tune-up session. I like to normalize inevitable client slips by saying to the family, "We could not have had a slip if we had not already made headway." I also like to refer to slips as a temporary derailment or an opportunity for comeback practice (Tomm & White, 1987). I explore with the family the steps they have already taken prior to our tune-up session to get back on track again. It is also helpful to ask family members:

- "What did you learn from this slip that you will put to use when you are faced with similar stressful situations in the future?"
- "What immediate steps will you need to take to get back on track quickly?"
- "What will you have to do to stay on track?"
- "What specifically will you need to do to get that to happen?"
- "What else will you have to do more of to stay on track?"

I may bring out my imaginary crystal ball and have family members gaze into it and describe in great detail what they are seeing themselves doing in a future place making further progress and staying on track. By the end of the tune-up session if there are still some minor concerns, I schedule a future appointment and send the family back on their vacation from therapy as a vote of confidence in them.

WORSE FAMILIES

When families return for the second and subsequent sessions reporting that their problem situation has gotten worse, I respond to this important client feedback by doing something different therapeutically. The use of pessimistic questions (Berg & Miller, 1992; Berg & Gallagher, 1991) may be an effective pathway to pursue to help foster a better cooperative relationship.

Besides assessing with family members whether we need a smaller or new treatment goal, I also explore with them who else we need to have present in our therapy sessions, including involved helpers from larger systems, inspirational others, or other key members of their social network. If the family has not responded well to solution-focused experiments (de Shazer, 1991; Gingerich & de Shazer, 1991; Molnar & de Shazer, 1987) or pattern intervention (O'Hanlon, 1987), I externalize the problem (White & Epston, 1990). With some families, however, the small changes that such strategies might have produced are not differences that are clearly registering with the family. Therefore, with these families it can be quite useful to slow things down by assigning weekly experiments and giving family members more room to share their problem-saturated stories and concerns. Asking conversational questions (Anderson, 1997; Anderson & Goolishian, 1988a) can open up space for family members to tell their story without any editing on the part of either the therapist or the consultation team. This can lead to the generation of new meanings and possibilities for action.

Kelly, a white 17-year-old, was court-ordered to therapy for shoplifting, chronic violation of parental rules, school truancy, and substance abuse. In the first session, the team and I offered to the parents the do something different task (de Shazer, 1985). One week later, the family returned reporting no progress at all. In fact, Kelly's acting-out behavior had gotten worse. The parents' goal for Kelly was for her to "come home on time at least one time" over the next week. Kelly would not commit to her parents' goal and could not identify anything she really wanted to get out of therapy or from her parents. According to the parents, Kelly had not come home on time once, and they were "furious at her." I tracked the problem sequence and discovered that the major family arguments occurred in the kitchen after Kelly returned home late at night. Kelly usually won these family arguments because she was "more awake" than her parents. She typically ended up cussing them out and locking herself in her bedroom. The team and I recommended to family members that they schedule their family arguments in the living room earlier in the evening when the parents were "more awake." Our rationale for having the family arguments was that this was the best way each family member could convey his or her "concern and emotional connection" to the others. We instructed them to take turns arguing with one family member for only 5 minutes at a time. They were to use the kitchen timer to accurately keep track of the time. Any leftover topics were to be written down on a piece of paper and discussed in the next scheduled arguing session.

When the family returned for our third session, they reported a major decrease in the family arguments and some behavioral improvement with Kelly. I amplified all of the changes. However, Kelly looked depressed and was shaking in her chair. There seemed to be some tension between Kelly and her father. The team picked up on these important nonverbal signs and commented on them as part of their reflection when the family and I went behind the one-way mirror at the intersession break. Some of the team's reflections were as follows: "I wonder if there is some missing piece to this family puzzle that has not yet been talked about?"; "Yeah, despite all of the family's progress over the past week, there seems to be something that is putting a damper on the good feelings . . . "; "I wonder if Kelly is trying to tell us something, like what the missing piece of the family puzzle might be, but is not sure how the piece will fit for them as a family . . ."

After we switched rooms, the family reflected on the team's reflections. Kelly surprisingly took a risk and shared with us that her 24-year-old brother, who was home from college for the summer, had sexually abused her 3 years ago. The parents were totally shocked, particularly the father, who was very close to his son. According to Kelly, Alan (the older brother) had come home drunk from a party while the parents were out for the evening and forced her to have intercourse with him. Alan had threatened to "kill" her if she "spilled the beans." The mother hugged Kelly and told her that "this will never happen again" and "Alan will be dealt with." The father planned to confront Alan about the sex abuse incident and make him "go for therapy." The parents denied knowing anything about their daughter's sexual victimization. I shared with the family that, because I am a mandated reporter, we would have to call the child protective services department and report this incident. The father offered to call from my office. I told the family that I would collaborate with the child protective service worker and provide advocacy and family therapy for them during this crisis period.

Kelly and her parents decided to press charges against Alan. He was court-ordered to a sex offender's group. Future family sessions involved providing support for Kelly and her family and collaborating with the child protective service worker and the probation officer. I saw Kelly and her parents six more times. I also got Kelly into a special group for sexually abused girls. Kelly's behavior dramatically improved after her courageous disclosure to her parents.

Kelly's case is an excellent example of the importance of therapeutic flexibility. The team and I began therapy by using solution-focused brief therapy experiments, which failed to produce any significant changes in the family—in fact, things had gotten worse. We attempted to disrupt the problem-maintaining pattern of interaction around Kelly's constantly breaking curfew, which produced some changes, but they were not "newsworthy" to her because she had an important story to tell. Our original highly active therapeutic stance of zapping the family with a variety of interventions and keeping the session conversations sharply focused on "what was better" had been blocking Kelly from telling her story. It was clear that we needed to do something different. The use of a strict reflecting team format (Andersen, 1991) helped the family and me get unstuck and gave my colleagues the opportunity to pick up on some important nonverbal signs that were indicative of some family secret being hidden. They were free as a group to probe for undiscussables and speak metaphorically about the family secret from a meta-position, which paved the way for Kelly to disclose the "not yet said" (Anderson & Goolishian, 1988b). Kelly's courageous disclosure helped generate new meaning for the parents regarding her behavior and led to very dramatic individual and family changes.

DISCONNECTED FAMILIES

With some families, a change in one part of the family system may fail to produce changes in the other parts of the system. Family members and subsystems in these families tend to be disconnected from one another. In some cases, even altering the concerned parent's behavior in relationship to the adolescent does not produce change but rather tends to reinforce the adolescent's symptoms or further exacerbates them. I have witnessed this phenomenon with families in which there were multiple symptom bearers. One useful therapeutic strategy with disconnected families is to intervene separately through individual family members or subsystems. I establish separate treatment goals and work projects with family members. Another option is to use a one-person family therapy approach (Selekman, 2002; Szapocznik & Williams, 2000).

George, Iveson, and Ratner (1999) have found, with individual clients, couples, or families presenting with multiple problems that they wish to address simultaneously, that it is possible to "knit them together." They contend that, by scaling each one of these problem areas as if they were in isolation from one another, they can increase the likelihood of clients being able to identify and use their strengths and resources to resolve each one of these difficulties separately. At the end of the session, they ask the clients to consider what effect changes on one scale will have on the other scales. This helps to reconnect the clients' problems in a constructive way.

A former disconnected family case of mine illustrates how challenging these cases are to work with.

Sarah had brought her alcohol-abusing 17-year-old daughter, Wendy, in for therapy "out of fear" that she "will fail her senior year" of high school because of her heavy alcohol abuse. After three sessions of therapy, Wendy's alcohol abuse behavior and school problems got worse, despite Sarah's making remarkable changes, such as going to Al-Anon and not being superresponsible in relation to Wendy. I had failed to engage Wendy in the first interview, and she had decided to boycott our future therapy sessions. Because I was feeling "stuck" and I was teamless during the time that I saw this family, I decided to expand the system and have Sarah bring her husband and 26-year-old son to the next session. The father came to our next session smelling of alcohol and looking disheveled. Wendy's older brother had been arrested for cocaine dealing prior to our session. My attempts to engage the father proved to be futile. Sarah and I ended up having four more sessions together. She continued to go to Al-Anon for support, stopped being "super-Mom," and began taking evening college classes. Sarah eventually came to the realization in therapy that the only person that could change in her family was herself.

Although I failed to resolve Sarah's presenting complaint, I still consider this case to be a therapeutic success. Sarah took many courageous steps in therapy to empower herself and learn how to better cope with a very troubling family situation. In our last session together, I complimented her on successfully "mastering the art of detachment" and for utilizing the "serenity prayer's" wisdom to better cope with her family.

ONE-PERSON FAMILY THERAPY

With case situations where it proves to be counterproductive to do conjoint family therapy due to extreme and intense parent–adolescent conflicts, severe marital discord, or intense post-divorce parental conflict, the threat of family violence, or both parents appearing to be incapacitated due to severe mental health or substance abuse issues, I will offer to the adolescent a one-person family therapy approach (Selekman, 2002; Szapocznik & Williams, 2000). When using this treatment format, the adolescent becomes the agent of change. Through the use of a flip chart, we can map out the major problem-maintaining patterns of interaction in the family that the adolescent finds him- or herself getting embroiled in or playing an active part in family politics. This can be a "newsworthy" experience to see how his or her responses to the parents' or siblings' actions may be contributing to things getting worse at home. Solution-focused and pattern intervention experiments can be spearheaded by the adolescent to help disrupt these vicious problem-maintaining patterns. Role playing can be employed to help the adolescent gain more confidence and practice serving as a change agent. Other individual and family therapy strategies can be proposed as well. Finally, the one-person family therapy approach can be of benefit to older adolescents struggling to be more independent of their families.

SOLUTION-ORIENTED THERAPEUTIC EXPERIMENTS AND TEAM STRATEGIES

In this section of the chapter, I present 17 solution-oriented therapeutic experiments and team strategies that I typically use with families in second and subsequent sessions. I describe each therapeutic experiment and team strategy, offer helpful guidelines about how to match specific therapeutic experiments with key client intelligence areas (Gardner, 1993, 1999) and client cooperative response group categories they may be presently in, and provide some case examples.

The Secret Surprise

The *secret surprise* experiment (O'Hanlon & Weiner-Davis, 1989) consists of having the adolescent pick two surprising things to do in 1 week's time to shock the parents in a positive way. The adolescent is not allowed to tell the parents what the surprises are. The parents are instructed to pull out their imaginary magnifying glasses and try to identify what their adolescent's surprises were. This is a playful experiment that is useful for amplifying exceptions and changes. Sometimes I reverse the task and have the parents provide the secret surprises. Similarly, I have had teachers that the adolescent is in conflict with experiment with this intervention, as well, to help improve their relationship. I like to use this experiment with the *mixed-opinion* client groups as a playful way to further empower the adolescent to generate the kind of positive behaviors the parents would like to see happen more often and increase their hope and expectancy levels that these changes will persist over time. Adolescents strong in the *interpersonal intelligence area* (Gardner, 1993) will enjoy doing this experiment.

Solution Enhancement Experiment

For clients presenting with habit problems such as substance-abuse, eating-distressed, or self-harming difficulties, the *solution enhancement* experiment (de Shazer, 1985) can empower them to increase their awareness of their resourcefulness when standing up to their bad habits and managing to stay on track. The adolescent is instructed as follows: "Over the next week, I want you to notice all of the various things you will do to avoid the temptation to [in client language] get "high," to "pig out," "cut yourself," and so forth. This therapeutic experiment is useful with *mixed-opinion* clients to help generate more exceptions and further enhance their problem-solving capacities. With some substance-abusing clients, I encourage them to write down their useful solutions on blank cards and carry them around in their purses and wallets. I have had some former adolescent clients tell me that they have found their "solution cards" helpful to them in stressful situations and times of crisis.

Adolescents who are highly skilled on the computer and shine in the *logical–mathematical intelligence area* (Gardner, 1993, 1999) may like to keep track of their progress and *what works* on a sophisticated graph. One adolescent I worked with established a very elaborate graph on his computer to quantitatively measure his parents' progress at reducing their "nagging behavior" with him over time. In response to his parents reducing their nagging behaviors, he took responsibility for completing his homework assignments.

Creating Your Own Superhero Cartoon Character

When working with adolescents that have been oppressed by their problem situations for a long time, one way to externalize their problems (White & Epston, 1990) is to have them draw them as supervillains in a cartoon strip format. They are to come up with a name for the supervillain, describe its magical powers and how it outsmarts the law and other kids just like them. After they have drawn their supervillains, I have them think about a new superhero they could create that would be capable of defeating their supervillains. As with the supervillains, I have them identify what their superheroes' names are, what their magical powers are, how they are clever, and what their potential strategies might be for defeating their supervillains. I give the adolescent a long sheet of paper to draw the boxes for the cartoon strip on. Sequentially, the adolescent is to depict in the boxes how his or her superhero will defeat the supervillain. He or she has to come up with dialogue to place in the bubbles over the cartoon characters' heads. Most adolescents have a lot of fun with this in-session art experiment and gain courage and wisdom from identifying with their superheroes, as well as important insights about how their problems operate and the tricks they employ, which can empower them to conquer their problems. Adolescents strong in the *visual–spatial intelligence area* (Gardner, 1993) will enjoy doing this experiment. This experiment can be useful with adolescents in the *same* or *worse* client category groups.

The Strengths-in-Action Project

Ben Franklin—diplomat, author, inventor, and business strategist—would be considered by many to be one of the most important and talented figures in American history. Franklin had undying curiosity, strived to further his knowledge, fine-tuned his interpersonal skills, and constantly engaged in a variety of experiments and projects. One of his most challenging projects was his "moral perfection project." Franklin created a list of 13 virtuous behaviors and attitudes that he would adopt, which he believed would help him "arrive at moral perfection" (Isaacson, 2003). Each week, for 13 weeks straight, he committed to engaging in and adopting one of these virtuous behaviors and attitudes. Apparently, Franklin completed the 13-week cycle four times in 1 year! Some of these virtuous behaviors and attitudes were *justice*, *sincerity*, *industry*, and *resolution* (Isaacson, 2003). In a similar fashion, I have an adolescent conduct a *strengths-in-action project* for 1 week. I first have the adolescent identify his or her three major strengths. As an experiment, I have the adolescent on a daily basis practice applying his or her strengths at school and in social interactions with peers and family members. While using each of their strengths, the adolescents keep track of the positive responses they trigger in others on a daily basis. Once clients discover the benefits of tapping and using their strengths more, we can explore with them what other areas of their lives or other settings might benefit from use of their key strengths to make their lives more meaningful and enjoyable. I have gotten good results by using this experiment with adolescents strong in the *interpersonal*, *linguistic*, *bodily–kinesthetic*, and *logical–mathematical intelligence areas* (Gardner, 1993) as well as with adolescents in the *mixed-opinion* or *same* client category groups.

Habit Control Ritual

The *habit control ritual* (Durrant & Coles, 1991) can be useful with families that have been oppressed by a particular problem for a long time. Once the family's problem has been externalized (White & Epston, 1990), family members can be instructed to keep track on a daily basis of the various things they can do to stand up to the problem and not allow it to get the best of them. They are also asked to keep track of the problem's victories over them—that is, how they accept invitations or are brainwashed by it to lock horns with one another. Nightly family meetings are scheduled for strategizing until the oppressive problem has been conquered by the family. If the adolescent and involved helping professionals in school or other social contexts are being pushed around by the problem, I have the client and the concerned helpers team up and implement this ritual in these other settings. This experiment is particularly useful with families that are in the *same* or *worse* categories in second or subsequent sessions. Adolescents who are strong in the *visual–spatial* and *interpersonal intelligence areas* (Gardner, 1993, 1999) will respond well to this ritual.

Imaginary Time Machine

The *imaginary time machine* experiment (Selekman, 1997, 2002) invites adolescents and other family members in the *mixed-opinion, same*, or *worse* client categories and are strong the in the *visual–spatial intelligence area* (Gardner, 1993, 1999) to take a trip in a make-believe time machine anywhere in time they wish to travel to. Once they have arrived at their destination, they are to describe in great detail where they went, who they are with, what they are doing, and apply all of their senses to their descriptions, including color and motion, which helps bring the traveling experience more to life for them. If the adolescent went back in time to meet with a historical figure that he or she always admired, after they got acquainted and did something special together, I would have him or her invite the historical figure to hop into the time machine, travel back together, and join our family meeting as a guest consultant. For example, if the adolescent brought back Martin Luther King, Jr., I would pose the following questions to the adolescent: "What advice would Martin Luther King, Jr., have for you and your parents to help the three of you get along better?" and "Let's say you brought Martin Luther King, Jr., to school with you. What would he encourage you to do differently in Miss Shaw's class [*the teacher he is in conflict with*] that would help you do better in her class?" Often, with the help of our historical figure guest consultant, creative and effective solution strategies are generated.

This in-session therapeutic experiment can also be used to help foster connection building and facilitate the mourning process with complicated unresolved grief case situations. In terms of connection building, I like to have the adolescent go back in time to a place where he or she felt more emotionally connected with the parent he or she presently feels disconnected from and is longing for more closeness in their relationship. Once the adolescent identifies the period of time, what he or she and the parent are doing together, and why this experience was so meaningful, I then invite the parent to reflect on his or her adolescent's time traveling experience and see what key aspects and important activities they used to do together he or she would be willing to reinstate to help strengthen their relationship in the present time. Often, parents are emotionally moved by their adolescents' time traveling experiences and respond by making themselves more consistently available to their kids for a closer emotional connection.

Many adolescents have grave difficulties mourning the loss of their parents, close relatives, or close friends who have moved away. When the loss of a parent or other family member occurs unexpectedly, the adolescent can become emotionally paralyzed by this experience. With the help of the imaginary time machine, the adolescent can have the opportunity to go back in time and relive his or her relationship with the departed loved one and officially say "good-bye." It is important, however, to carefully assess with the adolescent if he or she feels emotionally strong enough to handle this powerful experiment and to get parental permission to try it out. This should never be done with an adolescent who has been experiencing suicidal thoughts. The case below illustrates how this therapeutic experiment can help facilitate the mourning process with a highly depressed adolescent who experienced the tragic loss of her father.

Janet, a white 16-year-old, was referred to me by her psychiatrist for severe depression following the recent loss of her father. According to Sue, Janet's mother, she was "a daddy's girl" and used to spend "lots of quality time" with her father, Robert. Apparently, Robert had gone out to run some errands on a stormy evening, was not wearing his seat belt, lost control of his car, and crashed into a telephone pole and was killed instantly. Since losing her father, Janet was not able to function well enough to go to school, isolated herself in her bedroom, and was experiencing severe vegetative depressive symptoms. The psychiatrist had placed Janet on Zoloft and had spoken to the mother about wanting to hospitalize her if Janet's depressive symptoms did not stabilize. Both the mother and Janet wished to try outpatient counseling first. After three sessions of unsuccessfully helping Janet get to a better place and begin to process the painful loss of her father, I proposed to the family the imaginary time machine option to experiment with. Intuitively something was telling me that in order for Janet to be able to truly say "good-bye" to her father she had to say "hello" to him first. They agreed to try it out. Janet took the time machine back to a wonderful picnic she and her father had had a year earlier in a scenic park. Janet described how they were dressed, what they were eating, what they were talking about, the greenery, the birds, and the flowers surrounding them. Her description was so crystal clear that it was as if the mother and I were sitting across from them watching them enjoy this memorable experience. After about 25 minutes of being in a trance-like state, sharing her wonderful picnic experience, I had Janet hug and kiss her father and say "good-bye" to him. When Janet rejoined us in the session, she began to cry and talk about the loss of her father for the first time. The mother cried and gave Janet a big hug. In future sessions, the family brought in photos of the father to help them continue mourning and processing his death.

Invisible Family Inventions

The *invisible family inventions* (Selekman, 1997) can be used with clients in the *mixed-opinion*, *same*, or *worse* client group categories. Adolescents that are strong in the *visual–spatial* and *logical–mathematical intelligence areas* (Gardner, 1993, 1999) respond well to this experiment also. The adolescent is asked to think about and describe a gadget or machine that he or she would invent that would benefit other kids and families just like them. I ask the adolescent the following: "What would it look like?"; "How would it work?"; and "How specifically would it benefit you and other family members?" The added bonus with this experiment is that some adolescents are so enthusiastic about the prospect of inventing something that they go home and try and build their gadgets or machines. The parents and other family members are often impressed by the adolescent's creativity and other strengths and, under his or her leadership, offer to help him or her build it. If the inventions are not too large, I have the adolescent bring it in. Otherwise, a photograph of the invention will suffice. In many cases, the adolescent and his or her family use the invention to help further improve their situation at home.

Maria, a 12-year-old Latina adolescent, was brought in for family therapy by her father Sam for "depression" and "fears" of her "beginning to experiment with alcohol and drugs." Her school grades had greatly declined, she appeared "real nervous" all of the time, and she was "isolating herself more from the family." Sam proudly pointed out Maria used to be an A student and could be a "big help around the house." Maria had four other siblings. Her twin brothers were 11 years old, and she had a 6-year-old brother who had fetal alcohol syndrome. Carmen, 9 years old, who accompanied them to the session, also looked very depressed. According to Sam, Maria's mother, Juanita, had a "severe alcoholism" problem, and she "refused to go to any more counselors or treatment programs" for help. Apparently, she had been observed to "blackout regularly," "pass out" on "the living room sofa," and "scream at the kids when real drunk." Alcoholism problems ran in her family. Sam also shared his catastrophic fears about Maria's "gravitating toward alcohol and drugs as a teenager." Earlier in the session, Carmen, in a sad tone of voice, was able to verbalize her fears of her "mother dying soon" when processing some of the art experiments I had given her to do. Surprisingly, Maria did not show any emotional reaction to Carmen's concerns about their "mother dying soon." In fact, Maria had grave difficulty talking about her mother's alcoholism problem for the bulk of our family session. However, once I introduced the invisible family inventions experiment, Maria was better able to talk about what she would invent that would benefit not only her siblings but also her mother.

Her invention would be called "the family helper machine." It would be "a tall square-shaped machine with a door on it" that family members could "enter at any time of the day" when they were "stressed out," "sad," or "mad." The machine had a device inside it that could alter one's moods and "make you feel happy" when you exit it. Maria pointed out that her machine could "do something to my mom's brain and make her not want to drink when she went in there." I went down the line with Maria, having her describe how each family member would benefit from her invention. She said her father would be "less nervous" and "do more fun things" with them. Carmen would "be happier" and "go out and play with her friends more." Maria also saw herself "doing better in school" and socializing more with her friends. The family left our session in much better spirits and more hopeful about their situation.

Much to my pleasant surprise, Maria, Carmen, and her father went home and built "the family helper machine" prior to our second family session. They took an old refrigerator box, made a door on it, and wrote over the doorway in big bold letters "The Family Helper Machine." They brought in a photograph to show me what the machine looked like. Maria taught the other family members how and why they should use it. Apparently, Carmen and Maria were able to get their mother to go into the machine a few times. According to Maria, her mother seemed to function "better on those days."

Thanks to Maria's brilliant invention, she successfully got her mother to come to our third family session and begin to look at the devastating emotional effects her drinking was having on her kids and her own functioning. In responding to Maria's invention and Carmen's drawings about her feelings and the depressing family situation, Juanita shared with us, "It really breaks my heart." Once I was able to develop a solid therapeutic alliance with the mother, I was able to get her to agree to an outpatient detoxification, to be monitored by my psychiatrist colleague who was an addictionologist, and to work with me on relapse prevention. As Juanita continued to improve, the children's symptoms stabilized as well.

Famous Guest Consultant Experiment

The *famous guest consultant experiment* (Selekman, 2002) is particularly useful with *same* or *worse* client group categories and adolescents that are strong in the *visual–spatial* and *interpersonal intelligence areas* (Gardner, 1993, 1999). I like to use this therapeutic experiment with the following case situations: when the adolescent remains symptomatic due to entrenched family disconnection or invalidating interactions; when the family has not been responsive to solution-focused and other pattern interventions (Gingerich & de Shazer, 1991; O'Hanlon & Weiner-Davis, 1989); when working individually with adolescents or when using a one-person family therapy format with them; or when the treatment system is stuck and we need a playful thinking-out-of-the-box experiment to help move us forward. To begin this therapeutic experiment, I have each family member write down on a piece of paper two or three names of famous people that they have always admired or were inspired by. These can include historical figures, famous authors or artists, or sports, music, TV, and movie celebrities. After generating their lists, family members are to take turns sharing with one another the names they wrote down, why they selected these specific people, and what they have found to be most meaningful or inspirational about them. Next, family members are to imagine putting themselves into the heads of these famous people in terms of the creative ideas they would recommend for resolving the family's difficulties. With the help of these famous people, family members often generate several high-quality creative solutions.

Anna, a 16-year-old Russian adolescent, was brought in for family therapy by her parents, Boris and Hana, for "poor grades in school," "abusing alcohol and other drugs, "not respecting" their rules, and "associating with a loser group of peers." Apparently, Anna used to be a "good student" and was more cooperative with her parents until she entered high school. The family had lived in the United States for 10 years. The parents were given my name by Anna's school social worker. They were feeling totally frustrated and at their wits' end with Anna. Anna had been in individual therapy two times before for the same behavioral difficulties. Her biggest complaints about the parents were the following: "they yell and bitch too much," "they are too strict," and "I really hate when my mother calls my friends' houses to check up on me." According to the parents, "every day of the week" they "get into arguments and power struggles with Anna." Anna pointed out that she hates coming home after school because of her "parents' hassling" her "about every little thing." The parents and Anna were so pessimistic that they could not envision or even play around with the idea of a miracle happening (de Shazer, 1988). I got nowhere with the use of the coping and pessimistic questions (Berg & Miller, 1992). I was unable to establish a mutual treatment goal with Anna and her parents because they could not agree on anything together. During my subsystem session time, I gave Anna and her parents separately plenty of space to share their concerns and ventilate their frustrations. Anna's main wish was for me was to get the parents to "stop yelling and bitching" at her. The parents wanted to see all of Anna's negative behaviors changed all at once. Our first two family sessions were highly unproductive because of the intense conflict between Anna and her parents.

In our third session, however, I captured family members' interest and desire in working together in response to the famous guest consultant experiment. Since Boris was a university art history professor who favored modern art, he chose Pablo Picasso, René Magritte, and Andy Warhol as the famous people on his list. Hana's favorite pastime was reading, so on her list of famous people she had her two favorite authors, Agatha Christie and Isabel Allende. Anna had on her list the following famous people: Tom Cruise and the singer Pink. Each family member took a turn sharing why he or she had selected their famous people and how specifically they have been inspired by them. I then asked each family member to imagine putting themselves in the heads of these famous people and how they would solve their family difficulties. Thanks to Picasso, Magritte, and Warhol, Boris could see that "something novel and more creative" was needed with his parenting style. All of these artists were "quite skilled and versatile" in working with "a variety of art mediums" and "regularly reinventing themselves." With the help of Agatha Christie, Hana could see that she needed to "search for more clues" and "gain a better understanding of what was going on" with her daughter before she jumped to conclusions about how to best resolve her difficulties; she also recognized that "Agatha Christie would never nag at or yell at a potential suspect." For Anna, a lot of Pink's lyrics resonated with her about how she felt about her "own life." She began to cry and share with her parents a lot of the teen angst and sadness she was experiencing about the family situation. For the first time in one of our sessions, the parents reached out with affection to comfort Anna and convey their love to her. To close out our family session, the parents made a commitment to "stop yelling" and "be more supportive of Anna." Anna agreed to work on "following their rules better," let her "parents know more about what was going on" in her life, and try to "pick up" her "grades in school."

My Family Story Mural

The *my family story mural experiment* is particularly useful with adolescents strong in the *visual–spatial* and *intrapersonal intelligence areas* (Gardner, 1993, 1999) and *mixed-opinion*, *same*, or *worse* client group categories. This art experiment also is quite useful with adolescents who have a hard time expressing their thoughts and feelings. To begin the art experiment, I explain to adolescents that I would like them to use their artistic abilities and powers of imagination to draw with crayons or markers how they see the family drama or situation. They are then to give us a grand tour of their murals, explaining central family themes, the roles people play, family politics as they see it, and so forth. When processing their murals, they can also be asked what changes they would make in their murals and with their family stories or situations to make them better for them. Family members are asked to reflect on the adolescent's reflections about his or her mural. If there appears to be family disconnection issues, I may have the whole family group do the mural together. This can help foster connection building. I have used this art experiment in one-person family therapy with adolescents, as well. The my family story mural can be useful for uncovering potential barriers for change, family secrets, and bringing out the adolescent's voice more in the family drama. Often the parents and other family members learn a great deal from the adolescent about what he or she perceives as their family's major strengths as well as the most troubling aspects that he or she would like to see changed. This can dramatically alter family members' outmoded and unhelpful beliefs about the adolescent, change negative family interactions, and help improve their relationships with him or her.

Marne, a white 14-year-old severely depressed and self-harming adolescent, had grave difficulty in being able to tolerate family therapy sessions because of the intense conflict between her and her parents. According to Marne, her parents were always "stressed out" and "trying to play therapist" with her because in the past she had heavily brutalized her body with razors. Apparently, on a daily basis, "10 times a day," the parents would ask Marne, "How are you feeling? You're so quiet, what's wrong?" This annoyed her the most. When I saw Marne and her parents together, she would not open up about how she was doing or what she wished for them to change about their parenting styles.

Knowing that Marne was a gifted artist who excelled in the *visual–spatial intelligence area* (Gardner, 1993, 1999) and realizing that I had to do something different therapeutically, I took a risk and proposed the family story mural art experiment. Marne eagerly got to work and produced a very interesting and insightful product. She drew her parents and younger brothers large in the center of the sheet of paper. All the family members were closely and rigidly positioned next to one another, except for her mother, who was reaching out to touch Marne's father and her 12-year-old brother. Both the father and the brother had flat facial expressions with flat horizontal lines for mouths. Her mother was drawn wedged between the father and her brother. She was sporting a rigid semismile on her face. Her youngest brother was situated next to his older brother and had a smile on his face. Marne drew a tiny-sized version of herself, colored in gray, floating in space at a distance from her family. For the first time, Marne began to open up a great deal about the family patterns that troubled her the most, and she let me into her inner emotional world. When asked about the rigidity of family members' postures and their flat facial expression, she pointed out how family members were "depressed and worried about" her, her father was "depressed about his job situation," and the brother was also "bummed out" about the family atmosphere and worried about her. Marne pointed out that her mother's semismile represented her "putting up a good front to the outside world that her family is doing well." However, when there were "problems," she related, the mother became "highly worried." Out of all of the images Marne produced for her mural, the most troubling and striking one was her drawing of herself. When asked about drawing herself so small, she shared with me that she saw herself as "being insignificant." She drew herself in a gray color because she felt "dead inside." With the help of this art experiment, I gained a better understanding of Marne's oppressive life situation, learned about potential family target areas for intervention, and overall it helped to strengthen our therapeutic relationship.

The Imaginary Feelings X-Ray Machine

I like to use *the imaginary feelings x-ray machine experiment* with adolescents who are strong in the *visual–spatial* and *intrapersonal intelligence areas* (Gardner, 1993, 1999) and with *same* or *worse* client categories. This art experiment is particularly useful with adolescents who have grave difficulty in expressing their thoughts and feelings and may have somatic complaints. To begin with, I explain to the adolescent to imagine that I had a special x-ray machine that could show us pictures of what his or her feelings look like inside his or her body. The adolescent is to lie down on a long sheet of paper and pick a family member to draw the outline of his or her body when I turn the imaginary feelings x-ray machine on. Next, the adolescent is to draw pictures inside the outline of his or her body that depict how he or she thinks that his or her feelings look. When the x-ray is completed, he or she is to tell stories about each of the feelings. The pictures and their locations on the adolescent's body often are metaphors for their emotional reactions to past and present family difficulties. For example, one adolescent drew a sad face over her stomach to indicate how difficult it was to "digest" her "parents yelling at" her "all of the time." Throughout most of her adolescence, she was experiencing a "nervous stomach condition" without any physiological causes for it. Another adolescent, who was depressed and self-harming, drew flames burning near her heart to depict her "anger" with how she felt "jacked around" by past therapists, the psychiatric hospital staff she had worked with, and her school for "not listening" to her treatment expectations and not inviting her to take the lead in defining her goals for herself. This same client drew jagged lines "piercing into" her brain to represent her painful depressed feelings. Family members were then invited to reflect on the adolescent's x-ray. Similar to the my family story mural experiment, the adolescent's x-ray can have a profound impact on altering unhelpful family members' beliefs about him or her, and they can gain more insight into what has been troubling the adolescent the most with the family situation or in other social contexts. Often this can lead to improvements in family interactions and more support from family members. Adolescents' x-rays can also be used as a way to highlight changes in their coping abilities over time. An x-ray can be made at the beginning of treatment and further down the road, once change has occurred. Finally, the imaginary feelings x-ray experiment can also be used in individual sessions with the adolescent and in adolescent groups.

My Extraordinary Newspaper Headline

This fun in-session therapeutic experiment can be effective with adolescents strong in the *linguistic, visual–spatial,* and *interpersonal intelligence areas* (Gardner, 1993) and stretches their powers of imagination. I typically offer it to adolescents in the *same* or *worse* client category groups. The adolescent is to close his or her eyes and imagine three years from now picking up the front page of a major newspaper and reading a headline and an article about something extraordinary that they had done. The adolescent is to write down the headline and a few paragraphs about what they had done, the steps they had taken to achieve this great accomplishment or heroic act, how their incredible achievement or heroic act has benefited him or her and others, and so forth. This experiment can be quite effective with depressed or traumatized youth that have a hard time envisioning a brighter, more positive future. For them, it can inject positive emotion into their future realities and instill hope. Finally, the experiment may also offer the adolescent potential solution strategies for resolving his or her current difficulties.

Isabella, a 15-year-old Puerto Rican, was referred to me by her school social worker for depression and a major decline in her academic performance. Out of all of her major subjects, she was still able to maintain an A grade in her English class. Her parents had been divorced for 3 years, and she had very little contact with her father. Following her divorce, Patricia, the mother, actively dated and became a workaholic. Isabella complained about how her mother did not have much time for her. Although I had made some inroads in bringing Isabella and Patricia closer together, the former was still experiencing depressive symptoms. Knowing that Isabella was a gifted writer and an avid reader of science fiction and fantasy books, I offered her the extraordinary newspaper headline experiment to try during my individual session time with her. After 20 minutes, she came up with the following newspaper headline: "A Hispanic J. K. Rowling?" According to Isabella, the article stated at the age of 18 she had produced the first installment of a new Harry Potter-like book series. The writer of the newspaper article was comparing her writing abilities to those of J. K. Rowling and Lemony Snicket, author of the highly successful *Series of*

Unfortunate Events books. In addition, the writer stressed in the article how incredible it was that she was only 18 and the fact that she was the first Hispanic author to produce a new book series in the spirit of Harry Potter. When the writer asked how she had become such a talented writer, Isabella responded: "I express myself best in words and have a wild imagination." She further added, "I wanted to be the first Latina to write a Harry Potter-like book series. I also wanted the lead character to be a clever and strong teenaged girl." While describing her extraordinary headline and article, Isabella was smiling and her mood dramatically shifted for the better. Isabella spontaneously shared with me that this would be a good future goal for her to shoot for. From this session on, Isabella was propelled out of her depressive rut, picked up her grades, and stepped up her efforts to be an even better writer.

Adolescents' Mentoring Their Parents

When I am faced with adolescent case situations where the youth complains about feeling emotionally disconnected from or invalidated by one or both parents, I will introduce the *adolescents' mentoring their parents* connection-building experiment (Selekman, 2002). I have used this experiment with *mixed opinion*, *same*, or *worse* client category groups. After doing a careful assessment of what the adolescent's key intelligence and skill areas (Gardner, 1993, 1999) are, we will determine together how he or she can deploy them in a mentoring role in relationship to his or her parents. Adolescents who are strong in the *interpersonal intelligence area* (Gardner, 1993) particularly like this experiment. For 1 week, the adolescent will be put in charge of using his or her expertise in specific skill areas to teach one or both of his or her parents how to be more proficient in these skill areas or learn something completely new from their son or daughter that could benefit them. For example, a depressed and self-harming client longing to get closer to her father taught him how to bake bread and make a variety of cakes in 1 week's time. Apparently they had a lot of fun in the kitchen together. The father, a self-described "klutz," admitted that at the beginning of the week his baking projects were like "science projects that failed!" This powerful, fun, and meaningful experiment successfully strengthened the emotional connection between the father and daughter, which helped stabilize the adolescent's symptoms.

Interviewing the Problem

The *interviewing the problem experiment* was developed by Epston (1998, 2000) as a playful and effective method for liberating children and adolescents from the shackles of their oppressive problems. In addition, the in-session experiment can dramatically alter the adolescent's and family members' problem-saturated views and promote personal agency. I like to use this therapeutic experiment with adolescents who are strong in the *visual–spatial* and *bodily–kinesthetic intelligence areas* (Gardner, 1993, 1999) and with *same* or *worse* client category groups. After carefully co-constructing the family's presenting problem into an objectified tyrannical thing that has been getting the best of them, I have the adolescent pretend to play the role of the problem by stepping into its shoes and gaining a unique inside-looking-out perspective, seeing the world through its eyes and trying to think like it. I pretend to be a reporter for the local newspaper covering a story on the problem. Like a reporter, I want to get the "inside scoop" on the problem and secure answers to the following questions:

- "How did you get involved in this adolescent's life?"
- "Are you a friend or a foe?"
- "In what ways do you undermine this adolescent at school?"
- "What do you coach the parents to do that really pushes this adolescent's buttons?"
- "Why do you think you are the perfect problem for this adolescent and her family?"
- "I know that magicians don't like to share their secret tricks of the trade, but could you share one or two tricks you use with this adolescent that really gets the best of her?"
- "In what ways do the adolescent and her parents thwart your efforts to push them around?"
- "What would have to happen for you to leave this family for good?"

Tina, a 16-year-old white self-harming and depressed adolescent, was brought in for a family consultation by her therapist, who had been seeing them for 3 years. According to the therapist, Tina's "cutting" behavior and "depressive symptoms" had "increased over the past year." The therapist was feeling "very stuck." This coincided with the parents' divorcing and "continued warring after the breakup." Tina used to be very close to her father, however, this changed after he remarried. Nowadays they spent very little time together. Although the father, mother, and Tina's brother attended our meeting, only Tina and her mother felt like "the cutting was out of control." They spent a lot of time talking about the various ways the "cutting" was getting the best of them in different situations and contexts. For example, the mother talked about how the "cutting" situation with her daughter "consumed" her "mind at work" and affected her ability to "concentrate." Tina talked about how when she was "mad" or emotionally "hurt" by her dad or her friends her "mind would enter this zone" where "cutting" would take over and make her "carve on" her legs. In listening to how family members were describing the problem as if it had a life all of its own and knowing that Tina's strengths were drama, art, and athletics, I decided to try the interviewing the problem experiment. Tina thought this was a "cool idea." I had her put herself into the shoes of "cutting" and try to imagine how it thinks and in what ways it likes to brainwash Tina to self-injure and push her and her family, teachers at school, and her peer relationships around. In the process of interviewing "cutting," Tina became increasingly aware of how "cutting" was "ruining" her life by disfiguring her; for example, by leaving "bad scars" on her legs, it was preventing her from pursuing "the cheerleading squad" at her high school. She also got in touch with how "cutting" sabotaged a new relationship with a boy at school that she "really liked" who was "turned off by" her "scars." Family members spontaneously started asking questions of "cutting" as well. The mother asked in a sad tone of voice, "Why can't you leave Tina and me alone? I want to stop worrying about her all of the time." The father asked "cutting" what he did that "wasn't working." "Cutting" responded by saying, "It's what you *don't* do." Tina stepped out of her role and pointed out to her father that his lack of presence in her life was upsetting to her. When I asked "cutting" about the various ways Tina frustrates it, "cutting" gave some specific examples of what would be considered sparkling moments or personal victories for Tina. "Cutting" gets frustrated by Tina when she does the following: goes to "talk to" her "mother in privacy" about "what is bothering" her, calls "friends for support," or exercises "real hard" until she is "physically exhausted."

According to the therapist, this was the first time that Tina was able to open up about what was really bothering her and what coping strategies worked for her. By the end of the session, all family members agreed to work with Tina as a team to help support her continued efforts to conquer "cutting."

Visualizing Movies of Success

Visualizing movies of success (Selekman, 1997) is a useful visualization and coping tool to help adolescents disrupt oppressive self-defeating thoughts or to avoid the temptation to cave into problem patterns of behavior like self-harming, bingeing and purging, and substance abuse. This experiment is particularly effective with adolescents who are strong in the *visual–spatial* and *bodily–kinesthetic intelligence areas* (Gardner, 1993). I would also use this experiment with *mixed opinion*, *same*, or *worse* client group categories.

The adolescent is asked to close her eyes and capture a sparkling moment in the past when she performed with excellence in some activity, amazed herself with how well she handled a difficult situation, or that marked a major high point in her life. I have the adolescent apply all of her senses to the experience and describe in great detail everything she sees on the movie screen in her mind, including color and motion. This visualization experiment should be practiced once a day for 10–15 minutes until the adolescent can easily turn the movie on or off in her mind like a light switch.

Stephanie, a depressed and self-harming 16-year-old, was referred to me for her problems with "cutting." In the past, Stephanie used to be a star soccer player until she started to experience peer rejection issues and difficulties with depression. She felt like her cutting behavior was out of control. Whenever she would feel "real down" or experience some form of rejection from her peers, Stephanie would reach for "anything sharp" and begin cutting her "upper thighs." This would numb away her emotional distress. Since Stephanie was strong in the *visual–spatial intelligence area* (Gardner, 1993) and eager to learn some new coping skills, I taught her the visualizing movies of success tool. The sparkling moment that Stephanie projected onto her mind's movie screen was her scoring the winning goal for her team in front of her family and relatives. Apparently, the scoring kick she had made was from a severe angle to the right of the goal. In listening closely to Stephanie's very detailed movie of success, I could picture in my mind how difficult this shot was to make from that angle. I jokingly shared with her that even the English football star David Beckham would have found that kick to be difficult! Over time, Stephanie found this coping tool to be very useful in helping her better manage her "down" moods, peer difficulties, and overcome the urge to cut herself.

Therapeutic Letters

In addition to the gratitude letter (Seligman, 2002, 2003), I like to use letters in therapy as a way to engage important family members and to effectuate changes in larger systems in which the presenting problem is occurring, particularly in the school context. I typically use letters with families in the *same* or *worse* client group categories. When I have a case in which the adolescent is experiencing intense conflict with a particular teacher, I have the adolescent's parents prepare a letter for this teacher. The following case example illustrates the use of one of my client's letters to a teacher.

Ron had been referred to me for being disruptive in class and getting poor grades. He had a highly conflictive relationship with his English teacher. Ron's mother and I constructed the following letter to his English teacher that Ron was to hand-deliver.

> *Dear Miss Brown:*
>
> *I greatly appreciate your patience and concern with Ron. He can be really difficult to live with at times. I want to see him turn things around in your class-*

room too, so I gave him an assignment for the day in your class. I have asked him to notice what things you do in the class that he really likes and to write those things down and tell me about them tonight. Thank you for everything.

Sincerely,
Barbara Black

According to Barbara, Ron came home from school reporting "five" things that he liked about Miss Brown. In fact, the biggest exception or change was Miss Brown's praising him for coming up with the "right answer" in class. This therapeutic strategy had a major impact on Ron's relationship with Miss Brown. They had developed mutual respect for each other. Ron's disruptive behavior in the classroom stopped, and he ended up getting a B grade from Miss Brown.

The Therapeutic Debate and Splitting the Team

Sheinberg (1985) and Papp (1983) utilize the therapeutic debate as a team strategy with stuck and entrenched families. This team strategy is particularly useful with *same* or *worse* client group categories. Adolescents involved in their schools' drama programs and who excel in the *bodily–kinesthetic intelligence area* (Gardner, 1993, 1999) often enjoy the theatrics of the team members and join in on the debate. The therapist in the room always takes the prochange position and sides with the whole family group, while one team member takes the side of the parents and the other team member can take the side of the adolescent. More recently, to make the team debate more lively and interesting, I have added a third team member who will represent the identified presenting problem. This team member will provide an intriguing inside-looking-out perspective through the eyes and mind of the problem (Selekman, 2002). Family members are free to chime in and join the therapeutic debate when they hear something intriguing, feel misunderstood, agree with team members, learn something new about their situation, and so forth.

When working alone, I often bring my peer supervising colleague into the therapy room in spirit and enlist the family to work with me in proving him wrong. I have found this therapeutic strategy to be particularly effective with chronic adolescent substance-abusing and highly oppositional adolescents and their families (Todd & Selekman, 1991). Some of my most difficult adolescent clients have surprised me with their responses to my pessimistic peer supervisor's predictions about their relapsing in the future. After the first round of proving the pessimistic peer supervisor wrong, I tell the youth in the next session that the former is "still pessimistic" about him or her "remaining straight" and that "we made a lunch bet over our disagreement about your progress." Adolescents have responded to my pessimistic peer supervisor's grim predictions with comments like "I'll save you money on lunch!," "We will prove him wrong!," or "Where is that guy? He doesn't know a thing!"

Peer Reflecting Teams

With some stuck difficult adolescent cases, I explore with the parents and the adolescent whether we can enlist the services of the latter's peers who have experienced similar difficulties with their own parents, to serve as consultants to help us out (Selekman, 1995). This team strategy is particularly useful with adolescents strong in the *interpersonal intelligence area* (Gardner, 1993, 1999) and with families in the *same* or *worse* client group categories. Once the parents and youth agree to bring in the peers, I ask the parents to call the peers' parents and get their approval to have their son or daughter participate in the therapy. A special consent form will also be signed to protect client confidentiality and to get written permission from the peers' parents to involve them in the client's family therapy.

After the peers have been engaged for the consultation session, they either are positioned behind the family as a group in the therapy room or observe from behind the one-way mirror. Approximately 40 minutes into the hour, we will either turn our chairs around in the therapy room and listen to the peer group's reflections or switch rooms and go behind the one-way mirror to listen to their reflections. The family is in charge of deciding how the reflecting team will be positioned. Following the peer group's 10-minute reflections on our impasse situation, the family and I then reflect on their ideas. In using this peer team strategy, families and I have found the peers' ideas to be highly pragmatic and very creative. The case example below demonstrates the utility of this team strategy.

Polly had been referred to me by her school counselor for "cutting classes," "being truant" from school, and "conflicts with her teachers." The parents had decided to ground Polly for "2 months" as punishment for her school problems. My first two sessions with Polly and her parents were stormy. An intense blame–counterblame pattern of interaction occurred among the threesome. I was without a team on this case and could have greatly benefited from having one, particularly because I was feeling stuck. In each session, I broke up the family and met separately with the parents and Polly to help disrupt this vicious pattern of interaction. There were no exceptions identified, and the family could not envision possible future miracles ever occurring. Neither the parents nor Polly would budge from rigidly maintaining their polarized positions about how things should be. I was unable to negotiate any realistic or solvable treatment goals with the family. While meeting alone with Polly in the second session, I shared with her that I was feeling stuck and wondered if she had any girlfriends who had once had similar difficulties with their parents that we might want to invite to our next session. Polly became quite excited about the prospect of having her friends help us out with her parents. The parents were also receptive to the idea of doing something different and having Polly's friends come to our next family session to help us "brainstorm some new ideas."

In the third session the atmosphere was lighter in the room, and we all waited to hear the peer group's wisdom about what we needed to do differently. Two of Polly's closest friends came to our session. One peer used the metaphor of a "tug-of-war" match to describe what appeared to be going on between Polly and her parents. She also shared that the same "tug-of-war" situation had occurred with her and her parents. Her parents' solution had been to "let go of the rope" and make her fall on her "butt." At that point, she had begun improving her behavior, because "putting up a fight was not working." Another peer shared that when her parents had become "less rigid" with the consequences and were willing to make compromises, her behavior had turned around.

When asked to reflect on the peers' reflections, the parents and Polly found hearing their stories informative. Polly's parents began to spontaneously discuss with Polly whether she felt they were being too extreme with the "2-month grounding" situation. This was a different kind of interaction than the former blame–counterblame variety. The end result of this productive family discussion was a quid pro quo contract that I helped negotiate between Polly and her parents. Polly's original grounding period would be reduced to "2 weeks," provided that Polly would attend her classes and not "mouth off" to her teachers. The peer reflecting team helped us move from a stuck position in treatment and opened up space for new possibilities. Future therapy sessions involved amplifying changes, consolidating gains, and collaborating with school personnel.

TERMINATION IN SOLUTION-ORIENTED BRIEF FAMILY THERAPY

In my mind, when clients can make distinctions between their old problem-saturated beliefs and behavior and their new worldview and solution-maintaining patterns of interaction, change has clearly occurred. Consolidating questions are effective tools for eliciting family members' "news of a difference." Some helpful consolidating questions to ask in a final session with a family are "What would you have to do to go backwards?," "What will you have to do to prevent a major backslide?," and "What will you have to continue to do to keep these changes happening?" I also use my trusty imaginary crystal ball (de Shazer, 1985) and videotape metaphor (O'Hanlon & Weiner-Davis, 1989) to have clients share with me a detailed picture of what future changes they envision themselves making. To conclude this section, I address the controversial "flight into health" issue in brief therapy and discuss how I like to celebrate families' therapeutic changes.

Flight into Health or Satisfied Enough?

When working briefly with families, it is not uncommon, after rapid changes occur early in treatment or while on a longer time interval vacation from therapy, that clients drop out of treatment (Weiner-Davis et al., 1987). Is this a flight into unqualified ideal health? I do not think so. Clients are quick to tell us if they are experiencing difficulties while they are on a vacation from therapy. Parents do not hesitate to make an emergency appointment when the situation worsens or when a crisis occurs. In addition, if we were previously regularly eliciting from our clients feedback on the quality of our therapeutic relationship, their progress with goal attainment, and attended to their concerns, we were seeking thereby to maximize client satisfaction and solidify their treatment gains.

By sending families on vacations from therapy, I am conveying to them my confidence in their ability to cope and function well without me. Similar to my belief that clients should take the lead in determining what the goals of therapy should be, I believe that clients should be in charge of deciding when they would like to stop coming for therapy. As a solution-oriented therapist, I do not believe my job is to "cure" people but, rather, to help clients have more satisfactory life experiences. If clients call to cancel future scheduled appointments because they feel things are better for the time being, I always let them know that I have an open-door policy and if they need to schedule a future tune-up session they may feel free to call me.

Celebrating Therapy Changes with Families

Whenever possible, I like to make final therapy sessions memorable events. Different cultures worldwide celebrate rites of passage throughout the life cycle with ceremonies and the exchanging of gifts. I like to celebrate a family's rite of passage in moving from a problem-saturated context to a context of change. This end-of-therapy celebration ritual helps further empower families to take pride and joy in conquering their oppressive problems. I have thrown parties in probation officers' offices to celebrate my clients getting off of probation. Having been influenced by the innovative work of White and Epston (1990) and Durrant and Coles (1991), I will give family members certificates, pins, trophies, ribbons, and cakes to celebrate their victories over their oppressive problems. Another powerful way to celebrate families' goal attainment is to have them invite in for the last session an audience composed of key members of their social networks to reflect on their changes and honor their achievements (Selekman, 2002; Epston, 2000; White, 1995). By doing this, the therapist can be less central in the lives of his or her clients and hand them off to their social support systems. Finally, having clients prepare their own *reflection letters* from therapy, reflecting on the highlights of their change journey and what wisdom and new ideas they plan to take with them from your work together and continue to put to use in the future, can also help consolidate their gains. The family members' reflection letters can be read aloud to their invited guests from their social networks. The case examples below illustrate how I like to celebrate clients' changes at the end of therapy.

Bonnie, a 16-year-old, had been dragged into therapy by her parents for her chronic running away, heavy polysubstance abuse problems, and gang involvement. After eight sessions of therapy over 6 months, Bonnie had stopped running away and abusing chemicals. Because the family had had 16 past therapy experiences, the team and I were quite concerned that the family would spend the rest of their lives in therapy. In order to help break this pattern of family involvement with mental health professionals and to further empower the family, I had Bonnie and her mother write their own discharge summary from our therapy experience. In their discharge summary, they were instructed to list all of the changes they had made. They were also asked to mail copies of their discharge summary to all their former therapists. The family generated a list of six major changes they wanted former therapists to read about in their discharge summary, as follows: (1) "We have made it, in spite of all of your diagnoses!"; (2) "You can reason with Bonnie better"; (3) "No more knock-down, drag-out fights"; (4) "Bonnie doesn't run away"; (5) "Bonnie comes home on time a lot"; and (6) "Bonnie seems to have gone 'straight' [drug-free]." Surprisingly, the family did not mention how the running away problem had been resolved. To help make this latter change more "newsworthy," I presented the family with an achievement certificate for "Taming the Running Away Monster." Both Bonnie and her mother were touched by the achievement certificate they had received for conquering the Running Away Monster that had been oppressing them for 5 years. The next case example illustrates how I like to celebrate when adolescents get off probation in therapy sessions. In many cases, celebrating the termination of probation coincides with the conclusion of therapy.

Randy, a white 16-year-old delinquent boy, had been placed on probation for bicycle and car radio theft, marijuana abuse, and frequent police involvement. While on probation, Randy had violated a number of his probationary guidelines and ended up serving a month in the juvenile detention center. While in the "juvie" (Randy's language), Randy had gotten into a fight with a rival gang member. He was placed in solitary confinement for 3 days and was evaluated by the court-appointed psychologist. After completing his psychological testing session with Randy, the psychologist had shared with him that he would most likely end up back in the "juvie" 3 weeks after getting out.

In my first family session with Randy and his mother, I learned about the psychologist's grim prediction. I set up a theoretical bet between Randy and myself versus the pessimistic psychologist. Randy confidently vowed that he would prove the psychologist wrong by successfully terminating his probation 9 months later. I ended up seeing Randy and his mother six times over the 9-month period. In our sixth and final session together, I brought in a cake to celebrate the end of Randy's probation and the end of therapy. Prior to our last session together, Randy had written a beautiful letter that he planned to send to the psychologist in the "juvie." In the letter, Randy pointed out that he "remembered" the psychologist's prediction that he would end up back in the "juvie" 3 weeks after getting out. Randy also made it clear in his letter that the psychologist had underestimated his strengths and his ability to "turn things around" when the going "gets rough." After Randy read the letter, his mother and I gave him a standing ovation and encouraged him to mail the letter to the psychologist. The remainder of the session involved amplifying and consolidating family gains and having cake to celebrate Randy's great achievement.

Another way I celebrate clients' changes at the end of therapy is to induct them into my "Alumni Association." As part of the induction process, they have to agree when called upon to assist me in the future with my stuck family cases. I have found it quite useful to tap former clients' expertise and utilize them as guest consultants with other families I am working with or in the solution-oriented parenting groups I am running. The use of adolescent alumni has been most effective with youth that have been strongly affiliated with a negative peer group and desperately need a more positive peer support system until they can make some new friends.

SUMMARY

In this chapter, I have presented practical guidelines for selecting and matching therapeutic experiments with family members' key intelligence areas and cooperative response patterns in second and subsequent sessions. Seventeen therapeutic experiments were presented that tap family members' strengths and imagination powers and can produce rapid and transformative individual and relationship changes in the families. I also discussed the importance of therapists devoting ample session time for consolidating family members' gains, inquiring about and addressing any concerns they may have, and making the necessary therapeutic adjustments to better meet the clients' needs. By so doing, we can empower our clients to stay on track and make further meaningful future changes.

Ten

The Solution-Oriented Parenting Group

Empowering Parents to Be the Agents of Change

> Good parents give their children Roots and Wings. Roots to know where home is and wings to fly away and exercise what's been taught them.
>
> —JONAS SALK

With some families that are referred to us, despite our best efforts to engage their powerful and challenging adolescents, the only family members we may have available to us are one or both of their dethroned and pessimistic parents. These parents may report that they had had their adolescents in individual therapy for years or they had attempted family therapy a few times in the past and were left ill equipped to manage their adolescents' most challenging behaviors. Many therapists believe that if the powerful and reluctant adolescent cannot be engaged for treatment, family therapy will prove to be futile. However, parents also have a tendency to underestimate their resourcefulness and creativity and may have forgotten about their past successes in constructively managing their adolescents and other siblings' difficult behaviors. One treatment alternative that can be employed when the adolescent is reluctant to participate in family therapy despite the therapists' and parents' Herculean efforts to involve him or her in the treatment process is the solution-oriented parenting group (Selekman, 1991, 1993, 1999).

AN EVOLVING SOLUTION-ORIENTED PARENTING GROUP MODEL

The solution-oriented parenting group has been evolving since 1988. Unlike most parenting groups, the solution-oriented parenting group places a strong emphasis on the parents' strengths, resourcefulness, and creativity and arms them with "hands-on" therapeutic strategies and tools that they can put to immediate use. Parents are viewed as co-collaborators and the lead authors of the kind of solution-determined stories they would like to create with their adolescents. In addition to empowering parents as the agents of change, I have added a stronger educational component to the group, informing parents about important research findings regarding empirically based parenting tools, identifying and utilizing their adolescents' natural resiliency protective factors, learned optimism, positive emotion, and the characteristics of strong families. Finally, I have been making much more use of the group process over the years to encourage the exchange of novel and creative ideas from the parents and the normalization of common parenting struggles on the home front.

Like all parenting group therapy approaches, the original solution-oriented parenting group has had its limitations with certain parenting and family situations (Selekman, 1991, 1993, 1999). Some highly pessimistic and angry parents had felt that the solution-oriented parenting group was a very supportive context for the difficult situations they were grappling with, and they had not felt all alone with their plights; however, their adolescents had changed very little or not at all. In some cases, this was due to their teens' strong affiliation with negative peer groups and the need for direct intervention with them; or, another critical intervention area that had not been addressed and that was contributing to keeping things stuck and maintaining the status quo was the involvement of multiple helping professionals from larger systems. Other challenging parenting situations in the past have been engaging and retaining low-functioning parents and parents presenting with their own mental health and substance abuse issues. Finally, two other important parenting topic areas that had not been addressed in the past are helping parents to learn how to prevent emotional disconnection in their family relationships and empowering them as advocates for their adolescents in managing difficulties experienced in their schools or related larger systems.

In an effort to better meet the needs of contemporary parents, I have incorporated into this edition some new therapeutic strategies and tools and research-based educational material and have added two more group topic areas in the next section. This is followed by brief discussions on the mechanics of the group, the role of the group leaders, and a detailed session-by-session overview of the group.

EXPANDING THE PARENTING GROUP MODEL

In this section, I discuss six new components to the solution-oriented parenting group that have greatly contributed to better parental outcome results and helped make the group experience more meaningful for parents and the group leaders alike. Case illustrations are provided throughout this discussion.

Thinking in Circles

Often, when parents begin the solution-oriented parenting group, they come armed with a laundry list of behaviors they want to see changed; typically they have experienced treatment failure(s) with their adolescents, are pessimistic, and engage in a complainant style of interaction with the group leaders (Selekman, 1993, 1997; de Shazer, 1988). They are oblivious to the active support they provide in sustaining the problems in their families! Initially, these parents do not include themselves as part of the solution construction process. Most therapists have encountered parents who want to drop their adolescents off at the therapist's office to be *fixed* while they go off and run errands for the next hour. As early as the first group session we counter this parental pattern and way of thinking by introducing the parents to the system's concept of *circularity* (Palazzoli et al., 1980; Bateson, 1979). On a flip chart or blackboard, the group leaders map out a participant's circular problem-maintaining sequence of interaction. In Figure 10.1, I have mapped out a couple's problem-maintaining interaction with their recalcitrant and oppositional son. Readers can clearly see that the more divided parents are in how they manage their son's challenging behaviors, the more oppositional and disrespectful the son behaves toward them. For many parents, this exercise becomes a newsworthy experience for them. Parents begin to see as early as the first session that they not only have to change their ways of viewing problem situations but also have to alter their patterns of interactions with their adolescents in order to break up the problem life-support systems that they are very much a part of.

Since most people learn best through visual means, and 80% of our brain's activity is involved in visual processing (Ostrander, Schroeder, & Ostrander, 1994), mapping out parental problem-maintaining sequences of interactions or having the leaders role-play these issues can be a powerful and effective way to get parents to abandon unhelpful problem-solving efforts. My colleagues and I like to use the mapping out of circles and role playing throughout the course of the group training with parents stuck in unproductive behaviors. We invite other group participants stuck in similar interactive patterns with their adolescents to share their experiences and what they have done to break out of the vicious circles. We also invite group members who are making good progress or have already attained their goals to map out their solution-maintaining circles of success, an exercise that is highly informative and useful to other members of the group.

The mother attempts to set a limit on her son about his wanting to go out with his friends Friday night. He had been grounded for the weekend for curfew violation and getting a school detention.

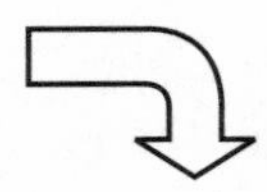

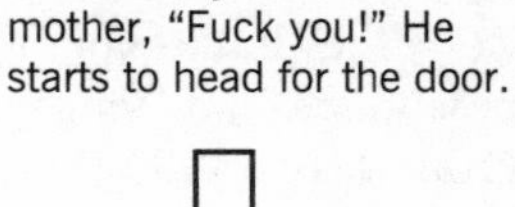

The son says to his mother, "Fuck you!" He starts to head for the door.

The mother screams at him for being so disrespectful and irresponsible.

The son continues to swear at her. They begin to argue.

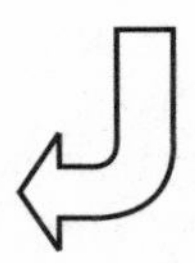

The father, in a laid-back fashion, tries to calm both of them down.

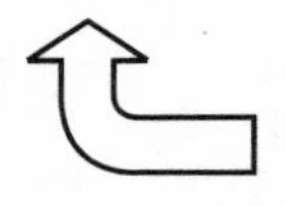

Feeling unsupported by her husband, she begins to blame him for not placing limits on the son.

The couple begin to argue in front of the son.

The son leaves the house to go rendezvous with his friends.

FIGURE 10.1. Mapping out a parent's problem-maintaining sequence of interaction.

Interestingly enough, the most frequently reported helpful aspect of the parents' group is learning how to "think in circles." One couple that found this to be the case used to lock horns and argue in front of their 16-year-old substance-abusing son while attempting to discipline him. Needless to say, these arguments would serve to neutralize the parents' authority and enable their son to continue abusing these drugs. After we mapped out the couple's problem-maintaining circle on the flip chart, they found themselves making a concerted effort in and out of group sessions to avoid arguing with each other. This paved the way for the couple to become a unified team, better enabling them to take a tough stance with their son about discontinuing his drug use.

Educating Parents about Important Research-Informed Ideas and Tools

Another integral component of the parenting group that has undergone expansion is the educational portions of the first, third, and sixth group sessions. In addition to teaching the parents the seven core solution-oriented parenting assumptions in the first group session, we like to educate them about important research findings on resilient children, learned optimism, positive emotion, and the characteristics of strong families.

Over the past 20 years, researchers have identified a number of core resiliency protective factors of at-risk children and adolescents who were living in high-stress family and community environments (Haggerty, Sherrod, Garmezy, & Rutter, 1994; Wolin & Wolin, 1993; Anthony, 1984, 1987). Some of the most critical resiliency protective factors cited by these researchers are:

- Strong parent–child relationship.
- Caring and supportive parents.
- Optimistic parental explanatory styles.
- Strong social skills.
- Effective and creative problem-solving abilities.
- Pronounced self-sufficiency.
- Good management of emotions.
- Low levels of family conflict.

My colleagues and I have found it to be quite useful to engage parents in a dialogue about which resiliency protective factors their adolescents and they possess and how they have put these natural abilities to good use to overcome adversity or crises in their lives. Not only does this discussion help make parents more aware of both these natural resources their adolescents and they possess, but it is a reminder of their past successes and abilities to cope with and resolve tough situations. In addition, helping parents become more aware of both their adolescents' and their own resourcefulness can boost their self-confidence, hope, and optimism levels. Finally, parents deadlocked in destructive interactions with their adolescents—such as constantly blaming them, not being supportive, or emotionally disengaging from them—may find these empirically based findings newsworthy and begin to change their interactions with their adolescents.

Seligman (2002, 2003) has demonstrated in his research that parental optimism can serve a protective function in helping to reduce the risk that adolescents will develop anxiety and mood disorders. His latest research indicates that the mean age for having a first depressive episode is 15 years of age. Seligman (2003) contends that one of the most important life skills we can teach children and adolescents is how to be "ace disputers." This entails teaching them how to search for evidence to counteract any self-defeating or pessimistic thoughts, to seek and entertain alternative explanations for negative experiences that occur, and to decatastrophize—that is, calm themselves down and think about constructive options to pursue—when experiencing stressful situations or being pushed around by self-defeating thoughts (Seligman et al., 1995). Once parents learn these helpful cognitive skills, they can practice using these skills to manage personal stressors, model their use for their adolescents when faced with life challenges and disappointments, and teach these tools to their adolescents. Through the use of role playing, we like to demonstrate for parents how to speak the language of change with their adolescents. The group leaders role-play a scene in which the adolescent has failed a test in one of her classes and is quite visibly devastated by this. The father begins the conversation by validating the daughter's feelings and offering empathy. This is followed by the father's saying: "I know this was a real disappointment for you, but I am confident that you will take the necessary steps to do better on the next test. After you do well on the next test, you will have picked up your grade and forgotten about this day." In the role play, the daughter responds to her father by holding her head up and being more hopeful. This role play often triggers group discussion, in that most parents have been faced with this situation with their adolescents; however, they often report having responded to their adolescents by lecturing them or yelling.

Positive psychologist Barbara Fredrickson's groundbreaking research has demonstrated that inducing positive emotions in individuals enables them to successfully achieve the following: strengthen their resiliency protective factors and coping abilities, greatly enhance their problem-solving abilities, build enduring personal resources (physical, psychological, intellectual, and social), loosen the grip of negative emotions on their minds and bodies, and produce upward spirals of personal growth over time (Fredrickson, 2002). Similarly, Gottman (1994) found in his research with 700 couples that those couples who were more likely to stay married 10 or more years engaged in 5 to 1 positive to negative interactions daily. With 94% accuracy, Gottman and his colleagues could predict which marriages would succeed or result in divorce based on their interactions. Both Fredrickson's and Gottman's research provides compelling evidence for the importance of parents constantly striving to create positive and inviting environments in their homes, to reduce the negativity and criticism, and to become more skilled at positive attending—that is, catching their adolescents at their best in terms of taking responsibility, being respectful, and making good choices. Whenever their adolescents are taking such positive steps, parents need to consistently respond with praise and encouragement to "keep up the good work." Finally we encourage parents in our groups to strive to achieve the daily goal of 5 to 1 positive to negative interactions with their adolescents.

Stinnett and O'Donnell (1996) interviewed a large sample of adolescents about what they would consider characteristics of strong families. The adolescents and researchers identified six characteristics:

1. Appreciation
2. Time together
3. Commitment
4. Communication
5. Dealing with crisis in a positive way
6. Spiritual wellness

Appreciation

The adolescents in the study reported that their families often expressed appreciation for them and acknowledged their accomplishments and positive qualities. The parental expression of appreciation was identified by adolescents as significantly contributing to their self-esteem and confidence building.

Time Together

One common theme in the study was that the adolescents' parents made themselves available to engage in quality time with their children. Often, the adolescents in the study felt that they had a key voice in determining the activity selected. Adolescent developmental research indicates that adolescents need to feel a strong sense of emotional and physical connection to their parents, despite their concurrent developmental need for more autonomy (Reimers et al., 1992; Papini & Roggman, 1992; Grotevant & Cooper, 1983).

Commitment

According to Stinnett and O'Donnell (1996), "the families of the adolescents possessing a high degree of wellness shared a special kind of love—a love that does not change with mood swings, hard times, or the passage of years. It is love that is conscious and unconditional. It says, 'I decide and promise to love you because of who you are, not because of what you do or how I feel'" (p. 46). Commitment was also reflected in family members' strong commitment to the well-being of the family.

Communications

Adolescents reported that their parents were able to keep the lines of communication open with them regardless of what issues or problems were presented to them. The adolescents in the study felt that their parents were good listeners and did not blame or attack them verbally.

Dealing with Crisis in a Positive Way

Another important characteristic of strong families identified by adolescents in the study was the way their families managed crisis situations in a positive manner. The parents maintained an optimistic stance in the face of crisis, and the families pulled together as a team to attack the issues or problems they were confronted with.

Spiritual Wellness

Stinnett and O'Donnell (1996) found in their study that strong families described their spiritual lives in various ways, including faith in God, a deep sense of purpose in life, concern for others, ethical and moral behavior, and a sense of unity with all living things. Spiritual wellness was identified as an important resource by many of the adolescents who participated in the study.

Externalizing the Problem and Coauthoring Parental Preferred Stories

My colleagues and I have found the innovative therapeutic ideas of Michael White and David Epston to be most helpful to use in our clinical work with adolescents and their families (White, 1985; White & Epston, 1990; Epston, 1998). We have particularly found the use of externalization of the problem (White & Epston, 1990; Epston, 1998), and unique account and redescription questions (White, 1988b) to be most effective with parents who have been oppressed by their problems for a long time. In one of our solution-oriented parenting groups, one parent was chronically oppressed by her tendency to "cave into nagging." After eliciting her emotionality and frustration around habitually "falling prey to nagging," the group leaders recommended that she keep track over the next week of what she does to "stand up to nagging and not allow it to push her around." In the next group session, this mother came up with three strategies to "avoid accepting invitations" from nagging: "Biting my tongue," "Being less reactive to small stuff," and "Creating a reward system for chore completion." These strategies proved to be helpful for the mother in gaining more cooperation from her oppositional 15-year-old son.

In second and subsequent sessions, we like to use unique account and redescription questions (White, 1988b) as a way to further amplify and consolidate the gains parents are making in their challenging roles as well as in the area of goal attainment. Some examples of these questions are:

- "How did you manage to take that step?"
- "What did you tell yourself to pull that off?"
- "How do you view yourself now, as a parent, as opposed to the former you before you began this group?"
- "What new ideas have you developed about yourself as a parent that you would want to share with other parents outside this group?"
- "As you continue to pioneer a new direction with your creative parenting, what will be the next step you will successfully accomplish?"

Externalizing and unique account and redescription questions have a liberating effect on parents paralyzed by their chronic problems. Through engaging in externalizing conversations with parents, we help them to re-story their lives and author more preferred stories of parenthood.

Using Group Process as a Resource

Over the years, my colleagues and I have come to recognize the therapeutic advantages of relying more heavily on the group process to empower its members. Parent participants never cease to amaze us with the sound wisdom, strengths, and resources they bring to the group. Therefore, by the third and later sessions, we have found it to be beneficial to the group for the leaders to be less central and less active in the group process. This is not to say that the leaders should be passive and not cheerlead and actively consolidate parental gains, but they should avoid overkill with this kind of therapeutic activity. The leaders use curiosity (Selekman, 1997) and open-ended conversational questions (Selekman, 2002; Andersen, 1991; Anderson & Goolishian, 1988a) with the parents to help elicit their support, as well as personal experiences in grappling with specific problems, and their expertise and past successes. Beside the upbeat and positive climate the leaders strive to create in the group, which promotes parental growth and change, we believe that any given solution-oriented parenting group possesses many of the curative factors described in Yalom (1975). Examples of these are cohesiveness, self-understanding, and instilling hope, altruism, and identification (pp. 83–100).

One of our solution-oriented parenting groups was conducted at a therapeutic day school for severely behavior-disordered adolescents. A mother who was regaining her authority and in a better place at managing her substance-abusing and oppositional son's behavior reached out to another mother in the group who was feeling "defeated" and "abused" by her "out-of-control" son who was exhibiting similar behavioral difficulties. Both parents had had their sons in every form of treatment, including residential. First, the more assured mother validated the defeated mother's feelings and self-disclosed that she had "been to hell and back" with her son "when things were at their all-time worst." Second, she invited the defeated mother to attend a family support group that she had been attending and found extremely supportive for parents who have experienced similar difficulties. We encouraged the helpful mother to share with the other mother and the rest of the group more information about this wonderful self-help group.

Connection-Building Parenting Practices

Nowadays, our media-driven and materialistic cultural landscape seduces young people into consuming recklessly, replaces human contact with a chat room or computer game, and greatly contributes to the disintegration of family relationships. Other aggravating factors contributing to the emotional disconnection process in families include our volatile economy and the high level of job lay-offs afflicting workers nationwide. Parents today are emotionally spent and scrambling to keep their families financially afloat. In some cases, it is difficult for parents to have anything left to give their children emotionally or to even have the energy to spend quality time with their families. However, parents need to find a way to actively and constructively manage these aggravating factors and stressors and be emotionally present for their adolescents.

As much as teenagers wish to have more independence, they also need to know that their parents are available to them for emotional support when they are struggling to cope with stressors in their lives. The stronger their attachments are and more positive involvement they have with their parents, the more self-confidence and self-worth they will have. Parents can further strengthen their relationships with their children by being good listeners, consistently validating their thoughts and feelings, showing empathy, conveying unconditional positive regard, and modeling optimism when their kids are having a rough time or get into trouble. Other effective connection-building practices we like to teach parents are the importance of regularly eliciting their adolescents' feedback on how well they are doing with their parenting, reinstating former parental behaviors that conveyed their love, appreciation, and commitment to their adolescents, and carving out weekly protected time together to engage in activities that their adolescents like to do with them.

Empowering Parents to Be Advocates for Their Kids in Larger Systems

One critical parental topic and skill area that has not been addressed in other parenting skills programs and is rarely covered in groups for parents is teaching them how to effectively collaborate with involved helping professionals from larger systems. Often, therapists assume that parents are deficient in this skill area and lack the appropriate negotiation skills and the resourcefulness to ensure that their adolescents' needs are being met rather than ignored or mismanaged in the various larger systems that affect them.

George and his colleagues (1999) empower parents by having them rehearse being successful in "doing justice" for themselves and their adolescents at a future scheduled school or other larger systems meeting with powerful and important helping professionals. Parents could be asked the following questions:

- "Let's say you already had the individual educational planning [IEP] meeting for your son with all of the big school district officials present, and it went really well and you know that you really did justice to yourself and got what you wanted for your son at the meeting. You're feeling a strong sense of pride in yourself and think back to how you pulled it off. What would you be remembering about how you were feeling and thinking before you went into the meeting?"
- "What steps will you tell me you took to get what you wanted for your son in the IEP meeting?"

Besides capitalizing on parents' natural negotiation and people skills that they are already using effectively at their workplaces or in the parenting realm, parents can be taught other helpful negotiation skills, such as how to honor helping professionals' problem views and *commitments* or positions that are driving their attempted solutions (Kegan & Lahey, 2001) and how to use *suspension* (Isaacs, 1999)—that is, how to suspend judgment—when faced with rigid or difficult helping professionals who are not supportive of their wishes for their adolescents. Once parents develop some confidence using these tools, they can intervene early and resolve any budding conflicts or difficulties between their adolescents and the helpers in these larger systems. Ideally, we want to help parents learn how to take the *third side* (Ury, 2000) in their interactions with larger systems professionals, which consists of:

- Seeking to understand both sides of the conflict or problem involving their adolescents.
- Encouraging a process of cooperative negotiation and speaking out about any blatant mismanagement of their adolescents' rights and needs.
- Supporting an inclusive solution that fairly meets the essential needs of both sides.

"The third side" negotiation framework, developed by master negotiator William Ury, is applicable not only to parenting, larger systems, and communities but to global disputes as well.

When parents are successful at mediating conflicts between their adolescents and school personnel and with other involved helping professionals, their adolescents appreciate their efforts. In addition, this parental activity also models for their adolescents how to constructively manage conflicts.

THE MECHANICS OF THE GROUP

The solution-oriented parenting group consists of eight 1½-hour sessions, which combines short didactic presentations by the leaders, in-session skill-building exercises, intersession refreshment breaks for the parents, editorial reflections by the leaders, and weekly skill-based therapeutic assignments for the parents to experiment with. The parents are often given longer time interval breaks, or vacations, between sessions 6 and 8 as a vote of confidence for their great progress and hard work put into achieving their goals.

We like to limit the group size to 8 parents. This may end up being a combination of couples and single parents. Once we have the maximum number of participants, it becomes a closed group. Often, we get more mothers than fathers attending our groups. We go to great lengths to try to engage reluctant fathers to participate in our groups. This includes making telephone calls, sending letters, and meeting the fathers at their workplaces or in their homes. We share with the fathers the following:

> "We can't do it without you. You are like the captain of the ship, and you and your partner can be like a dynamic duo when you are a unified team. We are very interested in your opinions, your and your partner's expectations of us, your creative ideas, and are totally com-

mitted to empowering you and your partner to resolve your adolescent's difficulties. Do you have any questions or concerns?"

Typically, once the leaders have demonstrated to these reluctant fathers their strong desire to have them participate in the group and address their concerns, the engagement process goes more smoothly.

My colleagues and I like to group the parents around the main presenting problems of their kids and their ages. For example, we will run a group for parents that have adolescents 15–18 years of age presenting with attention-deficit disorder. We have found it to be counterproductive to group parents around diverse presenting problems or radically different age ranges for their adolescents. However, if the group leaders, due to their agency or clinic's mandate, have to choose between grouping parents around the diverse presenting problems of their adolescents or the age range, it is better to group them together by the ages of their adolescents, since they are more likely developmentally in the same place.

THE ROLE OF THE GROUP LEADERS

Ideally, a male and female cotherapy team should run the group to provide gender balance. The group leaders are responsible for providing a safe, upbeat, and supportive therapeutic climate that is richly informative, that provides "hands-on" parenting tools the group members can put to immediate use, and that builds on the strengths and expertise of each participant to cocreate a context ripe for change. The leaders strive to connect in a meaningful way with each group member by using key language and belief system material, metaphors, validation, empathy, positive relabeling of negative behaviors, normalizing, humor, and compliments. The leaders also take the time to elicit each parent's expectations of them and to carefully assess each parent's current stage of readiness for change (Prochaska, 1999). This important information will help govern how the leaders interact with each parent, particularly with therapeutic questions and experiments employed.

Throughout the group process, the leaders use a variety of therapeutic questions geared to elicit the group members' expertise, to open up space for possibilities, and for goal-setting purposes. In addition, the leaders use role playing to teach the parents new skills and to dramatize how they get stuck with their kids and how to respond differently. The leaders regularly solicit the group members' feedback and creative ideas so they can share their expertise with one another. This is particularly helpful for stuck and pessimistic parents.

During the 15-minute intersession break, the leaders meet alone and construct the editorial reflection (Selekman, 1997, 2002) with compliments for the parents to underscore their creativity and resourcefulness, positively relabel both their negative behaviors as well as their kids', pose any questions we are curious about, and determine the therapeutic experiment that will be offered to the parents over the next week. Finally, at the end of every group session we solicit feedback from the parents regarding the quality of our relationships with them and how the group experience has been for them. We ask the following questions:

- "How did you find the group meeting today?"
- "What ideas did you find to be the most helpful that you plan to test out over the next week?"
- "Were there any topics or ideas discussed that you did not understand or you would like more clarification about?"
- "Are there any parenting topics that we did not cover today that you think are important that we address the next time we get together?"
- "Since we want to make sure that each of you feels supported and your expectations are met in our group, is there anything you would like us to change about our interactions with you or with the group format that would help you to feel more satisfied with our working together or your group experience?"

By eliciting this important feedback from the parents, the group leaders can adjust their stances, better cooperate with each member of the group, and maximize for successful parental treatment outcomes.

THE SOLUTION-ORIENTED PARENTING GROUP: SESSION-BY-SESSION PROGRAM

In this section, I describe the session content and activities for each of the eight sessions of the group. It is my hope that readers will find the following updated blueprint for conducting the greatly expanded and improved solution-oriented parenting group to be a helpful guide that better meets the needs of their parent clients struggling with their difficult adolescents.

Session 1. Solution-Oriented Parenting: Empowering Parents to Be the Agents of Change

In the first group session, the leaders introduce themselves and invite each one of the parents to respond to the following questions:

- "Imagine someone stopped you on the street and asked you what your strengths and talents were. What would you tell that person?"
- "How about if your adolescents were sitting next to you, and we asked them what they think two of your strengths were or what they appreciated the most about you. What do you think they would say?"

Each parent is given plenty of floor time to respond to these questions. Not only do these parents get to know one another better around their strengths, but also the positive nature of the questions takes the sting out of their difficulties and can be emotionally uplifting. For those parents that have difficulty responding to our questions, we encourage them to share how they think they shine in their parenting and work roles and in the hobbies they enjoy pursuing during their leisure time. This important information (parental key words, beliefs, metaphors related to their strengths and talent areas, themes of resilience) can be utilized by the leaders in the interviewing process, when complimenting the parents, and with prescribed therapeutic experiments.

The next important areas we like to explore with the parents are how the idea for pursuing our group evolved and what specifically triggered the decision to seek help at the present time. We also like to elicit from the parents what their expectations are of us, their theories of change, and if they had been in treatment in the past with their adolescents, what they disliked about those experiences, and what specifically was not addressed that would be important for us to know about. It also is most advantageous to the group leaders to explore with parents what elements of past treatment experiences they found most helpful. There may be a past treatment strategy they had learned that could be useful to them in trying to best manage their adolescents' current behavioral difficulties.

Often, parents are referred to the group by probation officers, school personnel, clergy, psychiatric hospitals, or their family physicians. A very small percentage of the parent participants are self-referrals. By securing a clear definition from each parent of what they view as the problem, the leaders will help ensure that they are focusing on the *right* problems to work on changing first. To help accomplish this and break the problem down into more solvable terms, we ask the following questions:

- "If there were one question you were dying to ask us and the group about this difficulty, what would that question be?"
- "Is there anything missing in your relationship with your adolescent that, if provided, would make a difference?"
- "What's your hunch or theory about why this difficulty exists?"

- "What do you think former therapists missed or overlooked with your situation that you wish to address in this group?"
- "What piece of this problem situation do you wish to work on changing first?"
- "If your kids were sitting next to you, what would they say is the number-one thing that you do that gets them the most upset?"

The answers to these questions can provide the leaders with a good understanding about the parents' beliefs, problem explanations, theories of change, and what specifically they would like to work on changing. In response to the last question, some parents will contract to work on changing their chronic nagging, yelling, or lecturing that they think could help improve their relationships with their adolescents.

After clarifying with each parent the *right* problem they wish to work on changing first, the leaders present the seven core solution-oriented parenting assumptions and the research material on resiliency protective factors, learned optimism, positive emotion, and the six characteristics of strong families. The seven *core* solution-oriented parenting assumptions are:

1. Change is inevitable.
2. Cooperation is inevitable.
3. Only a small change is necessary.
4. Clients have the strengths and resources to change.
5. Problems are unsuccessful attempts to resolve difficulties.
6. You do not need to know a great deal about the problem in order to solve it.
7. There are many ways to look at a situation, none more *correct* than others.

Each assumption is presented in a clear, concrete fashion, with disguised case examples provided by the leaders to help illustrate key points. For readers interested in learning more about these assumptions, see Chapter 2 (this volume), where a total of 10 "guiding assumptions" are discussed. With the fifth assumption, we like to present the theoretical ideas of the Mental Research Institute on how problems develop and are maintained (Fisch et al., 1982; Watzlawick et al., 1974). This involves a discussion about how parental action can contribute to the maintenance of the problem life-support systems in their families. To illustrate this assumption, we will map out on the flip chart a problem-maintaining sequence of interactions shared by a group member. Sometimes, the leaders will role-play a parent's problem-maintaining sequence of interactions with his or her adolescent. Finally, we show a picture of a tall mountain, which we call "the problem mountain." This picture serves as a metaphor for how parents get stuck viewing their adolescents and problem situations with tunnel vision, which prevents them from noticing exceptions, or sparkling moments. The educational portion of the session concludes with a discussion of the important research findings about resiliency protective factors, learned optimism, positive emotion, and the six characteristics of strong families.

The leaders end the group session by complimenting each parent on his or her strengths and resources and the valuable feedback everyone offered to other group members. Positive relabeling and normalization also are used to help create a climate ripe for change. One example of positive relabeling would be referring to a parent's labeled ADD (attention-deficit disorder) daughter as being active, dynamic, and determined. Another example of positive relabeling would be referring to a parent's son's "attitude problem" as his demonstrating his "assertiveness skills."

When presenting experiments to parents, the leaders change the inflection in their voices to further enhance parental cooperation with therapeutic experiment completion and to amplify embedded commands (note the words in italics in the quoted monologues). We also have found it beneficial to have the instructions for the therapeutic experiments written down on sheets so that parents will be better able to remember how precisely to implement the experiments, with space left for them to write down on the same sheets the results they achieve. The leaders offer the parents the *formula first session task* as their first experiment (de Shazer, 1985, 1988; Selekman, 1991b). The experiment is presented in the following way:

> "In order for us [the leaders] to have a more complete picture of your situations with your adolescents, we would like you over the next week to pretend to be Sherlock Holmes and Miss Marple detectives and with your imaginary magnifying glasses *notice* on a daily basis *what will be happening* in your relationships with your adolescents that *you would like to continue to have happen.* Please write your important discoveries down on your sheets and bring them into our next meeting."

This task is quite effective at helping parents to refocus their attention on what is *right* with their adolescents and going well in their relationships with them. The first session concludes with the leaders inviting group members to share their feedback on the meeting, such as what ideas or strategies they found most helpful, any adjustments or additional content material they would like the leaders to address, and any concerns or aspects of the group they would like us to change.

Session 2. Going for Small Changes

The second group session begins with the leaders inquiring with the parental detectives about what their positive discoveries were over the past week. The leaders ask the following questions to elicit and amplify these important exceptions and newsworthy gains:

- "While gazing through your imaginary magnifying glasses, what pleasant surprises did you observe happening with your adolescents that *you want to keep* having happen?"
- "Was that different for your daughter to do that?!"
- "Are you aware of how you got that to happen?!"
- "What did you tell yourself to pull that off?!"
- "How specifically did that help the two of you get along better over the past week?"
- "Now that you have a good solid stretch of days avoiding the temptation to blow up at your daughter, are you starting to view yourself differently as a parent now, as opposed to before when you found yourself blowing up at her all of the time?"
- "On a scale from 1 to 10—with 10 being your situation is better enough and 1 there is a great deal of work to be done—where would you have rated things 4 weeks before the group?"
- "At a 2. How about today?"
- "At a 7! The lucky 7! What further steps have you or your daughter taken to get up to the lucky 7?"

Every exception or change in parental self-perceptions and behaviors is responded to by the leaders with cheerleading and their making distinctions between old and new patterns of behavior.

The goal-setting process begins with the leaders asking the parents the miracle question (de Shazer, 1988; Selekman, 1997, 2002). After asking the miracle question and gaining a clear picture from the parents about what their ideal outcome pictures would look like, we ask them:

- "If your adolescents were sitting next to you, what would they say they were the most surprised or pleased with that changed with you in their ideal miracle pictures?"
- "How specifically will those changes be helping you get along better?"
- "We are curious: are there any pieces of the miracle already happening a little bit with you and your adolescents now?"
- "Are you aware of how you got that to happen?"

- "How has that made a difference in your relationship with your son?"

These latter questions elicit from parents important pretreatment changes that can be amplified, consolidated, and used as building blocks for solution construction. As part of the process of expanding the possibilities with the parents in the miracle inquiry, we invite them to describe in great detail what specifically they will be doing differently in their interactions with their adolescents and co-parents that will be making an important difference in their lives. Scaling questions (de Shazer, 1988, 1991; Selekman, 1997, 2002) are used to help negotiate with each parent a small and realistic behavioral goal. We like to ask parents the following questions when negotiating their goals:

- "If your adolescent were sitting right next to you and we asked him or her what behavior you engage in that gets him or her the most upset, what would he or she tell us?"
- "On a scale from 1 to 10—with 10 being that your nagging or yelling has been greatly reduced or eliminated, and 1 it is happening all of the time—where would he or she have rated your behavior 4 weeks before the group started?"
- "At a 1?! What about with your nagging today?"
- "At a 4! What steps would they identify that you took to get up to a 4?"
- "Let's say your son joined us at the next group, and I asked what steps you took over the past week to get up to a 5. What would he tell us you did?"
- "In what ways will he tell us that your cutting back on the nagging has made a big difference in your relationship with him?"

For many parents, this line of questioning will help them identify a specific parental behavior to target for intervention and serve as their initial treatment goal. Our belief is that parents should take the lead in defining their treatment goals. The leaders' job is to assist parents in negotiating small and realistic behavioral goals for themselves or their adolescents. Some parents may choose another treatment goal or may still be stuck, viewing the adolescent as the one who has to make all of the changes, and have grave difficulty articulating a realistic treatment goal in this group session.

For parents who report no changes at pretreatment or in the miracle inquiry or are still engaged in a complainant pattern of interaction with the leaders, we may try to externalize the particular adolescent behavior or patterns in their relationships with their adolescents that continue to push them around (White & Epston, 1990). One stuck parent in the group complained about how her son's "attitude" was getting the best of her. The leaders explored with the mother the various ways the "attitude" pushed her around and wreaked havoc even in her relationship with her 15-year-old *daughter*. The mother reported that the "attitude" would coach her to "scream at" her daughter, which in turn would lead to a "screaming match" during which her daughter would "win the argument." The mother was then asked percentage questions (Selekman, 1993) to help elicit from her quantitative measurements of how well she was defending herself *against* "screaming" prior to entering the group and presently. Before entering the group, the mother was being pushed around by "screaming 80% of the time." In our second group session, she rated her situation at "70% of the time caving into screaming." We explored what she was doing that helped her reduce the percentages. The mother reported that "avoiding power struggles" and "silently counting to 10 before I spoke" seemed to "help out a lot." When asked what her next steps would be to get down to a 60–65% rating, the mother replied that she would have to "increase" the frequency of the two strategies that were "working so well" for her. Through externalization of the problem (White & Epston, 1990), the leaders empowered the mother by helping her identify some important problem-solving and coping strategies that, by increasing their frequency, eventually led to her putting an end to the "attitude" problem in her family.

The leaders also may use coping, the pessimistic sequence, and subzero scaling questions (Selekman, 2002; Berg & Miller, 1992) to better cooperate with more pessimistic parents. We will ask these parents the following questions:

- "What steps have you been taking to prevent your situation from getting much worse?"
- "How specifically was that helpful?"
- "What else are you doing to prevent things from really escalating and getting much worse?"
- "Some parents in your situation might have thrown in the towel and dropped out of the group. What made you decide to keep coming and not give up?"
- "What would be the tiniest change that we can get going here over the next week that would give you an inkling of hope that things can improve a little bit?"
- "On a scale from –10 to –1—with –10 being your situation with your kid is totally hopeless and irresolvable, and –1 you have an inkling of hope that the situation could improve a little bit—where were you on that scale 4 weeks before starting this group?"
- "At a –9. How about 2 weeks ago?"

- "At a –5! What steps have you taken to get from a –9 to a –5?"
- "To get our baseline, where are you on the scale today?"
- "A –4! Are you aware of how you stepped up to a –4?"

Often these questions will increase parental hope levels and elicit from the parents important exceptions that we can capitalize on to help them to increase *what works.*

Once all of the parents have established initial treatment goals for themselves, the leaders compliment each parent on their good detective work and resourcefulness and offer them the *pretend the miracle happened task* (de Shazer, 1991; Selekman, 2002). The parents are told the following:

> "Over the next week, we would like you to pick 3 days to pretend to engage in the very miracle behaviors you think your adolescents would like to see you engaging in in relationship to them. While you are *pretending*, we would like you to *carefully notice* how your adolescents respond to you. Please write down your observations on your sheets, and bring this information into our next meeting. Have fun with this experiment, and strive for Academy Award performances!"

When parents are assigned this experiment, they often smile and appear to be eager to test it out.

Session 3. Connecting from the Heart: Meaningful Pathways for Further Strengthening Your Relationships with Your Teens

The third group session begins with the leaders exploring with the parents what further progress they made in achieving their treatment goals. Scaling questions can be used to secure a quantitative measurement of each parent's progress toward the goal's attainment. Every reported change is responded to with cheerleading and the amplification and consolidation of parental gains. Often, the parents are eager to share with the leaders and the group how pretending to engage in their adolescents' miracle-like behaviors produced great results in their adolescents' behavior over the past week. Scaling questions (de Shazer, 1988, 1991; Selekman, 1997, 2002) can be used to get a quantitative measurement of the parents' movement toward achieving their treatment goals. Presuppositional questions (O'Hanlon & Weiner-Davis, 1989; Selekman, 1997, 2002) are used to further empower parents by having them visualize future realities of continued success. Some examples of presuppositional questions are:

- "In our next group session, what further steps will you tell us you took to get up to an 8?"
- "Let's say we had you gaze into our imaginary crystal ball 3 weeks down the road. What further steps do you see yourself taking to improve your relationship with your daughter?"
- "While gazing into the crystal ball, how is your daughter responding differently to you since you stopped the nagging completely?"
- "What do we see you and her doing together in the crystal ball that would have been completely impossible to pull off prior to joining our group?"
- "Let's say we [the group leaders] ran into you and your son at the local shopping mall 1 month from today, and we asked your son what changes he has appreciated the most that you made. What will he tell us?"
- "Let's say in our future conversation at the shopping mall that we asked you to describe the steps you took to eliminate your chronic yelling habit with your son. What will you tell us you did to pull that off?"
- "What will your son tell us he saw you do that worked?"

Consolidating questions (Selekman, 1997, 2002) are used by the leaders to help solidify parental gains. Some examples of consolidating questions are as follows:

- "What would you have to do to go backwards?"
- "What will you have to *keep doing more of* to stay on the road to success?"
- "Let's say we were to invite you to our next solution-oriented parenting group as guest consultants. What helpful pointers would you share with those parents?"
- "On a scale from 10 to 1—with 10 being your situation is better enough, and 1 there is further work to be done—where were you at the start of the group on that scale?"
- "Where would you rate your situation on the scale today?"

Another useful strategy for consolidating parental gains is to have a parent who is succeeding at achieving his or her goals map out on the flip chart the circular solution-maintaining pattern of interactions. This exercise proves to be a newsworthy and informative experience for the other group members.

For parents still feeling stuck and frustrated, we offer them the opportunity to have their problem-maintaining interactions mapped out on the flip chart and invite other group members to offer problem-solving ideas and words of wisdom. Often, these stuck parents find this exercise to be quite helpful and emotionally uplifting. We have been quite amazed how creative and supportive parents can be in our groups, particularly with more stuck group members. Coping and pessimistic sequence questions (Berg & Miller, 1992; Selekman, 1997, 2002) can also be used with highly pessimistic and stuck parents. By the third group session, parents spontaneously use normalization, instill hope, and compliment one another.

Another important topic area covered in this group session is parental connection-building practices (Selekman, 2002). Parents are exposed to important Buddhist principles about connecting with their adolescents from the heart. This takes the form of *speaking and listening with compassion* and *practicing loving kindness* (Hanh, 2001, 2003a). The leaders model these principles through doing a role play of one or more of the group members' situations with his or her adolescent on how to speak and listen deeply in a compassionate way and respond with loving kindness even if his or her son or daughter was being difficult or had done something wrong. We teach parents that the anger they experience within themselves in response to their adolescents' button-pushing or challenging behaviors is an indication that their adolescents are suffering in some way and requires their compassion and loving kindness, not negative reactivity or aggression. In addition, we teach parents simple *mindfulness meditations* that they can use to "cool the flames" of their anger (Hanh, 2001). One simple mindfulness meditation we teach parents is a *sound meditation*. We have them find a quiet place in their houses to do the meditation. After getting comfortable in a chair, they are to close their eyes and for 15 minutes carefully listen to and focus all of their attention on the different sounds they hear around them, not getting too attached to any one sound. They are to label in their minds only the various sounds they hear. We have the parents practice this meditation in the group and ideally twice a day over the next week as an experiment. Many parents have shared with my colleagues and me that the mindfulness meditations they learned in the group helped them to better manage their anger and feelings of frustration when their adolescents were trying to get the best of them.

As part of this discussion, we stress to the parents the importance of their teens experiencing a *sense of place* in their hearts and teach them a variety of strategies for strengthening their emotional connections with them (Selekman, 2002). Besides encouraging parents to practice using empathy, validation, being active listeners, consistently showing pride and joy in their sons' and daughters' accomplishments, and conveying their love and appreciation for their adolescents, we have them regularly elicit their adolescents' feedback on their parenting and carve out protected time spent together engaging in a weekly activity of their adolescents' choice. The leaders have the parents do the following exercise as a way of getting them into the spirit of connection building. They are asked:

> "We would like you to imagine taking a trip in a time machine back to a time when you felt a very strong emotional connection with your adolescents. We want you to apply all of your senses to the experience, including color and motion. How many years back would you go? Where are the two of you? What are you doing with your adolescents? What is most special or important about this experience? How can you tell that he or she feels really close to you or is enjoying himself or herself with you in this activity or situation? How are you feeling emotionally and about your relationship with your son or daughter in this situation? If you were to bring back to the here and now any elements of these special experiences with your adolescents or ways of relating to them that you think could further strengthen your relationships with them, what would those elements or experiences be?"

Prior to the leaders taking their intersession break, they process their time traveling experiences with the parents and explore with them what helpful ideas were sparked and how they plan to begin implementing them over the next week. The third session concludes with the leaders complimenting the parents on their hard work and important gains. In addition to having the parents begin to reinstate or implement new ideas gained from their time traveling experiences, they are given the following *compliment box experiment* (Selekman, 2002):

> "Over the next week, we would like all of you to find an old shoebox and cut a slit in the box top. On a daily basis, we would like you and your partner to write down on slips of paper any responsible steps you see your adolescents take that you are pleased with and things that you really appreciate about them as people. After dinner each night, we would like you to have your sons and daughters blindly reach in and read off your compliments for them. Keep track of which compliments they were the most surprised about, found to be the most meaningful to them, and in what ways your interactions improved over the week. We would like you to bring in your compliment boxes (Selekman, 2002) to the next group meeting and be prepared to share with us what *further progress* you made in improving your relationships with your adolescents."

Session 4. If It Works, Don't Fix It

The group leaders begin the fourth group session by reviewing how the parents' experiments went. Not only do the leaders amplify and cheerlead for the parents, but the group members spontaneously do this for one another as well. Parents often report quite a lot of success with their compliment box experiment. One single-parent mother in the group had a very stormy relationship with her daughter in which they were constantly getting into power struggles and verbal jousting matches with each other. Not only was the daughter pleasantly surprised to read how much her mother appreciated her "tremendous courage" in picking herself up and making new friends after being suddenly rejected by two of her closest friends, but equally she was impressed by her mother's crediting her with doing "a great job straightening up" her "bedroom." Each day, the mother came up with new compliments for her daughter, and she found herself more regularly noticing what was *right* with her daughter than focusing on the negatives. Apparently, there was not even one power struggle or argument between them over the entire week!

Next the leaders follow up with the parents about what past successful patterns of behavior and fun and meaningful activities they reinstated with their adolescents, based on the last session's time traveling experiences. Finally, the leaders explore with the parents how they found the use of mindfulness meditation as a tool for helping them better cope with the stressors in their lives.

After processing with all of the parents how their experiments went, the leaders do a short presentation on the importance of continuing to increase solution-maintaining patterns that promote the kind of responsible, respectful, and cooperative behaviors that they wish to keep repeating with their adolescents. Often, the leaders will ask a parent who is well on his or her way to goal attainment to map out on the flip chart one of the solution-maintaining circular interactions with her adolescents that he or she would recommend. This exercise offers the other members of the group the opportunity to learn from one another novel and creative parental solution-maintaining strategies. We like to point out to the parents in the group how easy it is to get derailed or discontinue *what works* when they lose their tempers, are highly stressed out, or when spontaneous crises or difficulties occur with their adolescents. It is strongly recommended to the parents that they keep track on a daily basis of *what works* and *do more of it!* One tool that we introduce to the parents to help them keep track of and daily document what works is the *My Past and Present Parenting Successes Worksheet* (see Figure 10.2). The worksheet serves as a confidence booster and reminder of their successes and what they need to keep doing.

Instructions: List any past and present parenting strategies you have employed to successfully manage your teen's challenging behaviors.

1.

2.

3.

4.

5.

6.

7.

8.

9.

10.

FIGURE 10.2. My Past and Present Parenting Successes Worksheet.

After the group leaders compliment the parents on their positive gains with their kids, they are given the following experiment:

> "As a way to further empower all of you to continue to *do what works*, we would like you on a daily basis to list on the *My Past and Present Successes Worksheet* every solution-maintaining response that promotes the kind of responsible, respectful, and cooperative behaviors you want from your adolescents. Also, think about any past parenting responses or strategies that worked at resolving other difficulties with your adolescents or other children that may be worthwhile to use in experimenting with your adolescents' present challenging behaviors. Remember: *do more of what works!*"

Session 5. If It Doesn't Work, Do Something Different

In the fifth group session, the leaders begin the meeting by finding out from the parents what further progress they made. We amplify and consolidate their gains with the use of scaling and presuppositional questions (de Shazer, 1988, 1991; Selekman, 1997; O'Hanlon & Weiner-Davis, 1989). The leaders review with the parents their *My Past and Present Successes Worksheets*. As part of this discussion, we will have a few of the parents map out on the flip chart some of their most effective solution-promoting responses or strategies. In addition, we like some of the parents to share with the group some examples of past successful solution strategies that they reinstated with their adolescents that generated positive outcomes with their adolescents.

For those parents still feeling pessimistic or stuck, we use the brainpower and creativity of the group to come up with some ideas or suggestions for what he or she should try to experiment with. The group's recommendations will be listed on the flip chart for this parent to review and select those strategies that he or she feels most comfortable testing out over the next week.

Following this discussion, the leaders provide a short presentation on the importance of parents being flexible, on their toes, and be willing to do something *outside the box* when their attempted solutions are not working for them. We point out to the parents that they have become far too predictable to their adolescents with their vocal tones, body language, and verbal responses. In many ways, these outmoded responses have become like a broken record to their adolescents. Furthermore, the leaders stress that the more they persist in actions that are not working, the more they will further compound or exacerbate their adolescents' most problematic behaviors.

After the intersession break, the leaders compliment each parent on their gains and they are given the *do something different task* (de Shazer, 1985, 1988; Selekman, 1997, 2002). The experiment is presented to the parents in the following way:

> "Your adolescents have gotten your number. They can tell by the tone of your voices and the looks on your faces what is coming next. You guys are far too predictable! Over the next week, whenever your adolescents are pushing your buttons or you are tempted to be too superresponsible and go the extra mile for them, we would like you to *do something different!* It can be something nutty or off-the-wall, as long as it is *different* from your usual course of action. We want you to really blow your adolescents' minds!"

When given this experiment, parents often smile and are eager to have fun with it over the next week. For those parents who have already achieved their goals and are on the road to success, we encourage them to *do more of what works* and not deviate from this course of action.

Session 6. Collaborating for Success: Empowering Your Teens in Larger System Mazes

In our sixth group session, we begin by amplifying and consolidating each parent's progress. This group session tends to be quite upbeat and filled with a lot of laughter and positive emotion. Parents often come in reporting some very creative and outrageous novel behavioral responses they presented to their adolescents when the latter were being difficult. For the sake of brevity, I will only mention a few examples of the things parents have done in our groups to blow their difficult adolescents' minds!

A highly conservative Orthodox Jewish couple in their late 50s decided to surprise their 16-year-old highly oppositional daughter who was chronically truant and repeatedly violated their curfew rule by "lying in her bed armed with squirt guns." When, on a school night, the daughter entered her bedroom and turned on her light at 1:00 A.M., the parents showered her with squirt gun water from their strategic bed location. The daughter was "totally stunned" and nearly "had a coronary" from this experience. Although she was too tired to go to school the next day, from that day on she "attended school without any battles in the morning" and was "much more cooperative." The parents would "flash" their "trusty squirt guns" whenever the daughter would show any signs of going backwards, which seemed to help keep her on track with her "responsibilities."

A single-parent mother who was playing the human alarm clock role in trying to wake up her recalcitrant and highly oppositional 17-year-old son in the mornings to get up for school bought five alarm clocks with very loud ringers, set them for 6:30 A.M., and hid them all over his bedroom. According to the mother, her son "blasted out of bed like a rocket" when the alarms went off. Much to the son's dismay, he could not find all of the clocks and his mother had to come into his bedroom and help him find them. Apparently, that day, the son not only had "breakfast" with his mother but he "caught the school bus on time," which was "a personal first for him."

Another mother successfully neutralized her 14-year-old son's "button-pushing" problem and attempts to engage her in power struggles with him by responding in a variety of "crazy ways." On one occasion, she "rapidly recited the alphabet backwards." She also had success with asking her son "questions" that would have "nothing to do with the topic" at hand, such as "Do you know what your astrological sign is?" Finally, she became more "unpredictable and mysterious" with her daily routines and comings and goings from the house. By changing her interactive steps in relationship to her son, the latter became much more cooperative minus the "button pushing" and the power struggles.

One father, who was a criminal attorney, used to employ the Socratic method of questioning every time his daughter wanted to go out with friends. His daughter had described his behavior as being like a "police officer interrogating a suspect" every time she wanted to go out. This would lead to the daughter's lying, her engaging in more risky behaviors, or getting into trouble. The father had decided to experiment with the suggestion of one of the parents in the group as his novel and different way of interacting with his daughter. The other parent, a mother in the group, had recommended that he refrain from asking any questions of his daughter when she wanted to go out and instead wait for her to take responsibility by providing such important information as: whom she was going out with, where they were going, what they were going to do, and agreeing to come home by her curfew time. According to the father, if he avoided trying to be "the famous TV lawyer Perry Mason" and instead insisted on keeping his daughter "*off* the witness stand" every time she wanted to go out, she would readily produce all of the details he wanted to hear. He also observed that, as a consequence of changing his behavior, his daughter was being more responsible with her chores, doing her homework, and not getting into trouble as much.

The leaders stress to the parents that they should *continue doing what works* and using their creative parental responses until their adolescents' problematic behaviors have been eliminated. It is clear that the *do something different task* (de Shazer, 1988, 1991; Selekman, 2002) not only helps parents enhance their reflective skills—that is, pause and think about their options in particular situations—but also it appears to stimulate and strengthen their creative problem-solving capacities. Once parents have met with success using this experiment, they report enjoying their parenting roles and becoming more flexible and playful with their adolescents.

Midway into the group session, the leaders do a short presentation on negotiation skills and the importance of parents serving as their adolescents' advocates in the various larger systems they are experiencing trouble in. We expose the parents to *win–win* negotiation skills (Follett, 1995) and *The Third Side* negotiation framework of William Ury (Ury, 2000). Parents are taught that often the larger systems their adolescents are experiencing difficulties in are like mazes with lots of red tape, and the professionals involved may have a variety of different agendas, expectations, or concerns. Because of this, parents are encouraged to adopt a one-down position in relationship to these helpers and listen intently to their problem concerns or *commitments* (Kegan & Lahey, 2001), expectations for their adolescents' behaviors, and what helpers would like from them as their parents. The leaders teach parents how to defer judgment, use curiosity, and contain their negative emotional reactions or defensiveness with more rigid or pessimistic helpers. By conveying a strong desire to understand and address the helpers' concerns with their adolescents as well as the necessity of collaborating together—viewing them as potential allies supporting their causes—the parents will be able to foster cooperative relationships with them and open the door for meaningful dialogue and the co-construction of mutually desired solutions.

The leaders find it very useful to invite the parents to share their own personal experiences successfully collaborating or negotiating with colleagues at work, with family members, and people in their communities. Any past successful strategies the parents had employed when collaborating with others or using their negotiation skills in difficult situations may be worthwhile experimenting with in their present interactions with involved helping professionals from larger systems. Some parents have a knack for effectively negotiating with teachers and other school personnel for the special resources or assistance their adolescents require. We also like parents to share with the group some of their negative past experiences dealing with larger systems professionals and point out how their style of negotiating may have backfired on them. For example, one father of a 15-year-old boy repeatedly complained to the school principal about "how unfair" two of his son's teachers' grading systems were. The result: because the teachers were quite angry about the father's failure to first meet with them individually to share his concerns, instead complaining to their boss, the son's grades declined further, a victim of the "teachers' hit lists." Finally, we can employ the "back from the future" parental empowerment strategy of George and his colleagues (1999), in which parents project themselves into a future place where they successfully negotiate in a school or other larger systems meeting what they had advocated for their adolescents. The parents are then to walk themselves back to the here and now, spelling out the steps they took to be successful in the meeting.

After the leaders compliment each parent in the group on their great progress or for having achieved their goals, they are given a 2-week vacation from the group as a vote of confidence. While on vacation, the parents are asked to do the following:

> "While vacationing from the group, we would like you to keep track on a daily basis of what *further progress you are going to make* at maintaining and generating new solution interactions with your adolescents. Additionally, we would like you to practice using the negotia-

tion and collaboration skills you learned in today's group or experimenting with your past successful negotiation and collaborative strategies with involved helping professionals, your adolescents, and other family members. We look forward to hearing your stories of success!"

Session 7. Pioneering New Parenting Directions

The leaders begin the seventh group session by eliciting from the parents their stories of success. Every exception or positive step each parent took is met with cheerleading and consolidating questions by the leaders, such as:

- "Are you aware of how you did that!?"
- "Is that different for you to respond to your son in that way!?"
- "Did he faint when you did that!?"
- "Some parents would have gotten very defensive with your daughter's dean. How were you able to maintain your composure so well?"
- "Did you tell yourself anything to avoid 'losing it' with the dean?"
- "It sounds as though your son's probation officer is trying to find any possible way to get him placed in juvenile detention. How were you able to get him to see the light and that this would not be good for your son's emotional well-being?"
- "On a scale of 1 to 10—with 10 being your situation is better enough and 1 there is a lot further work to be done—where would you have rated your situation 2 weeks ago? How about today?"
- "What would you have to do at this point to go backwards?"
- "Let's say you experience a slip over the next few weeks. What steps will you take to quickly get back on track?"

For those parents who are still experiencing difficulties with their adolescents or who struggled in using the negotiation or collaboration skills taught in the last group session, we tap the resourcefulness and creativity of the group members to depict on the flip chart their recommended solution strategies. By this stage of the group experience, the group often is able to generate three or more high-quality solution strategies without the leaders' help that can empower the stuck parent to successfully better manage the difficulty with his or her adolescent or to interact differently with challenging involved helping professionals.

Again, as a vote of confidence for the parents' tremendous progress, they are given a 3-week vacation from the group. While on vacation, the leaders recommend to the parents, if they wish to do any work, they should just keep track of what further progress they are going to make.

Session 8. Celebrating Change: Honoring Your Solution-Oriented Parenting Successes

In the last group session, the leaders celebrate the parents' changes and hard work by giving them achievement certificates and a sheet cake that has written on it in icing "Congratulations, Solution-Oriented Parents!" As part of the celebration process, we invite each parent to give a speech reflecting on the differences between where they were prior to the group and how they view themselves and their relationships with their adolescents at the present time. The leaders also reflect on the parents' changes over time and invite them serve as guest consultants in our future parent groups. Unique redescription questions (White, 1988b; Selekman, 1997) are used to elicit the parents' *news of a difference* and to further consolidate their gains. Some examples of these questions are:

- "How are you viewing yourself differently as a parent now, as opposed to formerly, before you started in this group?"
- "Let's say we invited you to our next solution-oriented parenting group as an expert consultant. What helpful advice or pointers would you share with these parents?"
- "If your adolescent were sitting next to you, and we asked him or her what changes he or she appreciates the most that you made in the group, what would your teen say?"

Presuppositional questions (O'Hanlon & Weiner-Davis, 1989; Selekman, 1997, 2002) are also useful for consolidating parental gains. Parents are invited to gaze into the leaders' imaginary crystal ball 6 months into the future, spelling out as clearly as possible what further changes they see happening with themselves, their adolescents, and in their parent–adolescent relationships. We also ask parents to imagine what further changes they would report to the group at a 1-year anniversary party that was provided for them by the leaders.

The majority of our parent participants tend to achieve their treatment goals by the fourth or fifth group session. For those parents who are still struggling by the end of the group, the leaders make themselves available to them for family or marital therapy or advocacy or collaboration with some of the involved helping professionals they continue to experience conflicts with. My colleagues and I have found that one of the major bonuses of participating in this group is that conflictual couples at the start of the group often become a unified team well before our last group session.

Another important bonus of this group is that powerful and reluctant teenagers who balked at participating in family therapy in the past frequently contact one of the leaders for counseling for themselves. They subsequently have reported in their individual therapy sessions their appreciation to the therapists for having helped their parents make some meaningful and quite dramatic changes. Some of these adolescents have pointed out that their parents' changes helped them to see the benefits of counseling. This includes adolescents that have had extensive treatment and are involved with street gangs. One parent in our group had a son who was gang-involved and had many long-term stays in juvenile correctional facilities; he sought treatment for himself 1 week after his mother had completed the group. According to the mother, her son had refused to go for any form of treatment in the past.

SUMMARY

The solution-oriented parenting group has shown good clinical results with parents of adolescents diagnosed with oppositional defiant disorder, attention-deficit disorder, substance abuse, eating-distressed, self-harming, and violent and aggressive behavioral difficulties. The group also serves as an effective alternative to family therapy when adolescents refuse to attend sessions with their parents. Although past parent participants interviewed at posttreatment have indicated that this group has empowered them to resolve their difficulties with their kids and they learned a variety of effective parenting tools, future research is needed employing rigorous quantitative evaluative methods to empirically support its efficacy with challenging adolescent treatment populations.

Eleven

Solution-Oriented Brief Family Therapy and Beyond

We have tomorrow bright before us like a flame.
—LANGSTON HUGHES

PATHWAYS TO CHANGE REVISITED

Throughout this book, I have presented many innovative ideas and therapeutic strategies that can increase our effectiveness when working with difficult adolescents and their families. I have also stressed the importance of therapists needing to be much more sensitive to wider societal aggravating factors that both contribute to the development of and further exacerbate many of the problems youth and their families struggle with today. Our media-driven and consumerist cultural landscape has served as fertile soil for a significant increase in adolescent stress-related problems, peer difficulties, and family disconnection. Today's teenagers are constantly told by every form of the media that they live in an unsafe world, are struggling to cope with excessive homework loads, are being pushed to grow up way too fast, are constantly being bombarded with far too many choices, and have to be skilled human chameleons to fit in and keep up with their peers. Additionally, computers, high-tech gadgets, and other popular possessions among teens have replaced the need for family involvement or, in extreme cases, the need for social contact. As therapists, we need to serve as catalysts for connection building with adolescents and their parents and across other social contexts that our clients are experiencing difficulties in. Furthermore, we need to encourage parents to provide firm guidelines regarding computer, TV, videogame, cell phone, and gadget usage, set limits when necessary, and make family involvement both an attractive alternative and a priority.

Over the past 12 years, I have greatly expanded the original solution-oriented brief family therapy model described in the first edition of *Path-*

ways to Change to better address a lot of the stressors, societal aggravating factors, and complex issues and challenges adolescents and their families have been increasingly facing. At this point, I will review and summarize some of the major themes discussed in this book. To begin with, one of the central themes of this volume is my strong belief that all adolescents and their families have the strengths and resources to change, no matter how chronic their difficulties may be. In my view this is one of the most important assumptions for therapists to adopt with *all* families who walk through their office doors. In trying to co-create a therapeutic climate ripe for change, I believe that the most important therapeutic objective to accomplish in the first interview is to identify with our clients what their key intelligence areas (Gardner, 1993) are so that we can accurately match our therapeutic questions and experiments with what they do best, gain their cooperation, and collaboratively co-construct solutions together.

Another important theme pervading this text is the need for therapists to use the key findings of recent psychotherapy studies as a guide to doing scientifically *what works* with our clients, particularly adolescents presenting with serious behavioral and family difficulties. As reflected in the case examples and therapeutic ideas I present in this book, many of these key empirically based findings have helped to guide and inform my clinical thinking.

Therapists need to actively collaborate with involved helping allies from larger systems and key resource people in the adolescent's social ecology, such as peers and adult inspirational others. Having regular family–multiple helper collaborative meetings can empower the family and all members of the helping system, potentially greatly reducing lengths of stay in treatment. Numerous case examples have demonstrated how the involvement and expertise of peers and inspirational others in family therapy sessions and collaborative meetings greatly contribute to positive treatment outcomes. These important resource people in the life of adolescents help us to generalize and consolidate their gains outside of our offices. The key members of the adolescents' social networks and involved helping professionals deserve the same kind of respect that we give our clients. They are valuable allies that can offer wisdom, expertise, and the added support we can use when faced with challenging and complex adolescent case situations.

When working with difficult adolescent cases, therapists need to be able to serve as intergenerational negotiators working both sides of the fence. Once we can find out *what's in it for them* in terms of what privileges they want from their parents or what they want to see changed the most in their parents' behaviors, we can better appreciate our roles as intergenerational labor relations arbitrators as it were and set up *something-for-something* contracts with the parents. Far too many therapists invest most of their therapeutic energy in empowering the parents without attending to the goals and expectations of the adolescents in their cases, which can lead to immediate disaffection by the adolescents, often even dropping out of treatment. Most adolescent clients, no matter how difficult, will tell us directly or offer us clues for how *best* to cooperate with them. With those adolescent clients who have had past therapy experiences, it is crucial to tap into their expertise about what they liked and disliked about former therapists, so as to avoid making the same mistakes.

A final idea I wish to touch on is my belief that therapy is a creative art form. The therapeutic context is a stage for improvisation, creativity, and playfulness on the part of the therapist. For any one family story, there is a multiplicity of ways the therapist can improvise. Similar to a skillful jazz saxophonist, I like to begin an interview playing the family's central theme, gradually blowing notes that are outside the family's musical score through the use of humor and storytelling and eventually to co-create with the family a new musical score that combines elements from the old and new scores. At times, I will really push the limits of my playing to generate laughter among family members, which helps them experience themselves and their relationships differently, thus opening up space for new possibilities.

IMPLICATIONS FOR THE FUTURE

The groundbreaking positive psychology research of Seligman (2003), Peterson and Seligman (2004), Csikszentmihalyi (1997, 2003), and Fredrickson (2002, 2003) provides a great deal of support for important elements of solution-oriented therapy approaches, such as creating a positive and hopeful therapeutic climate and keeping the main therapeutic emphasis on client strengths and virtues. These researchers also have field tested effective methods for empowering clients to have more fulfilled and meaningful lives as well (Peterson & Seligman, 2004; Seligman, 2002, 2003). In addition, there is quite a lot of overlap between positive psychology's theoretical assumptions and methods and what we do as solution-oriented therapists. I believe the leading theorists and researchers of this new psychology movement have a lot to offer us in helping make our therapeutic approaches much more comprehensive and effective. Some of my clients have experienced great clinical results using some of the positive psychology field-tested experiments. Finally, Peterson and Seligman's (2004) important text *Character Strengths and Virtues: A Handbook and Classification* offers therapists practical guidelines for identifying clients' key signature strengths and how clients can successfully deploy them in specific ways to lead more meaningful and productive lives. Unlike DSM-IV, this handbook solely focuses on client strengths and offers treatment planning recommendations.

Although there have been numerous qualitative studies and follow-up telephone interviews conducted by solution-focused brief therapy institutes and teams around the world, there have not been any well-controlled experimental studies with large culturally diverse adolescent samples using both qualitative and quantitative research methods to demonstrate this model's efficacy with this treatment population (Beyebach, Rodriguez-Sanchez, Arribas de Miguel, Herrero de Vega, Hernandez, & Rodriguez-Morejon, 2000; Gingerich & Eisengart, 2000; Stalker et al., 1999; George et al., 1999; Lindforss & Magnussen, 1997; DeJong & Hopwood, 1996; Metcalf, Thomas, Duncan, Miller, & Hubble, 1996). Clearly, more scientific and rigorous treatment outcome studies are needed to truly demonstrate the efficacy of solution-oriented therapy approaches. It would be interesting to see how well either the base solution-focused brief therapy or the solution-oriented brief family therapy models would compare with such empirically validated family therapy approaches as functional family therapy (Sexton & Alexander, 2002) and multisystemic therapy (Henggeler et al., 2002).

SUMMARY

In this book, I have presented a strength-based and collaborative family therapy approach that offers clinicians multiple pathways for providing effective treatment with difficult adolescents and their families. It is my hope that the ideas discussed in this book will help therapists find their creative edge in challenging family sessions and provide them with a renewed sense of optimism in their day-to-day clinical work in the trenches with difficult adolescent clients and their families.

References

Alexander, J. F., & Parsons, B. V. (1982). *Functional family therapy: Principles and procedures.* Carmel, CA: Brooks & Cole.

Alexander, J. F., Barton, C., Schiavo, R. S., & Parsons, B. V. (1976). Systems-behavioral intervention with families of delinquents: Therapist characteristics, family behavior, and outcome. *Journal of Consulting and Clinical Psychology, 44,* 656–664.

Alexander, J. F., Pugh, C., & Parsons, B. (1998). *Blueprints for violence prevention: Vol. 3. Functional family therapy.* Boulder, CO: Center for the Study and Prevention of Violence.

Allgood, S. M., Parham, K. B., Salts, C. J., & Smith, T. A. (1995). The association between pretreatment change and unplanned termination in family therapy. *American Journal of Family Therapy, 23,* 195–202.

Allman, L. R. (1982). The aesthetic preference: Overcoming the pragmatic error. *Family process, 21*(1), 43–57.

American Psychiatric Association. (1994). *Diagnostic and statistical manual of mental disorders* (4th ed.). Washington, DC.

Andersen, T. (1987). The reflecting team: Dialogue and meta-dialogue in clinical work. *Family Process, 26*(4), 415–428.

Andersen, T. (1991). *The reflecting team: Dialogue and dialogues about the dialogues.* New York: Norton.

Anderson, H. (1997). *Conversation, language, and possibilities: A postmodern approach to therapy.* New York: Basic Books.

Anderson, H., & Goolishian, H. (1988a). *Changing thoughts on self, agency, questions, narrative and therapy.* Unpublished manuscript.

Anderson, H., & Goolishian, H. (1988b). Human systems as linguistic systems: Evolving ideas about the implications for theory and practice. *Family Process, 27,* 371–393.

Anderson, H., & Goolishian, H. (1991a). Thinking about multi-agency work with substance abusers and their families: A language systems approach. *Journal of Strategic and Systemic Therapies, 10*(1), 20–36.

Anderson, H., & Goolishian, H. (1991b, October). *"Not-knowing": A critical element of a collaborative language systems therapy approach.* Plenary address presented at the 1991 Annual American Association for Marriage and Family Therapy Conference, Dallas, TX.

Anderson, H., Goolishian, H., Pulliam, G., & Winderman, L. (1986). The Galveston Family Institute: Some personal and historical perspectives. In D. Efron (Ed.),

Journeys: Expansion of the strategic–systemic therapies (pp. 97–125). New York: Brunner/Mazel.

Anthony, E. J. (1984). The St. Louis risk project. In N. K. Watt, E. J. Anthony, L. C. Wynne, & J. Roth (Eds.), *Children at risk for schizophrenia: A longitudinal perspective* (pp. 105–148). Cambridge, UK: Cambridge University Press.

Anthony, E. J. (1987). Risk, vulnerability, and resilience: An overview. In E. J. Anthony & B. J. Cohler (Eds.), *The invulnerable child* (pp. 3–48). New York: Guilford Press.

Argyris, C. (1987, September–October). Skilled incompetence. *Harvard Business Review*, pp. 1–7.

Aronson, E. (2000). *Nobody left to hate: Teaching compassion after Columbine*. New York: Freeman.

Asay, T. P., & Lambert, M. J. (1999). The empirical case for the common factors in therapy: Quantitative findings. In M. A. Hubble, B. L. Duncan, & S. D. Miller (Eds.), *The heart and soul of change: What works in therapy* (pp. 33–57). Washington, DC: American Psychological Association.

Auerswald, E. H. (1968). Interdisciplinary versus ecological approach. *Family Process, 7,* 202–215.

Auerswald, E. H. (1972). In A. Ferber, M. Mendelsohn, & A. Napier (Eds.), *The book of family therapy* (pp. 684–706). New York: Science House.

Barton, C., & Alexander, J. F. (1981). Functional family therapy. In A. S. Gurman & D. P. Kniskern (Eds.), *Handbook of family therapy* (pp. 403–443). New York: Brunner/Mazel.

Bateson, G. (1972). *Steps to an ecology of mind.* New York: Ballantine Books.

Bateson, G. (1979). *Mind and nature: A necessary unity.* New York: Ballantine Books.

Baumrind, D. (1991). The influence of parenting style on adolescent competence and substance use. Special issue: The work of John P. Hill: I. Theoretical, instructional, and policy contributions. *Journal of Early Adolescence, II, 5695.*

Beavers, W. R., & Hampson, B. (1990). *Successful families.* New York: Norton.

Bennett-Goleman, T. (2001). *Emotional alchemy: How the mind can heal the heart.* New York: Harmony.

Bennett-Goleman, T., & Goleman, D. (2001, February). *Emotional alchemy: How the mind can heal the heart.* Workshop presented at Transitions Learning Center, Chicago, IL.

Bennis, W. (1976). *The unconscious conspiracy: Why leaders can't lead.* New York: American Management Association.

Berg, I. K., & Gallagher, D. (1991). Solution-focused brief therapy with adolescent substance abusers. In T. C. Todd & M. D. Selekman (Eds.), *Family therapy approaches with adolescent substance abusers* (pp. 93–111). Needham Heights, MA: Allyn & Bacon.

Berg, I. K., & Miller, S. D. (1992). *Working with the problem drinker: A solution-focused approach.* New York: Norton.

Beutler, L. E., & Harwood, M. T. (2000). *Prescriptive therapy: A practical guide to systematic treatment selection.* New York: Oxford University Press.

Beutler, L. E., Moliero, C. M., & Talebi, H. (2002b). Functional impairment and coping style. In J. C. Norcross (Ed.), *Psychotherapy relationships that work: Therapist contributions and responsiveness to patients* (pp. 145–175). New York: Oxford University Press.

Beyebach, M., Rodriguez-Sanchez, M. S., Arribas de Miguel, J., Herrero de Vega, M., Hernandez, C., & Rodriguez-Morejon, A. (2000). Outcome of solution-focused brief therapy at a university family therapy center. *Journal of Systemic Therapies, 19*, 116–128.

Black, E. I. (1988). *Families and larger systems*. New York: Guilford Press.

Bodin, A. (1981). The interactional view: Family therapy approaches of the Mental Research Institute. In A. S. Gurman & D. P. Kniskern (Eds.), *Handbook of family therapy* (pp. 267–309). New York: Brunner/Mazel.

Bogdan, J. (1984). Family organization as an ecology of ideas. *Family Process, 23*, 375–388.

Bohart, A. C., & Tallman, K. (1999). *How clients make therapy work: The process of active self-healing*. Washington, DC: American Psychological Association.

Bohm, D. (1980). *Wholeness and the implicate order*. London: Routledge.

Bohm, D. (1985). *Unfolding meaning*. London: Routledge.

Boscolo, L., Cecchin, G., Hoffman, L., & Penn, P. (1987). *Milan systemic family therapy: Conversations in therapy and practice*. New York: Basic Books.

Breggin, P. R. (2000). *Reclaiming our children: A healing plan for a nation in crisis*. Cambridge, MA: Perseus.

Brown, S. (2003). *How to negotiate with kids . . . even when you think you shouldn't*. New York: Penguin.

Clifton, D. O., & Nelson, P. (1992). *Soar with your strengths*. New York: Delacorte Press.

Conoley, C. W., Ivey, D., Conoley, J. C., Schmeel, M., & Bishop, R. (1992). Enhancing consultation by matching the consultee's perspective. *Journal of Counseling Development, 69*, 546–549.

Coppersmith, E. I. (1985). Families and multiple helpers: A systemic perspective. In D. Campbell & R. Draper (Eds.), *Applications of systemic family therapy: A Milan approach*. London: Grune & Stratton.

Cox, D., Cox, A. D., & Moschis, G. P. (1990). When consumer behavior goes bad: An investigation of adolescent shop-lifting. *Journal of Consumer Research, 17*(2), 149–160.

Csikszentmihalyi, M. (2003). *Good business: Leadership, flow, and the making of meaning*. New York: Penguin.

Csikszentmihalyi, M. (1997). *Finding flow*. New York: Basic Books.

Csikszentmihalyi, M. (1990). *Flow*. New York: Harper & Row.

Curtis, C. (1995). Outward bound. *Saturday Evening Post*, November 21 (267), p. 74.

DeFrain, J., & Stinnett, N. (1992). Building on the inherent strengths of families: A positive approach for family psychologists and counselors. *Topics in Family Psychology and Counseling 1*(1), 15–26.

Deissler, K. G. (1989, Fall). Co-menting: Toward a systemic poietology? *Continuing the Conversation, 18*, 1–10.

Deissler, K. G. (1992). *Systemic studies of cooperation in the context of a mental state hospital*. Unpublished manuscript.

DeJong, P., & Hopwood, L. E. (1996). Outcome research on treatment conducted at the Brief Family Therapy Center 1992–1993. In S. D. Miller, M. A. Hubble, & B. L. Duncan (Eds.), *Handbook of solution-focused brief therapy* (pp. 272–298). San Francisco: Jossey-Bass.

Dembo, R. (1992, June). *Plenary overview of consensus panel on screening and assessment of substance-abusing adolescents*. Consensus panel address for "Treatment of Substance-Abusing Adolescents," Office for Treatment Improvement, Alcohol, Drug Abuse, and Mental Health Administration, Washington, DC.

de Shazer, S. (1982). Some conceptual distinctions are more useful than others. *Family Process, 21*, 71–84.

de Shazer, S. (1984). The death of resistance. *Family Process, 23*, 79–93.

de Shazer, S. (1985). *Keys to solution in brief therapy.* New York: Norton.
de Shazer, S. (1988). *Clues: Investigating solutions in brief therapy.* New York: Norton.
de Shazer, S. (1991). *Putting difference to work.* New York: Norton.
de Shazer, S., Berg, I. K., Lipchik, E., Nunnally, E., Molnar, A., Gingerich, W., & Weiner-Davis, M. (1986). Brief therapy: Focused solution development. *Family Process, 25,* 207–222.
Dimeff, L., Baer, J., Kivlahan, D., & Marlatt, G. (1998). *Brief alcohol screening and intervention for college students: A harm-reduction approach.* New York: Guilford Press.
Dishion, T. J., & Kavanagh, K. (2003). *Intervening in adolescent problem behavior: A family-centered approach.* New York: Guilford Press.
Dodge, K. A. (1991). The structure and function of proactive and reactive aggression. In D. J. Pepler & K. H. Rubin (Eds.), *The development and treatment of childhood aggression* (pp. 201–218). Hillsdale, NJ: Erlbaum.
Duncan, B. L., & Miller, S. D. (2000). *The heroic client: Doing client-directed, outcome-informed therapy.* San Francisco: Jossey-Bass.
Durrant, M., & Coles, D. (1991). The Michael White approach. In T. C. Todd & M. D. Selekman (Eds.), *Family therapy approaches with adolescent substance abusers* (pp. 135–175). Needham Heights, MA: Allyn & Bacon.
Eastwood, M., Sweeney, D., & Piercy, F. (1987). The "no problem-problem": A family therapy approach for certain first-time adolescent substance abusers. *Family Relations, 36,* 125–28.
Efran, J., & Lukens, M. (1985, May–June). The world according to Humberto Maturana. *Family Therapy Networker,* pp. 23–28, 72–75.
Epston, D. (1998). *Catching up with David Epston: Collection of narrative practice-based papers, 1991–1996.* Adelaide, South Australia: Dulwich Centre Publications.
Epston, D. (2000, May). *Crafting questions in narrative therapy practice.* Workshop presented at the Evanston Family Therapy Institute, Evanston, IL.
Erickson, M. H. (1954). Pseudo-orientation in time as a hypnotic procedure. *Journal of Clinical and Experimental Hypnosis, 2,* 161–283.
Erickson, M. H. (1964). The confusion technique in hypnosis. *American Journal of Clinical Hypnosis, 6,* 183–207.
Erickson, N. H. (1965). The use of symptoms as an integral part of therapy. *American Journal of Clinical Hypnosis, 8,* 57–65.
Erickson, M. H. (1980a). The nature of hypnosis and suggestion. In E. L. Rossi (Ed.), *The collected papers of Milton H. Erickson* (Vol. 2). New York: Irvington.
Erickson, M. H. (1980b). Hypnotic alteration of sensory, perceptual, and psychosocial processes. In E. L. Rossi (Ed.), *The collected papers of Milton H. Erickson* (Vol. 3). New York: Irvington.
Erickson, M. H., & Rossi, E. (1983). *Healing in hypnosis.* New York: Irvington.
Erickson, M. H., Rossi, E., & Rossi, I. (1976). *Hypnotic realities.* New York: Irvington.
Fisch, R., Weakland, J., & Segal, L. (1982). *The tactics of change.* San Francisco: Jossey-Bass.
von Foerster, H. (1981). *Observing systems.* Seaside, CA: Intersystems.
Follett, M. P. (1995). Constructive conflict. In P. Graham (Ed.), *Mary Parker Follett: Prophet of management* (pp. 53–77). Boston: Harvard Business School.
Frank, J. D., & Frank, J. B. (1991). *Persuasion and healing: A comparative study of psychotherapy* (3rd ed.). Baltimore, MD: John Hopkins University Press.
Fredrickson, B. L. (2002). Positive emotion. In C. R. Snyder & S. J. Lopez (Eds.), *Handbook of positive psychology* (pp. 120–135). New York: Oxford University Press.

Fredrickson, B. L. (2003, July–August). The value of positive emotions. *American Scientist, 91*, 330–335.

Friedman, S. (Ed.). (1995). *The reflecting team in action: Collaborative practice in family therapy.* New York: Guilford Press.

Gardner, H. (1993). *Multiple intelligences: The theory in practice.* New York: Basic Books.

Gardner, H. (1999). *Intelligence reframed: Multiple intelligences for the 21st century.* New York: Basic Books.

Gardner, H. (2004). *Changing minds: The art and science of changing our own and other people's minds.* Boston: Harvard Business School.

George, E., Iveson, C., & Ratner, H. (1999). *Problem to solution: Brief therapy with individuals and families* (rev. ed.). London: Brief Therapy Press.

Gergen, K. J., & McNamee, S. (2000). From disordering discourse to transformative dialogue. In R. A. Neimeyer & J. D. Raskin (Eds.), *Constructions of disorder: Meaning-making frameworks for psychotherapy* (pp. 333–349). Washington, DC: American Psychological Association.

Gilligan, S. (2002). *The legacy of Milton H. Erickson: Selected papers of Stephen Gilligan.* Phoenix, AZ: Zeig, Tucker, & Theisen.

Gingerich, W., & de Shazer, S. (1991). The BRIEFER project: Using expert systems as theory construction tools. *Family Process, 30,* 241–249.

Gingerich, W., de Shazer, S., & Weiner-Davis, M. (1988). Constructing change: A research view of interviewing. In E. Lipchik (Ed.), *Interviewing* (pp. 21–31). Rockville, MD: Aspen.

Gingerich, W., & Eisengart, S. (2000). Solution-focused brief therapy: A review of the outcome research. *Family Process, 39*(4), 477–498.

Glassner, B. (1999). *The culture of fear.* New York: Basic Books.

Glassner, B., & Loughlin, J. (1987). *Drugs in adolescent worlds: Burnouts to straights.* New York: St. Martin's Press.

Goleman, D. (2003). *Destructive emotions: How we can overcome them.* New York: Bantam.

Goolishian, H. (1991, October). *The dis-diseasing of mental health.* Plenary address presented at the Houston–Galveston Institute's Conference II, San Antonio, TX.

Goolishian, H., & Anderson, H. (1981). Including non-blood related persons in family therapy. In A. S. Gurman (Ed.), *Questions and answers in the practice of family therapy* (pp. 75–80). New York: Brunner/Mazel.

Goolishian, H., & Anderson, H. (1988, November). *The therapeutic conversation.* A 3-day intensive training sponsored by the Institute of Systemic Therapy, Chicago.

Gordon, D., & Meyers-Anderson, M. (1981). *Phoenix: Therapeutic patterns of Milton H. Erickson.* Cupertino, CA: Meta.

Gottman, J. (1994). *Why marriages succeed or fail . . . And how you can make yours last.* New York: Fireside.

Gottman, J., Katz, L. F., & Hooven, C. (1997). *Meta-emotion.* Mahwah, NJ: Erlbaum.

Greene, R. W. (1998). *The explosive child: A new approach for understanding and parenting easily frustrated, "chronically inflexible" children.* New York: HarperCollins.

Grotevant, H. D., & Cooper, C. R. (1983). *Adolescent development in the family.* San Francisco: Jossey-Bass.

Gurin, J. (1990, March). Remaking our lives. *American Health,* pp. 50–52.

Haggerty, R. J., Sherrod, L. R., Garmezy, N., & Rutter, M. (1994). *Stress, risk, and resilience in children and adolescents.* Cambridge, UK: Cambridge University Press.

Hanh, T. N. (2001). *Anger.* New York: Riverhead.

Hanh, T. N. (2003a). *Creating true peace: Ending violence in yourself, your family, your community, and the world.* New York: Free Press.

Hanh, T. N. (May, 2003b). *Building a century of peace*. Public presentation at Loyola University, Chicago.

Hammerschlag, C. (1988). *The dancing healers: A doctor's journey of healing with Native Americans.* New York: Harper & Row.

Hargrove, R. (1999). *Masterful coaching: Extraordinary results by impacting people and the way they think and work together.* San Francisco: Jossey-Bass.

Havens, R. A. (1985). *The Wisdom of Milton H. Erickson: Human behavior and psychotherapy.* New York: Paragon.

Henggeler, S. W., Schoenwald, S. K., Rowland, M. D., & Cunningham, P. B. (1998). *Multisystemic treatment of antisocial behavior in children and adolescents.* New York: Guilford Press.

Henggeler, S. W., Schoenwald, S. K., Rowland, M. D., & Cunningham, P. B. (2002). *Serious emotional disturbance in children and adolescents: Multisystemic therapy.* New York: Guilford Press.

Henggeler, S. W., & Sheidow, A. J. (2002). Conduct disorder and delinquency. In D. H. Sprenkle (Ed.), *Effectiveness research in marriage and family therapy* (pp. 27–51). Alexandria, VA: American Association for Marriage and Family Therapy.

Hoffman, L. (1988). A constructivist position for family therapy. *Irish Journal of Psychology, 9,* 110–129.

Hoffman, L. (2002). *Family therapy: An intimate history.* New York: Norton.

Hubble, M. A., Duncan, B. L., & Miller, S. D. (Eds). (1999). *The heart and soul of change: What works in therapy.*Washington, DC: American Psychological Association.

Isaacs, W. (1999). *Dialogue and the art of thinking together.* New York: Currency.

Isaacson, W. (2003). *Ben Franklin: An American life.* New York: Simon & Schuster.

Jones, R. A. (1977). *Self-fulfilling prophecies: Social, psychological and physiological effects of expectancies.* Hillsdale, NJ: Erlbaum.

Jung, C. (1923). *Psychological types.* London: Kegan Paul.

Kabat-Zinn, J. (1990). *Full catastrophe living.* New York: Delacort.

Kabat-Zinn, J. (1995). *Wherever you are there you are: Mindfulness meditation in everyday life.* New York: Hyperion.

Katz, S. J., & Liu, A. E. (1991). *The co-dependency conspiracy.* New York: Warner Books.

Kearney, P., Byrne, N. O., & McCarthy, I. M. (1989). Just metaphors: Marginal illuminations in a colonial retreat. *Family Therapy Case Studies, 4*(1), 17–33.

Keeney, B., & Ross, J. (1983). Cybernetics of brief family therapy. *Journal of Marital and Family Therapy, 9,* 375–382.

Kegan, R., & Lahey, L. L. (2001). *How the way we talk can change the way we work: Seven languages for transformation.* San Francisco: Jossey-Bass.

Keith, D., & Whitaker, C. (1981). Play therapy: A paradigm for work with families. *Journal of Marital and Family Therapy, 7*(3), 243–255.

Keyes, C. L. M., & Haidt, J. (2003). *Flourishing: Positive psychology and the life well-lived.* Washington, DC: American Psychological Association.

Khan, M. T. (2001, April 4). Voyage to maturity. *Birmingham Post*, p. 43.

Kilbourne, J. (1999). *Deadly persuasion: Why women and girls must fight the addictive power of advertising.* New York: Free Press.

Kissen, B., Platz, A., & Su, W. H. (1971). Selective factors in treatment choice and outcome in alcoholism. In N. K. Mello & J. H. Mendelsohn (Eds.), *Recent advances in studies of alcoholism* (pp. 781–802). Washington, DC: U.S. Government Printing Office.

Kivlahan, D., Marlatt, G., Fromme, K., Coppel, D., & Brand, E. (1990). Secondary prevention with college drinkers: Evaluation of an alcohol skills training program. *Journal of Consulting and Clinical Psychology, 58*, 805–810.

Klein, G. (1998). *Sources of power: How people make decisions*. Cambridge, MA: MIT Press.

Klein, G. (2002). *Intuition at work*. New York: Currency Doubleday.

Koch, R. (1998). *The 80/20 principle: The secret to success by achieving more with less*. New York: Currency Doubleday.

Lambert, M. J. (2003, March–April). The power of client feedback. *Psychotherapy Networker*, p. 16.

Lambert, M. J., & Barley, D. E. (2002). Research summary on the therapeutic relationship and psychotherapy. In J. C. Norcross (Ed.), *Psychotherapy relationships that work: Therapist contributions and responsiveness to patients* (pp. 17–37). New York: Oxford University Press.

Leake, G. J., & King, A. S. (1977). Effect of counselor expectations on alcoholic recovery. *Alcohol, Health and Resource World, 11*(3), 16–22.

Lebow, J., & Gurman, A. S. (1996, January–February). Making a difference: A new research review offers good news to couples and family therapist. *Family Therapy Networker*, pp. 69–76.

Lewin, T. (2003, December 9). Raid at high school leads to racial divide, not drugs. *New York Times*, p. A20.

Liddle, H. A. (2002). *Multidimensional family therapy for adolescent cannabis users* (Cannabis Youth Treatment Series, Vol. 5). Rockville, MD: Center for Substance Abuse Treatment.

Lindforss, L., & Magnussen, D. (1997). Solution-focused therapy in prison. *Contemporary family therapy, 19*, 89–104.

Lipchik, E. (1988, Winter). Interviewing with a constructive ear. *Dulwich Centre Newsletter*, pp. 3–7. Available from Dulwich Centre Publications, Hutt Street, P.O. Box 7192, Adelaide, South Australia 5000.

Lipchik, E., & de Shazer, S. (1986). The purposeful interview. *Journal of Strategic and Systemic Therapies, 5*(1), 88–99.

Lussardi, D. J., & Miller, D. (1991). A reflecting team approach to adolescent substance abuse. In T. C. Todd & M. D. Selekman (Eds.), *Family therapy approaches with adolescent substance abusers* (pp. 227–240). Needham Heights, MA: Allyn & Bacon.

Lyotard, J. F. (1996). *Just gaming*. Minneapolis: University of Minnesota Press.

MacMaster, S. A., (2004). Harm-reduction: A new perspective on substance abuse services. *Social Work, 49*(3), 356–364.

Madanes, C. (1984). *Behind the one-way mirror*. San Francisco: Jossey-Bass.

Maddux, J. E. (2002). Stopping the "madness": Positive psychology and the deconstruction of the illness ideology and the DSM. In C. R. Snyder & S. J. Lopez (Eds.), *Handbook of positive psychology* (pp. 13–25). New York: Oxford University Press.

Maraniss, D. (1999). *When pride still mattered: A life of Vince Lombardi*. New York: Simon & Schuster.

Maruyama, M. (1974). The second cybernetics: Deviation-amplifying mutual causative processes. *American Scientist, 51*, 164–179.

Maturana, H., & Varela, F. (1988). *The tree of knowledge: The biological roots to human understanding*. Boston: New Science Library.

McCarthy, I. M., & Byrne, N. O. (1988). Mistaken love: Conversations on the problem of incest in an Irish context. *Family Process, 27*, 181–199.

McDermott, D., & Snyder, C. R. (1999). *Making hope happen: A workbook for turning possibilities into reality*. Oakland, CA: New Harbinger.

McKeel, A. J. (1999). *A selected review of research of solution-focused brief therapy.* Available online at *www.enabling.org/ia/sft*

Metcalf, L., Thomas, F. N., Duncan, B. L., Miller, S. D., & Hubble, M. A. (1996). What works in solution-focused brief therapy. In S. D. Miller, M. A. Hubble, & B. L. Duncan (Eds.), *Handbook of solution-focused brief therapy* (pp. 335–349). San Francisco: Jossey-Bass.

Miller, W. R. (1985). Motivation for treatment: A review with special emphasis on alcoholism. *Psychological Bulletin, 98,* 84–107.

Miller, W. R., & Rollnick, S. (2002). *Motivational interviewing: Preparing people for change* (2nd ed.). New York: Guilford Press.

Miller, W. R., & Sovereign, R. G. (1989). The checkup: A model for early intervention in addictive behaviors. In T. Loberg, W. R. Miller, P. E. Nathan, & G. A. Marlatt (Eds.), *Addictive behaviors: Prevention and early intervention* (pp. 219–231). Amsterdam: Swets & Zeitlinger.

Milner, M. (2004). *Freaks, geeks, and cool kids: American teenagers, schools, and the culture of consumption.* New York: Routledge.

Minuchin, S. (1974). *Families and family therapy.* Cambridge, MA: Harvard University Press.

Minuchin, S. (1986, May). *Week-long live family therapy training.* Sponsored by Gestalt Integrated Family Institute, Chicago.

Minuchin, S., & Fishman, H. C. (1981). *Family therapy techniques.* Cambridge, MA: Harvard University Press.

Mipham, S. (2003), *Turning the mind into an ally.* New York: Riverhead.

Mitchell, S. (1988). *Tao Te Ching: A new English version.* New York: HarperCollins.

Molnar, A., & de Shazer, S. (1987). Solution-focused therapy: Toward the identification of therapeutic tasks. *Journal of Marital and Family Therapy, 13*(4), 349–358.

Moore, M. (2002). *Bowling for Columbine* [Film]. United Artists.

Newfield, N. A., Kuehl, B. P., Joanning, H. P., & Quinn, W. H. (1991). We can tell you about "psychos" and "shrinks": An ethnography of the family therapy of adolescent drug abuse. In T. C. Todd & M. D. Selekman (Eds.), *Family therapy approaches with adolescent substance abusers* (pp. 277–310). Needham Heights, MA: Allyn & Bacon.

Norcross, J. C. (Ed.). (2002). *Psychotherapy relationships that work: Therapist contributions and responsiveness to patients.* New York: Oxford University Press.

Nylund, D., & Corsiglia, V. (1994). Becoming solution-focused forced in brief therapy: Remembering something important we already know. *Journal of Systemic Therapies, 13*(1), 5–13.

O'Hanlon, W. H. (1987). *Taproots: Underlying principles of Milton H. Erickson's therapy and hypnosis.* New York: Norton.

O'Hanlon, W. H., & Weiner-Davis, M. (1989). *In search of solutions: A new direction in psychotherapy.* New York: Norton.

Orford, J., & Hawker, A. (1974). An investigation of an alcoholism rehabilitation halfway house: II. The complex question of client motivation. *British Journal of Addiction, 69,* 315–323.

Ostrander, S., Schroeder, L., & Ostrander, N. (1994). *Superlearning 2000.* New York: Dell.

Palazzoli, M. S. (1980). Why a long interval between sessions? The therapeutic control of the family–therapist suprasystem. In M. Andolfi & I. Zwerling (Eds.), *Dimensions of family therapy* (pp. 161–171). New York: Guilford Press.

Palazzoli, M. S., Boscolo, L., Cecchin, G., & Prata, G. (1980). Hypothesizing—circularity—neutrality: Three guidelines for the conductor of the session. *Family Process, 19*(1), 3–13.

Papini, D. R., & Roggman, L. A. (1992). Adolescent perceived attachment to parents in relation to competence, depression, and anxiety: A longitudinal study. *Journal of Early Adolescence, 12*, 420–440.

Papp, P. (1983). *The process of change.* New York: Guilford Press.

Parker, M. W., Winstead, D. K., & Willi, F. J. (1979). Patient autonomy in alcohol rehabilitation: Literature review. *International Journal of the Addictions, 14,* 1015–1022.

Parsons, B. V., & Alexander, J. F. (1973). Short-term family intervention: A therapy outcome study. *Journal of Consulting and Clinical Psychology, 41,* 195–201.

Patterson, G. R., & Forgatch, M. I. (1985). Therapist behavior as a determinant for client noncompliance: A paradox for the behavior modifier. *Journal of Consulting and Clinical Psychology, 53,* 846–851.

Peele, S. (1989). *Diseasing of America: Addiction treatment out of control.* Lexington, MA: Lexington Books.

Penn, P. (1985). Feed forward: Future questions, future maps. *Family Process, 24*(3), 299–310.

Perez-Bouchard, L., Johnson, J. L., & Ahrens, A. H. (1993). Attributional style in children of substance abusers. *American Journal of Drug and Alcohol Abuse, 19,* 475–489.

Peters, T. J., & Waterman, R. H. (1982). *In search of excellence: Lessons from America's best-run companies.* New York: Warner Books.

Peterson, C., & Park, C. (1998). Learned helplessness and explanatory style. In D. F. Barone, M. Hersen, & V. B. van Hasselt (Eds.), *Advanced personality* (pp. 287–310). New York: Plenum Press.

Peterson, C., & Seligman, M. E. P. (2004). *Character strengths and virtues: A handbook and classification.* New York: Oxford University Press.

Prochaska, J. O. (1999). How do people change and how can we change to help many more people? In M. A. Hubble, B. L. Duncan, & S. D. Miller (Eds.), *The heart and soul of change: What works in therapy* (pp. 227–259). Washington, DC: American Psychological Association.

Prochaska, J. O., & Norcross, J. C. (2002). Stages of change. In J. C. Norcross (Ed.), *Psychotherapy relationships that work: Therapist contributions and responsiveness to patients* (pp. 303–315). New York: Oxford University Press.

Prochaska, J. O., Norcross, J. C., & DiClemente, C. C. (1994). *Changing for good.* New York: Morrow.

Rackham, N., & Carlisle, J. (1978). The effective negotiator: The behavior of successful negotiators. *Journal of European Industrial Training,* 2(6), 6–11.

Reimer, M. S., Overton, W. F., Steidl, J., Rosenstein, D. S., & Horowitz, H. (1996). Familial responsiveness and behavioral control: Influences on adolescent psychopathology, attachment, and cognition. *Journal of Research on Adolescence,* 6, 87–112.

Reimers, T. M., Wacker, P., Cooper, L. J., & De Raad, A. O. (1992). Acceptability for behavioral treatments for children: Analog and naturalistic evaluations by parents. *School Psychology Review,* 21, 628–643.

Reivich, K., & Shatte, A. (2002). *The resilience factor: Seven essential skills for overcoming life's inevitable obstacles.* New York: Broadway.

Rimer, S. (2004, January 4). Unruly students facing arrest, not detention. *New York Times*, pp. A1, A15.

Rowe, C. L., & Liddle, H. A. (2002). Substance abuse. In D. H. Sprenkle (Ed.), *Effectiveness research in marriage and family therapy* (pp. 53–89). Alexandria, VA: American Association for Marriage and Family Therapy.

Sanchez-Craig, M., & Lei, H. (1986). Disadvantages of imposing the goal of abstinence on problem drinkers: An empirical study. *British Journal of Addiction, 81*, 505–512.

Schon, D. (1983). *The reflective practitioner: How professionals think in action*. New York: Basic Books.

Schwartz, B. (2004). *The paradox of choice: Why more is less*. New York: HarperCollins.

Seikkula, J., Alakare, B., & Aaltonen, J. (2000). A two-year follow-up on open dialogue treatment in first episode psychosis: The need for hospitalization and neuroleptic medication decreases. *Social and Clinical Psychiatry, 10*(2), 20–29.

Seikkula, J., & Olson, M. (2003). The open dialogue approach to acute psychosis: Its poetics and micro-politics. *Family Process, 42*(3), 403–419.

Selekman, M. D. (1989a). Taming chemical monsters: Cybernetic-systemic therapy with adolescent substance abusers. *Journal of Strategic and Systemic Therapies, 8*(3), 5–10.

Selekman, M. D. (1989b). Engaging adolescent substance abusers in family therapy. *Family Therapy Case Studies, 4*(1), 67–74.

Selekman, M. D. (1991a). "With a little help from my friends": The use of peers in the family therapy of adolescent substances abusers. *Family Dynamics of Addiction Quarterly, 1*(1), 69–77.

Selekman, M. D. (1991b). The solution-oriented parenting group: A treatment alternative that works. *Journal of Strategic and Systemic Therapies, 10*(1), 36–49.

Selekman, M. D. (1993). *Pathways to change: Brief therapy solutions with difficult adolescents*. New York: Guilford Press.

Selekman, M. D. (1995). Rap music with wisdom: Peer reflecting teams with tough adolescents. In S. Friedman (Ed.), *The reflecting team in action: Collaborative practice in family therapy* (pp. 205–223). New York: Guilford Press.

Selekman, M. D. (1996). Turning out the light on a seasonal affective disorder. *Journal of Systemic Therapies, 15*(3), 40–52.

Selekman, M. D. (1997). *Solution-focused therapy with children: Harnessing family strengths for systemic change*. New York: Guilford Press.

Selekman, M. D. (1999). The solution-oriented parenting group revisited. *Journal of Systemic Therapies, 18*(1), 5–24.

Selekman, M. D. (2002). *Living on the razor's edge: Solution-oriented brief family therapy with self-harming adolescents*. New York: Norton.

Selekman, M. D. (2004, January–February). The therapeutic roller coaster: Working with self-harming teens is dramatic and unpredictable. *Psychotherapy Networker*, pp. 77–87.

Selekman, M. D., & Todd, T. C. (1991). Crucial issues in the treatment of adolescent substance abusers and their families. In T. C. Todd & M. D. Selekman (Eds.), *Family therapy approaches with adolescent substance abusers* (pp. 1–20). Needham Heights, MA: Allyn & Bacon.

Seligman, M. E. P. (1998). *Learned optimism: How to change your mind and your life*. New York: Pocket Books.

Seligman, M. E. P. (2002). *Authentic happiness*. New York: Free Press.

Seligman, M. E. P. (2003). *Nine-month vanguard master class in authentic happiness coaching and positive psychology*, Bethesda, MD.

Seligman, M. E. P., Reivich, M. A., Jaycox, L., & Gillham, J. (1995). *The optimistic child*. New York: Houghton-Mifflin.

Sexton, T. L., & Alexander, J. F. (2002), Functional family therapy: An empirically supported family-based intervention model for at-risk adolescents and their families.

In T. Patterson (Ed.), *Comprehensive handbook of psychotherapy, Volume II: Cognitive, behavioral, and functional approaches* (pp. 117–140). New York: Wiley.

Shedler, J., & Block, J. (1990). Adolescent drug use and psychological health. *American Psychologist, 45*(5), 612–30.

Sheinberg, M. (1985). The debate: A strategic technique. *Family Process, 24*(2), 259–271.

Sherman, S. J., Skov, R. B., Hervitz, E. F., & Stock, C. B. (1981). The effects of explaining hypothetical future events: From possibility to probability to actuality and beyond. *Journal of Experimental Social Psychology, 17,* 142–157.

Siegel, S. (1999). *The patient who cured his therapist and other stories of unconventional therapy.* New York: Marlowe.

Simon, H. A. (1955). Rational choice and the structure of the environment. *Psychological Review, 63,* 129–38.

Simon, H. A. (1956). A behavioral model of rational choice. *Quarterly Journal of Economics, 69,* 99–118.

Simmons, R. (2002). *Odd girl out: The hidden culture of aggression in girls.* New York: Harcourt.

Snyder, C. R., & Lopez, S. J. (Eds.). (2002). *Handbook of positive psychology.* New York: Oxford University Press.

Snyder, C. R., Michael, S. T., & Cheavens, J. S. (1999). Hope as a psychotherapeutic foundation of common factors. In M. A. Hubble, B. L. Duncan, & S. D. Miller (Eds.), *The heart and soul of change: What works in therapy* (pp. 179–201). Washington, DC: American Psychological Association.

Snyder, C. R., Rand, K. L., & Sigmon, D. R., (2002). Hope theory: A member of the positive psychology family. In C. R. Snyder & S. J. Shane (Eds.), *Handbook of positive psychology* (pp. 257–277). New York: Oxford University Press.

Snyder, J., & Patterson, G. R. (1995). Individual differences in social aggression: A test of the reinforcement model of socialization in the natural environment. *Behavior Therapy, 26,* 371–91.

Snyder, M., & White, P. (1982). Moods and memories: Elation, depression, and the remembering of the events of one's life. *Journal of Personality, 50*(2), 149–167.

Spanos, N. P. (1990). Imagery, hypnosis and hypnotizability. In R. G. Kunzendorf (Ed.), *Mental imagery.* New York: Plenum Press.

Spanos, N. P., & Radtke, H. L. (1981). Hypnotic visual hallucinations as imaginings: A cognitive–social psychological perspective. *Imagination, Cognition and Personality, 1*(2), 147–170.

Stalker, C. A., Levene, J. E., & Coady, N. F. (1999). Solution-focused brief therapy: One model fits all? *Families in Society: The Journal of Contemporary Human Services, 80*(5), 468–477.

Steinberg, L. D., Darling, N., Fletcher, B., Brown, B., & Dornbusch, S. (1995). Authoritative parenting and adolescent adjustment: An ecological journey. In P. Moen, G. H. Elder, & K. Luscher (Eds.), *Linking lives and contexts: Perspectives on the ecology of human development.* Washington, DC: American Psychological Association.

Stinnett, N., & O'Donnell, M. (1996). *Good kids: How you and your kids can successfully navigate the teen years.* New York: Doubleday.

Stone, D., Patton, B., & Heen, S. (2000). *Difficult conversations: How to discuss what really matters most.* New York: Penguin.

Szapocznik, J., Kurtines, W. M., Foote, F. H., Perez-Vidal, A., & Hervis, O. (1983). Conjoint versus one-person family therapy: Some evidence for the effectiveness of conducting family therapy through one person with drug-abusing adolescents. *Journal of Consulting and Clinical Psychology, 51*(6), 889–899.

Szapocznik, J., Kurtines, W. M., Foote, F. H., Perez-Vidal, A., & Hervis, O. (1986). Conjoint versus one-person family therapy: Further evidence for the effectiveness of conducting family therapy through one person with drug-abusing adolescents. *Journal of Consulting and Clinical Psychology, 54*(3), 395–397.

Szapocznik, J., & Williams, R. A. (2000). Brief strategic family therapy: Twenty-five years of interplay among theory, research, and practice in adolescent behavior problems and drug abuse. *Clinical Child and Family Psychology Review, 3*(2), 117–134.

Taffel, R. (2003, November–December). Confronting the new anxiety. *Psychotherapy Networker*, pp. 33–37, 59.

Taffel, R., & Blau, M. (2001). *The second family: How adolescent power is challenging the American family.* New York: St. Martin's.

Thornton, C. C., Gottheil, E., Gellens, H. K., & Alterman, A. I. (1977). Voluntary versus involuntary abstinence in the treatment of alcoholics. *Journal of Studies on Alcohol, 38,* 1740–1748.

Todd, T. C., & Selekman, M. D. (1991). Beyond structural–strategic family therapy: Integrating other brief systemic therapies. In T. C. Todd & M. D. Selekman (Eds.), *Family therapy approaches with adolescent substance abusers* (pp. 241–271). Needham Heights, MA: Allyn & Bacon.

Tomm, K. (1987). Interventive interviewing: II. Reflexive questioning as a means to enable self-healing. *Family Process, 26,* 167–183.

Tomm, K., & White, M. (1987, October) *Externalizing problems and internalizing directional choices.* Paper presented at the Annual American Association for Marriage and Family Therapy Conference, Chicago.

Trungpa, C. (1988). *Shambhala: The sacred path of the warrior.* Boston: Shambhala.

Ury, W. (2000). *The third side: Why we fight and how we can stop.* New York: Penguin.

von Glasersfeld, E. (1984). An introduction to radical constructivism. In P. Watzlawick (Ed.), *The invented reality* (pp. 17–40). New York: Norton.

Watzlawick, P., Weakland, J. H., & Fisch, R. (1974). *Change: Principles of problem formation and problem resolution.* New York: Norton.

Weakland, J. H., & Jordan, L. (1990). Working briefly with reluctant clients: Child protective services as an example. *Family Therapy Case Studies, 5*(2), 51–68.

Weiner-Davis, M. (1992). *Divorce busting.* New York: Simon & Schuster.

Weiner-Davis, M., de Shazer, S., & Gingerich, W. (1987). Building on pretreatment change to construct the therapeutic solution: An exploratory study. *Journal of Marital and Family Therapy, 13*(4), 359–363.

Weiss, R. L., Halford, W. K., & Kim, W. (1996). Managing marital therapy: Helping partners change. In V. B. van Hasslet & M. Hersen (Eds.), *Sourcebook of psychological treatment manuals for adult disorders* (pp. 489–537). New York: Plenum.

Whitaker, C. A. (1975). Psychotherapy of the absurd: With a special emphasis on the psychotherapy of aggression. *Family Process, 14,* 1–16.

White, M. (1984). Pseudo-encopresis: From avalanche to victory, from vicious to virtuous cycles. *Family Systems Medicine, 2*(2), 150–160.

White, M. (1985). Fear-busting and monster taming: An approach to the fears of young children. *Dulwich Centre Review,* pp. 29–33. Available from Dulwich Centre Publications, Hutt Street, P.O. Box 7192, Adelaide, South Australia 5000.

White, M. (1986). Negative explanation, restraint and double description: A template for family therapy. *Family Process, 25*(2), 169–184.

White, M. (1987/Spring). Family therapy and schizophrenia: Addressing the in-the-corner lifestyle. *Dulwich Centre Newsletter,* pp. 14–21. Available from Dulwich Centre Publications, Hutt Street, P.O. Box 7192, Adelaide, South Australia 5000.

White, M. (1988a). Anorexia nervosa: A cybernetic perspective. In J. E. Harkaway (Ed.), *Eating disorders* (pp. 117–129). Rockville, MD: Aspen.

White, M. (1988b, Winter). The process of questioning: A therapy of literary merit? *Dulwich Centre Newsletter,* pp. 8–14. Available from Dulwich Centre Publications, Hutt Street, P.O. Box 7192, Adelaide, South Australia 5000.

White, M. (1995). *Re-authoring lives: Interviews and essays.* Adelaide, South Australia: Dulwich Centre Publications. Available from Dulwich Centre Publications, Hutt Street, P.O. Box 7192, Adelaide, South Australia 5000.

White, M., & Epston, D. (1990). *Narrative means to therapeutic ends.* New York: Norton.

Whitfield, S. (1992). *Magritte.* London: South Bank Centre.

Wolin, S. (1991, October). *The challenge model: How children rise above adversity.* Plenary address presented at the 1991 Annual American Association for Marriage and Family Therapy Conference, Dallas.

Wolin, S. J., & Wolin, S. (1993). *The resilient self: How survivors of troubled families rise above adversity.* New York: Villard.

Yalom, I. P. (1975). *The theory and practice of group psychotherapy.* New York: Basic Books.

Index

f indicates figure